Anonymous

A Memorial of Constantine Hering

Born January 1st, 1800 ; died July 23d, 1880

Anonymous

A Memorial of Constantine Hering
Born January 1st, 1800 ; died July 23d, 1880

ISBN/EAN: 9783337746155

Printed in Europe, USA, Canada, Australia, Japan

Cover: Foto ©ninafisch / pixelio.de

More available books at **www.hansebooks.com**

A

MEMORIAL

OF

CONSTANTINE HERING

BORN JANUARY 1ST, 1800
DIED JULY 23D, 1880

PHILADELPHIA

Press of GLOBE PRINTING HOUSE.

I
Biographical Sketch

II
Literary Life

III
In Memoriam

PREFACE

AT the Memorial Meeting, held in Philadelphia, October 10th, 1880, the undersigned were requested to edit and publish a Biographical Sketch of Dr CONSTANTINE HERING, together with the Addresses and Eulogies pronounced over him, and whatsoever details of his professional life and works as might be deemed worthy of preservation; the whole thus constituting an enduring Memorial of our revered friend and master.

In the accomplishment of their task the Editors cannot but confess, that, as this fine life revealed itself page by page, they found no small satisfaction in the contemplation of the benison to the world which its history would prove.

The speakers and writers whose words are recorded in the following pages, all bear witness to the deep impression which the grand traits of Dr HERING's character, not only as a physician but as a man, produced on all with whom he came in contact. With 'charity for all and malice towards none,' the whole of his long, laborious, and blameless life was spent in laying broad and deep the enduring principles of Homœopathy.

For the assistance rendered by the Rev. WILLIAM H. FURNESS, D.D., in preparing the Biographical Sketch, the editors are deeply indebted; and are grateful likewise for the services rendered by others in translating foreign papers.

CHARLES G. RAUE,
CALVIN B. KNERR,
CHARLES MOHR.

BIOGRAPHICAL SKETCH.

BIOGRAPHICAL SKETCH.

THE ancestors of Dr. Hering came from Moravia. They wrote the family name Hrinka. His father, a gentle natured man, educated first at the Fürstenschule in Meissen, the same in which Hahnemann received his early education, and then at the Universities of Leipzig and Würtemberg, was devoted to teaching and to music. He published numerous works of instruction in the art of music, some of which passed through several editions, among them a collection of juvenile songs; some of these are still sung by children the world over. His method, resembling the Kindergarten mode of education, commended itself by its simplicity and practical character. In his humble home he strove to surround his little ones with refining influences. Books with poor pictures were not tolerated in the nursery. He maintained that early impressions were powerful in influencing later life, and zealously strove to banish from his home all that was not good, beautiful or true.

Before marriage he lived in Leipzig, which city he left to occupy the position of instructor in the family of Krug von Nidda. In 1795, he was given the position of conrector and organist of the church in Oschatz with the title of Magister, equivalent to Doctor of Philosophy. Sixteen years later he moved to Zittau, a beautifully situated town in the Oberlausitz, where he became principal of the public school and later professor of music in the seminary. In 1836, he was partly emerited, wholly so eight years later, and the remainder of his life, which ended January 4th, 1853, was devoted to his favorite art, music. His family consisted of three daughters and four sons. One of the sons, Carl Eduard, was pronounced by Mendelssohn the strongest musician on counterpoint in Europe.

Dr. Hering was born on the first day of January, A.D. 1800, consequently he could claim to be one of the first men of the century. His father was seated at the organ when word was brought to him of the birth of a son, whereupon pealed forth a burst of praise: *Nun danket alle Gott.* The trumpet angels, attached to the organ, sent forth their hallelujahs, heralding the advent of a new century and the birth of a son. The child was carried the next day into the open air, his father believing in the hardening process. A day or two afterwards he was baptized and named Constantine. In giving him this name which had been borne by a child that had died, the father showed himself above a popular superstition.

Oschatz, the birth-place of Dr. Hering, is a small town situated between Dresden and Leipzig. As the diligence passed through it, it happened occasionally that some traveller of note stopped over night and spent the evening with Magister Hering, widely known for his position in the musical world. Dr. Hering preserved the memory of these guests. They did much, doubtless, to determine his way of thinking. He remembered sitting on the knee of Chladni and listening to the wonderful account of the *Klangfiguren* (sound figures). Seume, a literary man of that day, was one of those evening visitors, whose talk about America and democracy inspired the listening child with the love of freedom and the hatred of privileged classes.

The early teachers of Dr. Hering were persons of a like character to his father. One in particular, August Rudolph, an excellent mathematician, he always spoke of with veneration. Lehrer Rudolph taught him to love mathematics as a science, not merely of dry formulas, but as a revelation of the laws of being. The boy had no liking for history, "a collection of foolish and horrible things," as he called it to his father, who told him he should write it after a better fashion. But he preferred to study plants, insects, stones. He incurred a reproof from his beloved teacher, Herr Rudolph, by refusing to call Peter of Russia, Peter *the Great*, preferring to say, in the course of a composition condemnatory of the Russian ruler, "Peter, whom *fools* call great."

It was in the boyhood of Dr. Hering that the Old World was all in a tremble under the bloody footsteps of the First Napoleon. Dr. Hering had vivid recollections of the time before and after the battle of Jena, and of the march to Russia and the disastrous retreat. A portion of the French army on its way to Russia passed through Saxony, a small company halted before the house of Magister Hering and demanded food; Constantine, a lad of twelve, ran out with a fresh loaf of black bread (rye bread), which an officer took only to fling it on the ground where it was kicked about by the soldiers. "It's good bread," cried the boy, "my mother made it; don't you know God will punish you for throwing bread away?" The men said nothing and passed on. By and by rumors came of the great catastrophe, the fatal retreat. As it chanced the same squad came to the Magister's begging food. Again the same boy came out to help the poor wretches, taking white bread to them this time; the same officer, wasted, in rags, with his arm in a sling met the boy. "Ah! my boy," he exclaimed, "the curse you told us of has fallen upon us."

The first stimulus to a love of the natural sciences the boy received when he found on his father's grapevine the caterpillar named *Sphynx atropos*. This *Atropos*, followed in later years by the *Lachesis*, called to his mind the three weird sisters who were supposed to determine the course of human life. He often said: "The destinies have come to me in reverse order." First came Atropos, the inflexible, who cuts the thread of human life, next Lachesis who spins it, and finally Clotho holding the distaff. He likened his work of writing the Materia Medica to the spinning of threads for a fabric, and when the web was well begun, he said: "When I shall be called hence the work will be left on the loom for other hands to weave." When the boy's mind had received the impulse to study Nature's works he became enthusiastic in pursuit of knowledge. The collection of insects, stones, and plants busied him in all the hours that could be spared from school. He made long excursions to the neighboring hills and valleys and returned laden with minerals for his cabinet, or plants for his herbarium. He was wont to stop at inns to arrange his collections, and it was in those places that he picked up the popular forms of speech which he was so fond of using. Nothing was more distasteful to him than empty, high-sounding phrases; both in conversation and in writing he clung to the Anglo-Saxon.

Among the books in his library is a small work on botany numbering eighty-eight pages and bearing the title, "Systematisches Verzeichniss der in der Oberlausitz wildwachsenden Pflanzen von M. Karl Christian Oettel, 1799." On the fly-leaf, in the boy's handwriting, in which is recognizable a strong similarity with the man's, are written the words: "My first book on botany." The interlinear marks, the underscorings and marginal notes on the well-worn pages of this little book show how diligently Constantine used it.

Although at this early age he was eager in the pursuit of scientific knowledge, he was alive to the importance of acquiring a skillful use of his hands.

Surgery seems to have been in his mind. This is shown by an anecdote he was fond of relating descriptive of his first operation. A younger sister, who occasionally accompanied him on his rambles through the woods, was so unfortunate as to have one of those troublesome ticks which infest the woods become fastened upon her. No other help being at hand, and the little girl declaring she would not see a doctor, Constantine had to perform the operation of extracting the tick from his sister's back; this the young surgeon, who was averse to shedding blood when it could be avoided, accomplished by gently but firmly grasping the insect's body and pulling with steady but almost imperceptible force. At first the insect, feeling opposition, began to tighten its hold, but it could not long resist the very *gradual* but *unrelenting* force which was brought to bear upon it and compelled it to release its victim. The boy had made an observation which was of use in after life, for he often successfully employed the "gradual force method" in practice, and sometimes when harsher means had been tried in vain.

In 1817, young Constantine was sent to an academy in Dresden where he studied surgery. A year later a copy of Euclid literally fell into his hands at an old book stall; the volume deeply interested him at once. He resolved to go home and give himself to Greek and Mathematics, which he did until 1820, when he went to Leipzig where he studied seven courses in medicine.

He next went to Würzburg, attracted to the seat of learning in this place by the fame of Schönlein, the pathologist, with whom he formed a friendship which his conversion to the doctrines of Hahnemann never disturbed. He was graduated at Würzburg with the highest honors. His medical examination was very severe—all the more so for his well-known devotion to Homœopathy.

For nine years, from 1817 to 1826, Dr. Hering's life was the life of a student. By his fellow-students he was nick-named "*Wisent*" on account of his energetic application to study. He struggled long with poverty. His privations were many. He first became interested in Homœopathy by engaging to write against it. His work was to be published by Baumgaertner. In it he first endeavored to define what is *similar* in the Homœopathic sense. Then he examined the Materia Medica of Hahnemann. "Beginning with the chapter headed Sensorium, I found," he said, "under every remedy *Schwindel*. I began to think it was all Schwindel!" When the book was nearly done he came across Hahnemann's challenge: "Disprove, ere you condemn!" He continued his investigations. Some mysterious agency seemed to him to lead him on to the belief that Hahnemann had found the truth. The book was never published. An old friend, an apothecary, was delighted to hear that he was writing against the new school, but when he went to this friend one day for a tincture of Peruvian bark, wanting it, as he told the apothecary, for a homœopathic proving, the man of the shop exclaimed: "My young friend, don't you know there is danger in that?" The young doctor replied that he was a student of mathematics and believed he could distinguish the true from the false. From that moment his old friend and other friends turned their backs on him. It was said by the more charitable that he was going crazy. In truth he became, as he said, a fanatic in the cause of homœopathy and preached it in season and out of season like a very apostle.

A remarkable personal experience had a decisive effect in his conversion to the new theory of therapeutics. In making an autopsy on the body of a suicide exhumed by the authorities, he was so unfortunate as to take into his system, through an abrasure on one of his fingers, some of the poison engendered in the decomposition of the dead. After some days the wound became gangrenous. Leeches, calomel and caustics were of no avail. Amputation as a last resort was rejected, as the loss of his hand would be fatal to his profession, and he would rather die than suffer it. He was at the time still under the old impression that it was absurd to suppose external diseases to be within reach of internal remedies, and he met with ridicule the proposition of an older disciple of Hahnemann to treat him with homœopathic pellets. Nevertheless, to please his friend, but with no idea of receiving any benefit, he consented to take minute doses of Arsenic. With the sense of relief that came to him as the wound began to heal, the light of the new art of healing broke upon him, he said, in all its fulness. "I owed to it far more than the preservation of a finger. To Hahnemann who had saved my finger, I gave my whole hand, and to the promulgation of his teachings, not only my hand, but the entire man, body and soul."

From studying homœopathy there was but a step to the practice of it. His success was cheering. He no longer suffered want.

He next became a teacher of natural sciences and mathematics in the Blochmann Institute in Dresden. Upon the recommendation of Blochman he was sent by the King of Saxony on a botanical and zoological expedition to Surinam and Cayenne. He made the expedition in company with his friend Weigel who was to attend to the botanical work while he was to have charge of the zoological department. He remained six years in Surinam. His zoological researches were extended over the full period of his stay, but only a portion of this time in the interest of the king. His love for homœopathy had by no means lessened in the pursuit and study of Nature's tropical wonders. The Moravian colony in which he resided offered every inducement for the practice of the new healing art. Although the scientific work had not suffered thereby, for he had sent many new and interesting specimens to the museum, and had assisted his friend Weigel in the preparation of a herbarium containing three thousand specimens of plants, letters to the king, written by enemies to homœopathy, reported him negligent in his trust, and sharp orders came to abandon homœopathy and attend to his specified duties. The unjust censure of the government made him decide to throw up his commission, which he did by return of mail. He now by no means relinquished his study of natural history, for he made many more curious and valuable discoveries, collected plants, reptiles and animals, sent numerous interesting contributions to the Academy of the Natural Sciences in Philadelphia, and practiced homœopathy at his own sweet will. He made many converts to the cause and educated a student, Dr. Bute, whom he sent North at the time of the outbreak of cholera in 1832, to try his skill against the epidemic. While his student was successfully battling with the cholera in Philadelphia, he went among the lepers who were colonized in the vicinity of Surinam, outcasts from society, and although unable to cure more than a few he did much to relieve the sufferings of many, and by his observations enriched the therapeutics of that dread disease, leprosy. He sent numerous medical articles to his friend Stapf in Germany who published them in his journal, "The Archives." He studied the habits and customs of the creoles, mulattoes, negroes and Arrowackian Indians. It was at the risk of his life that he penetrated into the forests to become acquainted with this wild tribe, and we owe to his affiliation with the sons of the tropical forest the discovery of the healing virtues that lay hidden in the poison bag of the Surukuku snake. Besides the serpent-virus he tested upon his own person a large number of hitherto unproven drugs, thereby enriching the Materia Medica. He married, but lost his wife soon after the birth of a son. This bereavement and the hope of finding a wider field for homœopathy, induced him to direct his steps to the North.

After a residence of more than six years in Surinam, his love of personal liberty, of freedom of speech and of thought, had so strengthened, that he was drawn, naturally, toward the United States, the country in which the freedom he loved was most ample.

His fellow-countrymen of the Moravian colony in Surinam were loath to have him leave them, and, as their custom was, invoked the Bible test in the matter. The book opened and the finger pointed to the text: "Well done, thou good and faithful servant; * * * enter thou into the joy of thy Lord." So, heavy of heart, yet seeing in his going, as they believed, the will of Providence, they sped his parting and gave him many things useful for the voyage. But whatever the omen given by the test might have been, Dr. Hering would not have suffered his purpose to have been changed by it. His strong nature resented any interference with his free will, least of all by an appeal to chance. He believed that each man must learn to judge and to decide for himself, and he lived up to this belief his life long.

The ship in which he sailed from Surinam was old, badly handled and ill-found. She was bound for Salem, in Massachusetts, but after going ashore upon the Rhode Island coast, she finally put into Martha's Vineyard. Here, on a beautiful Sunday morning, in January, 1833, he landed. On the ground lay the white snow, the first that he had seen for seven years, and the sight of it rejoiced his heart. "I took it up," he said, "and was happy." In a little while he came to Philadelphia, the city in which for nearly half a century his home was destined to be.

Dr. Hering was one of the pioneers of homœopathy in America. Eight years earlier Dr. Gram, the herald of the new school in the United States, had established himself in New York, and when Dr. Hering came to Philadelphia there were a dozen, perhaps a score, of homœopathic physicians scattered over the whole country.

He had to fight prejudice as well as disease, but his skill and his strength in the faith were great and he prevailed. His practice increased so largely and so rapidly that within a year after his arrival he engaged an assistant, and in this first year of his residence in America he took to himself a German wife, Marianne Hussman, daughter of George Hussman, of Philadelphia. Indeed, at last fortune seemed to show him heartily her favor.

A little less than a year after his arrival in Philadelphia, Dr. Hering was waited upon by a committee from the "Homœopathic Society of Northampton and Counties Adjacent," consisting of Drs. W. Wesselhoeft, H. Detwiller and J. Romig who were appointed to confer with him on the establishment of a homœopathic school of instruction, and on January 1st, 1834, Dr. Hering's thirty-fourth birthday anniversary, was proposed and adopted a plan, the result of which was the institution of the "North American Academy of the Homœopathic Healing Art," to be located at Allentown, Pennsylvania, with Dr. Hering as President and principal instructor.

This institution, the first of its kind in the world, was founded April 10th, 1835—Hahnemann's birthday—and in the following month Dr. Hering's connection with it began. The academy was started with much enthusiasm and with a fair prospect of success. A stock company was formed for the purpose of raising a fund to purchase a lot and building and to support the institution. About one hundred subscribers from Allentown, Bethlehem, Philadelphia and New York and in various parts of the country, raised a fund sufficient to buy a tract of land comprising a square block of ground in the centre of Allentown. A large proportion of this fund was raised in Philadelphia, and we must not here omit to make mention of the hearty cooperation of a valued friend of Dr. Hering, Mr. William Geisse, the introducer of homœopathy in Philadelphia; also of Dr. Geo. H. Bute who brought all the influence of his extensive practice to bear in favor of the new institution. Seven thousand dollars were subscribed by its promoters in a single day—such was their eagerness that the new school should be founded.

On May 27th, 1835, the corner-stone for the two wings of the main building was laid in the presence of a large concourse of people and friends of the undertaking. At the same time Dr. Hering delivered in the court-house the inaugural address, in the German language, entitled, "A few words concerning the necessity and usefulness of homœopathy;" his text, so to speak, being the words of George Washington: "*There is but one right way: to seek the truth and steadily to pursue it.*" The funds that were believed to be quite sufficient to provide for the maintenance of the Academy until such time as it should become self-supporting had been raised, but, unfortunately, this well-intended scheme miscarried; not, however, from intrinsic weakness, nor yet from any fault of those who had its management in charge. In the troublous period that ended in the financial crash of 1837, the banker with whom the endowment fund was deposited made a bad failure, and the money upon which the academy depended for its immediate support was lost. So the buildings which had been erected, and used but so short a time, were sold; and for the time being the collegiate teaching of homœopathy in America came to an end.

Dr. Hering had not labored in vain. During his connection with the institution his efforts to disseminate the germs of homœopathy were indefatigable. He taught the principles of Hahnemann, practiced them on the sick, wrote books and pamphlets, caused the German text books to be translated so as to bring their contents within the reach of all, and thus "became the cornerstone around and upon which his associates and colaborers clustered and leaned for support." He made many warm friends both among the laity and his professional brethren. At the instigation of his friend Wesselhoeft and with his help he labored extensively with the clergy who sought instruction and practised the new art *con amore* upon their parishioners who lived far away from the new doctors. With one of these clergymen, the Rev. John Helfrich, Dr. Hering formed a deep and lasting friendship, and before the close of his life he had the satisfaction of seeing no less than seven of this man's descendants, sons, grandsons and nephews, join the ranks of homœopathy.

While somewhat disheartened by this financial failure, Dr. Hering was far from being cast down. The active practice of his profession in Philadelphia remained to him, and in his work he found a substantial profit as well as a constant pleasure. A far more serious sorrow fell upon him in 1840, in the death of his second wife; a sorrow that softened only with time.

His fame as a leader in the new school of medicine by this time was established in Europe as well as in America. Several years after the collapse of the Allentown Academy he received an invitation from Hahnemann's widow to come to Paris and succeed to her late husband's practice; and later he was invited to establish himself in London. Honorable and tempting as these invitations were, he refused them both. After several years he felt, however, the need of change, of recreation after the sorrowful experiences through which he had passed; and his longing was great to see his Fatherland once more. So, giving to his brother-in-law, Dr. Hussman, the charge of his Philadelphia practice, he went over to Germany to visit his father in the old home. Here he remained until May, 1846, and here he married again. His third wife was Fräulein Therese Buchheim, daughter of Dr. Christian Friedrich Buchheim of Bautzen, Saxony, who remained the faithful partner of his life to its close. His visit to Germany was shortened by the news that came to him of the death of Dr. Hussman. On receiving this news he decided at once to return to America; and he came back with the full determination to make Philadelphia his permanent home. In the year 1852, he bought the house in Twelfth street, where he thenceforward lived and where he died.

From the time of his return to Philadelphia until close upon the time of his death he led the active, trying life of a city physician in large practice; a life of much toil, of much responsibility, of little rest. And yet in the midst of this arduous practice of his profession he made time for other good work. The seeking out and proving of new remedies, which for years past had received much attention from him, was zealously continued; and true to his belief that he who finds must give, he was diligent in placing in print, and so within the reach of his professional associates, the results of his investigations. His highly important discoveries, both in therapeutics and in Materia Medica[*], recorded in his voluminous writings, remain a lasting testimony to his constant labors, and the fit memorial of his useful life. Much of what he discovered was immediately imparted orally to his class of students in the Hahnemann College. In this institution, which he helped to establish, he occupied the Chair of Institutes and Materia Medica, and

---

[*] For a detailed account of his works and writings see Part II, prepared by Dr. C. B. Knerr.

latterly the position of Dean until 1869, when, in order that he might gain time to finish the important literary work that he had in hand, his resignation was tendered and regretfully accepted.

During his later years, as age and his literary labors pressed upon him, as a further relief from the cares of his profession he admitted to the honor of partnership with him his pupil and son-in-law, Dr. Calvin B. Knerr. But until the very last he continued to treat a large number of patients in their homes as well as at the office, and was considered indispensable by his brother physicians of Philadelphia in all important consultation cases, and was consulted by mail or telegraph in critical cases by homœopathic physicians living in the United States as well as abroad. Indeed, he loved his profession so heartily that while strength remained to him he would not upon any consideration relinquish its active duties.

On March 23d, 1876, he celebrated, or rather his friends celebrated, the fiftieth anniversary of his graduation in medicine. An engrossed parchment, handsomely framed, was presented to him by his professional associates. This parchment bore the following inscription :

To Our Revered and Beloved Colleague,

Constantine Hering,

Who, having received the Degree of Doctor of Medicine from the University of Wurzburg, March 23d, 1826, to-day, by the favor of Heaven, witnesses the Fiftieth Anniversary of that occasion, we, the Homœopathic Physicians of Philadelphia, in Mass Meeting assembled, offer our affectionate congratulations and good wishes.

To his exceptional intellectual ability, untiring industry, broad culture and liberal spirit, Homœopathy pre-eminently owes her firm establishment and vigorous growth in America. The year of his Jubilee finds him still occupied, in the same spirit, in labors for the same end.

Passing in review the forty-three years of his fellow-citizenship with us, we regard with grateful admiration his labors in the broad field of science, his unselfish devotion to the advancement of the Art of Healing, his generous demeanor towards his fellow-workers, and the pure record of his spotless life.

May a kind Providence long spare him to a profession which he honors, and to colleagues in whose heart he is cherished.

Attest:
A. R. Thomas, M.D., *President*.
Robert J. McClatchey, M.D., *Secretary*.

Jacob Jeanes, M.D.,
A. W. Koch, M.D.,
C. Neidhard, M.D,
H. N. Guernsey, M.D,
C. G. Raue, M.D,
Richard Gardiner, M.D.,
Committee of Signers.

On the same occasion the following addresses were made by his friends Drs. P. P. Wells, H. N. Guernsey and Carroll Dunham.

Dr. P. P. Wells spoke as follows:

Gentlemen:—On the first day of January, in the year of our Lord 1800, in the town of Oschatz, in Saxony, there was a remarkable event. It was the *birth of a baby*. Do you say there was nothing uncommon in that? I reply, this was no common baby. It was a very remarkable baby, and this was soon manifest. For immediately on his finding himself thrust into a world where he was compelled to do his own breathing, he at once began, with ceaseless activity, endeavoring to *find out all about it*. In this he was probably the most active baby that ever was born. He was never quiet, but ever restless, day and night, sleeping but little, for the most part wide awake and busy, *finding it out*. Do you ask how I know this? I have it by infallible inference from the fact that they named this baby CONSTANTINE HERING. So the baby lived and grew, sturdy and strong, ever thus employed, till babyhood became boyhood, and even this, strange as it may seem, brought no change as to this singular idiosyncrasy, he was ever and incessantly trying to *find it out*. This boy expanded into the youth, and he was the same, still *finding it out*. The youth had just merged into early manhood, when in March, 1826, and on the 23d day of that month, the University of Wurzburg presented him to the world as a Doctor of Medicine, and by this time he had *found out* a good deal. In the May following he received the honorable appointment of Teacher of Mathematics and the Natural Sciences in Blochmann's Institute, in the City of Dresden. In connection with this Institute, and in the interests of Natural Science, the king of Saxony sent him to the Southern part of this continent, in November of the same year. In this new situation the habits of early life were equally conspicuous. Enquiry and experiment were his constant employment. In these he never grew weary, and from these he never ceased till he had accomplished the objects of his mission; work ever seemed his only rest. In these labors nothing by its minuteness escaped his observation; nothing by greatness his mastering; nothing by its evanescence eluded his grasp. The molecule, the planet, and the lightning even were each and equally compelled to stand and yield up their secrets to the mastering mind of this young man. He continued in these employments in Surinam, S. A., about seven years. There was but one thing in all the difficulties attending his pursuits which he never could find out. That was the practical meaning of the word *impossible*. I strongly suspect he never believed there was such a word.

But on the present occasion it is not so much the man of science as the physician with which we have to do. We have said he was made a doctor in 1826. The remarkable thing about this is, they made an old school doctor of him, and he survived it. Survived it, retaining his earliest, early and later thirst for knowledge, with increasing diligence in its pursuit. This is certainly very remarkable, in view of the known fact that a young doctor no sooner lays his hand on the precious parchment, than he is seized with the absorbing conceit that now he *knows all about it*. This is especially apparent in the case of old-school young doctors. Under the influence of this delusion they almost uniformly drift away together into a total darkness as to all laws which can throw light on the science of therapeutics or direct its practice. The escape of our young friend from this common fate can only be explained when we know the fact that previous to the reception of this doctorate, he had become a convert to the truths of homœopathy. This saved him. Anchored to these he went out to bless the world by teaching them to others, and in the exercise of his pristine restless activity, to advance from these to a knowledge of new facts and principles in harmony with them, till he had gathered from his survey of the broad field of nature before him, such stores of knowledge of phenomena of disease, the effects of external agents on the living organism, the relations of these latter to the former, which constitute them their curatives, that he soon stood before the profession an acknowledged master, the peer of the noblest of them all.

Having accomplished the objects of his mission to Surinam, he started for his native country, in his progress to which he landed in Philadelphia, in January, 1833, with the purpose of soon resuming his journey, and in Dresden again to return to his official duties in the Institute, to the official staff of which he was still attached. But this he was never more to do. Providence blessed us by permitting him, who had mastered the planets and the lightning, to be himself conquered by the conqueror of us all, sooner or later. I need not say that victor was a lovely woman. She cast her spell over him and he was bound by it and could go no further. She became his, and through her power over him he became hers and ours from thenceforth.

These were the circumstances and this the manner of the advent among us, now more than forty-three years ago, of the man from whom has gone out, more than from any and all others, light and teaching which have made homœopathy what it is in the land to-day, a recognized power of beneficence, which, whoever will, may hate, but only the recklessly daring will longer make the object of a sneer, as all did at the beginning of his career among us, even the most pusillanimous and contemptible.

It may be well to look a moment at the state of things in the country at that time, as to all belonging to his favorite doctrines and practice There were no text-books in the language of the country, from which, if any were desirous of doing so, they could learn its principles. There were no manuals of Materia Medica or repertories to aid any who might wish to make practical application of the law of cure which homœopathy had proclaimed. There was almost no literature from which a knowledge of that system of curing, so generally believed to be absurd and as generally ridiculed, could be obtained. There were no schools where the homœopathic system of medicine was taught. There was here and there one scattered over the Eastern part of the country (with one exception, not two in any one place), but few altogether, who were endeavoring to practice, in part or in whole, with the light which was in them, according to the law of healing which Hahnemann had promulgated. These, taken as a whole, were not sufficient to modify in a great degree the total darkness which prevailed, as to all knowledge of natural law or principles controlling therapeutics of the time. Now how different is all this. We have text-books, manuals, repertories, literature and schools. Instead of the few scattered struggling ones who then scarcely gave light enough to make the prevailing darkness apparent, now there are thousands of intelligent practitioners of the school, furnished with all needed helps to facilitate their labors and aid their success. Such is the contrast between 1833 and 1876·

Now, as we have said, from Constantine Hering more than from any other man or men, have gone out the forces which directly or indirectly have wrought this great change. He taught publicly and privately, and he has taught incessantly, because he could not help it. Publicly in Allentown and Philadelphia. Privately wherever he has been, in season and out of season, always teaching. Whatever may have been the value of his public instructions, and we esteem them at the highest, we have no doubt those which were more and most private, have contributed more to the spread and triumphs of homœopathy, and the increase of the number of its practitioners. The abundance of these, and their influence on the minds and practice of men, none but the Omniscient can ever know. No one who has been blest with their benefits will ever forget them. Rich, free, full, generous, abundant, asking no reward but a listening ear and an absorbing mind, he was never weary of instructing the ignorant, strengthening the weak, encouraging the doubting and fearing, and leading any who needed guidance into clearer light and a self-sustaining confidence.

Early in the history of this period of change, even in distant New England, whose inhabitants have a traditional reputation for a disposition to *find things out*, there was here and there one who had heard that there was a system of cure called homœopathy; that it gave increased power to cure, as compared with the ancient school of practice founded on mere hypothesis, and that there was a man in Philadelphia who knew something about it. These went there and to him, were taught, and returned with light, which they were, more than for any other thing, anxious to make known to their neighbors. These neighbors came, and they were in turn followed by others, till the number was great who came to this centre of light, as to the Mecca of the new faith, and Constantine Hering became their prophet. It was in this way that homœopathy spread so rapidly in those days, and this place and man became *the* centre of the great light. I myself was one of those pilgrims in 1842. I know no way in which I can show so satisfactorily the spirit and manner of this private teaching, the noble, generous heart of the teacher, his unparalleled unselfishness and his unwearied patience, as by relating my first introduction to him by letter, at his residence in Philadelphia, and what followed. After reading the letter he said, "how long do you remain in town?" When told, he said "come to me to-morrow afternoon at 3 o'clock, and I will see no one else." At this time his consultation room was thronged by such numbers as have rarely been found in any other. Of course I did not fail to keep the appointment. He took me to a private room, turned the key in the lock, heeded no taps at the door, and from this time till far into the small hours of the night he was telling me just what I needed to know, without the least cessation. This was only interrupted by my inability to endure longer absorption, being an invalid, and not in the least by his tiring of pouring from his overflowing fulness into my empty vessel. Apparently he was quite willing to go on to I don't know what limit. When told I must leave and the cause, he at once said " come to me to-morrow afternoon at 3 o'clock, and I will see no one else." The second call was a repetition of the first, in the matters of instruction given and received, duration into the small hours, and like the other was brought to an end only by my inability to endure longer. He not only told me just what I needed to know, but what has been of practical use to me from that day to this. And this was all with such an air of evident satisfaction and enjoyment on his part, that I have no recollection of thanking him for his kindness. He dismissed me with so much of the manner of one who had just been blessed himself, rather than of one who had been imparting his wealth to another, that the picture as it is now in my memory, is a living, pleasing illustration of the truth, it is more blessed to give than to receive. I don't believe I thanked you then, sir, for your abundant goodness. I do not remember that I did, but I do it now from the very centre of a warm, grateful heart. Be assured, sir, I have never ceased to hold in memory a sense of your great goodness, or of the greatness of the benefit you then conferred on me.

Gentlemen, I have no reason for supposing this to be an exceptional case at all. There was no cause for partiality on his part for me. He had never heard my name or seen it, till he read the note I handed him. I had no claim on him for the least favor. There was nothing in me personally to call out such unexampled beneficence. The whole was a spontaneous overflow of his generous nature, such as always blessed the needy who called on him. And it has been by a continuance of such acts that he has made the impress of his mind so broad and deep on the homœopathic profession in this country. First, directly on those who came into immediate contact with him; and second, and indirectly, on those who were influenced in turn by the truths and principles these visitors carried away with them. The extent of this has been so great that it is safe to affirm it surpasses that made by any other or all others of his cotemporaries. So quietly and unostentatiously has this process of private teaching been going on, that it may be there are few who are aware that we are indebted to this man more than to any others, for what homœopathy is in this land to-day.

And then, further, he has taught us by contributions to the literature of our school, to an extent surpassing those of any man. The importance of these contributions is equal to their extent. The writings of no other man are so compact with thought, so abounding with facts contributed to our knowledge, with suggestions of relationships of these to other facts and to each other, so luminous with the effulgence of genius, so astonishing by the great labors they disclose. The wealth of thought and suggestion in these is so great, that in view of it one of the ablest masters of our school, Haynel, said to me—"Other men are constantly catching up the sparks which Hering is constantly throwing off, and expanding them into great fires, and passing them off as their own." And this is true. Take from the literature of homœopathy the contributions of Hering, and you have robbed it of half its wealth.

And now, gentlemen, I thank you for honoring me with the pleasant duty of tendering our united homage to our loved master and friend. While doing this I am assured that in view of his life long labors and their results, of his never failing loyalty to truth, his unwearied and incessant endeavors for its advancement and defence, of his ever generous, abundant and free instructions to those who were in need, and above all, of his spotless example as physician, citizen and friend, you will join me as with one heart, while I say to him—WELL DONE, GOOD AND FAITHFUL SERVANT.

And to you gentlemen, I would say, when you regard whatever in his character, life-work and devotion to truth, that which is most worthy, remember the homage which his great and good heart craves most of all from you, is contained in an obedience to this brief exhortation—GO THOU AND DO LIKEWISE.

Dr. Henry N. Guernsey spoke as follows:

Gentlemen:—It is with feelings of veneration that I rise to respond to the toast *Homœopathy*—that cause for which our distinguished colleague, Dr.

Constantine Hering, in honor of whose jubilee we have assembled tonight, has devoted so much of his lifetime, so much of the severest labor, mental and physical, and for the advancement of which he has accomplished so much, that his name must be co-identical with the science for all coming time. For centuries back there has been a constant reform and progress for the better in all the arts and sciences. The great religious reformation of the fifteenth and sixteenth centuries, arising after the important discovery of the art of printing, were to be followed by reforms of none the less value to the human race.

Less than a century ago, people in every part of the civilized world were feeling the need of *another* reform—a grand reform in *medicine*. The barbarous modes of practice then in use, involving nauseous and poisonous doses, deleterious and disgusting mixtures, that loved ones were compelled to swallow, resulting in more harm than good, conspired to cause a cry to go forth: "O that the Lord would send us something—some little sweet something, that we may take when sick to make us well again!"

This prayer, so earnestly uttered, the Lord has answered, in sending us *homœopathy*.

Homœopathy is a divine institution, and should be most sacredly held in trust by all its votaries, even as it was held by Samuel Hahnemann, whom the Lord deputed to impart it, and by his faithful disciple, whom we have brought here to-night, to show our gratitude, and whom we delight to honor. Homœopathy has shed a new light upon the whole medical world, and is everywhere making apparent its beneficial results. It teaches us that diseases are not entities—that they are not open to the natural sight, touch or taste, neither are they subject to the effects of weights or measures.

The scalpel cannot reveal, nor can the microscope behold them. All diseases are morbid effects of disordered dynamic forces, and to cure such an effect we must seek a dynamic force from the medical kingdom, whose subtlety in degree and quality *equals* the subtlety in degree and quality of that dynamic force, producing the disease. *This*, and *this alone*, is *homœopathy*. This science, based upon the law *similia similibus curantur*, is as true as the Bible! It comes from the same source, and it must ever shine as the great beacon-light in medical science, as the Bible is the great beacon-light in the science of theology. It must ever continue to heal more and more the suffering of the human race, as we come more and more under its real influence. It must ever and ever continue to overcome all other methods of medical practice, until homœopathy reigns supreme, as the grand and only law of cure for all manner of diseases in all varieties of living creatures.

Dr. Carroll Dunham spoke as follows:

Gentlemen of Philadelphia:—An invitation to Philadelphia, the Mecca of American medicine, and especially of American homœopathic medicine, could not fail to meet a cordial response from every homœopathic physician. An invitation from so numerous a body of our colleagues, representing so worthily our schools, our literature and our press, and on an occasion so interesting as the celebration of the jubilee of our venerated colleague, Dr. Hering, so touches us, that I am sure I utter the sentiments of all of my associates, when I thank you, in their name and my own, with my whole heart, for this opportunity, to unite with you in your graceful testimonial of homage and love to our honored friend.

If the opportunity had been as great as your large-hearted hospitality, and could have embraced the wide expanse of our country, these walls could not have contained the legion of those who would have come up hither to honor themselves, by honoring your venerable guest.

Gentlemen, this banquet, which your hospitality and good taste have crowded with viands from the ends of the earth, and decorated with flowers of every variety of loveliness and fragrance, constrains me to speak of the banquet at which our friend Dr. Hering has been entertaining us all, and all of our school in every part of the world, for a far longer time than my personal memory can recall.

For forty years the feast of reason has been spread in his study. The bill of fare, in our English and in his native German, has been widely distributed. The strong meat of scientific reasoning, the choicest fruits of keen and sagacious observation, the wine of a cheerful, hopeful confidence in the unity and consistency of natural law, the salt and spices of a pungent wit and a wholesome satire, the milk of human kindness and the flowers of poesy, have loaded the table, at which every student has met with a princely welcome, the only condition being that he should *be hungry and should eat.*

Twenty-eight years have passed since I, a hungry student, knocked at Dr. Hering's door, asking for mental food, and daring to expect at best a crust, or a soup-ticket directing me to some college. I was welcomed to his festive board, and there I have feasted ever since.

There is this peculiarity about his banquet, that, whereas *here*, what was order an hour ago is now confusion and a mass of *débris*, *his* table, spread for forty years, is now fuller and richer than ever, though so many have partaken of his cheer! Nay, he has assured me that though guests come lean and hungry, *as I did*, and take their fill, as I did, yet they rather add to than diminish his store.

To one thing I *know* they add—to the blessed consciousness of having done great good, of having made the rough paths smooth for multitudes of his colleagues, and through them, to multitudes of the people; a consciousness which, under whatever trials, must gladden these years of our dear friend's life!

At a time when many men give up their labors, Dr. Hering is crowding his table with choicer viands than he has ever offered us; and his welcome is still extended, as heartily as ever, to those who hunger for knowledge.

Gratefully acknowledging the courtesy of your entertainment, we utter our fervent gratitude to him in whose honor you give it, and pray for his health and welfare among you in the many years which we hope are still in store for him.

For a number of years preceding his death, Dr. Hering was troubled with an asthmatic affection that, while not threatening his life, caused him much suffering. In June and July, 1872, he had a severe attack of gastric fever that lasted for more than four weeks, and that left him for a considerable time sensibly weakened. In the summer of 1876, during the session of the International Congress of Homœopathic Physicians, after exposure to the hot July sun, he fell seriously ill. This illness continued for several months, and before entire recovery was made one of his attacks of asthma came on. The attack seized him in November and did not entirely relinquish its hold upon him until the following March. During this long period of prostration his inability to work distressed him greatly. He spoke of sickness as a miserable state of existence, and for a long while he remained sad and depressed. In February, 1877, when he was beginning somewhat to revive, the death of his dear friend Dr. Carroll Dunham took place, and the lively sorrow caused by this loss again cast down his spirit and materially retarded his recovery. Excepting the recurring attacks of asthma, the last two years of Dr. Hering's life were unattended by any marked symptoms of illness; indeed, shortly before his death, which was sudden,—the manner of which will be described later on—he had tolerable health.

Dr. Hering's coming to the United States was the result of well considered intention. He came not to make an experiment, but to carry out a carefully matured plan. After his arrival here he continued the study of our national institutions that he had begun in Suriname; and so fitted himself thoughtfully and conscientiously to be a good citizen of his adopted country. In politics he early took an intelligent interest, which later— when the events which induced the civil war were crystalizing—developed into a fervent enthusiasm. When Fremont was nominated for the Presidency his whole soul was in the nomination. He earnestly upheld the principles which Fremont represented, and he warmly admired that gallant young officer "who displayed a noble courage in far-reaching undertakings; who braved the dangers of hunger and cold; who enriched all the branches of the natural sciences, and who threw light upon a vast and almost unknown territory." During the ensuing political campaign he went to the trouble of making elaborate comparative statistical tables in which he exhibited the proportion of whites to blacks; of whites who could read, to whites who could not, and of foreign born whites to native whites in the several States and Territories; and he gave also very heartily his personal influence toward securing Fremont's election. His earnestness in this matter was due in great part to his intense hatred of slavery; and this same feeling caused him to throw himself with the whole strength of his being upon the side of the North when the war at last came.

Dr. Hering identified himself with the country of which he had become a self-elected citizen. He took pleasure in promoting the cause of learning, both by acting in conjunction with the several learned societies of which he was a member, and also by personally aiding many deserving young men in their struggle for education. He belonged to various charitable organizations, which were the better managed for his advice, and the better enabled to carry out their purposes by his assistance; and he did the work of many charitable organizations himself—a more zealous, a more wisely liberal man than he never lived. He kept himself abreast of the news of the day, local, national and general, and founded upon his knowledge opinions — positive, clear-cut and usually sound. And when the opportunity arose for him to make his personal force felt in support of his opinions he acted as decisively as he was wont to speak.

Yet, while thus discharging faithfully and positively his duties as an American citizen, he never lost his love for his Fatherland. He was deeply interested in German affairs always, and even in his young manhood he had faith in the eventual accomplishment of German unity. In the year 1826, while on a visit to Cologne, he was present at a banquet at which he predicted the completion of the great cathedral. His prophecy was received with much mirth, but, undaunted, he arose and gave as a toast the sentiment: "The Cathedral of Cologne will be completed as surely as Germany will become one and united!" With a good deal of ironical laughter the toast was drunk, and the young doctor was not a little complimented upon his excellent skill as a satirist. But he meant no satire; he was in dead earnest, and before he died Germany in very truth was united, and the completion of the cathedral was assured. During all the years of weary waiting his faith in the accomplishment of German unity never wavered. Indeed, it strengthened with his strength. How well he foresaw what was to come is shown in a lecture that he delivered in the year 1860, on the Natural Boundary, an utterance most remarkable as it now is seen in the light of subsequent events.

A fit pendant to this lecture is the following

account* of the celebration which took place at Dr. Hering's house, ten years later, when the unity of Germany had ceased to be a hope and had become a fact.

The unity of the Germans was celebrated in a Family Festival at the residence of the venerable Dr. Constantine Hering, on Twelfth street to-day. The exercises began at 7 A. M. The following was the programme:

Music by a quartet band of brass instruments under the direction of Carl Gaertner.

Wie schœn leuchtet uns der Morgenstern. Nicolai, 1599. "How beautiful the Morning Star."

Dr. Koch, who was then introduced by Dr. Hering, said:

If in any family any great event takes place, be it happy or unhappy, joyful or sad, the friends of the house assemble and express their sympathy or love, as the circumstances may dictate; that is, they will either betray sorrow, grief and affection, or they will, on a different occasion, express their joy, happiness or gratitude. As single families, so are great families of nations subject to occurrences which, happy or unhappy, joyous or sad, exert an influence either advantageous and productive of good, or disturbing and prejudicial, not only upon the inner form and order of government, but also as the single members of the nation's family.

As you all know, seven weeks ago a family, ambitious, haughty, desirous of glory, and believing itself invincible—the French nation—without cause, threw the gauntlet jeeringly at the feet of the German family, with the vain presumption of dividing its members, taking possession of its country and plundering it. The infamous declaration of war was accepted. The whole German family, sire and son, husband and wife, brother and sister, united like molten metal into one solid mass, one gigantic body. Germany, the land which had so often been visited by sore affliction, its inhabitants disunited and robbed of its territory, but now a united Germany, without stooping to pick up the soiled gauntlet, grasped with power-

---

* From the Philadelphia *Evening Bulletin*, September 10th, 1870.

ful hand the sword, and not only repelled the haughty invader, but drove him back into his home, where he is now awaiting the course things will pursue.

In order to express our sympathy, joy and exultation with true German feeling and character, at the brilliant and unexpected success of our German brothers, we to-day assemble, at the invitation of our friend Dr. Hering, to celebrate a *Family Festival*, in which we gladly participate to express our warmest congratulations on the happy victories of the United German people, and sing hymns of Praise to the *Father of all*.

Thus shall it be: No Suabia-land; no Prussia-land; no Pomerania-land; no Bavaria-land; but *one* FAMILY-LAND—ONE STRONG, UNITED GERMAN FATHERLAND!!

Music.

Ein feste Burg ist unser Gott.—Luther, 1529. "A mighty fortress is our Lord."

Rev. Dr. Barrett said that he was pleased to meet with Dr. Hering and his friends, this morning, to render thanks to Almighty God for the wonderful things He had done for the cause of right and humanity in Europe; for we have seen, in six weeks, that imposter and miserable schemer, Louis Napoleon, overthrown, and his dynasty ended. He had only to regret that the republicans in France failed to see that this war had been brought upon Germany by the Emperor, who was indeed France, and that the Germans had been compelled in self-defence to invade the French territory. It was now the clear duty of the Republicans who had come in possession of the French Government to sue for peace, and beg the clemency of King William to give them the best terms possible under the circumstance. If they failed in this, the leader of the German people would be justified in prosecuting the war to a legitimate close. The German people have great reason to give thanks to the God of nations, to whom all the honor and glory of their success belongs; and he thought the opening of this day of thanksgiving was very properly made in the songs of praise used by the early German Christians.

Music.

Nun danket alle Gott—Rinkhart, 1649. "Now thanks be given to the Lord."

Mr. J. R. Sypher, introduced by Dr. Hering, said: We have reached the opening of a new era. We read in history that the German people were pioneers in the history of civilization, were celebrated for profound learning, practical discovery, and an earnest Christian spirit in the true worship of God. We learn from the newspapers of the day that the Germans are a Sabbath-breaking, beer-drinking, a carousing, noisy, lawless populace. To-day history repeats its lesson. This scum that has long appeared on the surface is swept away, and the bright metal beneath appears. The historic German again comes to the surface, and the world is reminded that this noisy element that has so loudly claimed to represent the German character in America has set up false pretenses. We have had the carousing celebrations of German victories in the beer-saloons; but we here have the substantial, Christian-loving German people meeting to give praise to God for the great things He has done for their nation. The pioneer Germans who came to Pennsylvania in 1683, came with ministers, school-teachers, and printing press. They were the first to print the Bible in America, the first to establish Sunday-schools, the first to issue Sunday-school tickets, the first to establish schools that were absolutely free, and the first to protest against holding human beings in slavery. They have always loved learning, free schools, and pure, simple Christian worship. And this is being made manifest in the progress of the German armies, and the daily thanksgivings that go up from the camps of the German soldiers west of the Rhine. For this we have reason to be thankful.

Music.

Allein Gott in der Hœh' sei Ehr'.—Decius, 1540. "Glory be to God on high."

The company was invited to partake of coffee and sandwiches, and after that ceremony had ended the band closed the morning exercises (it might with propriety be called service) by rendering the Americanized tune "Old Hundred."

The music for this evening's exercises will be sung by the Mannerchor, and is as follows :

The Song of the Fatherland,	. . .	Arndt & Reichard, 1813
As one man we will rise,	. . . .	Karl E. Hering, 1846
They ne'er shall have the Rhine,	. .	Becker & Stunz, 1830
The Watch on the Rhine,	. . .	W. Mueller & K. Wilhelm, 1854
Why from Rummers Rhenish Wine, .	.	Gœttling & Methfessel, 1829
When Noah left his floating frame,	. .	Kopisch and Reissiger, 1850

Dr. Hering was a man of strong resolution. Slow in forming his plans, he was very determined in executing them; and while he would accept placidly inevitable digressions and interruptions he never lost sight of the end that he had in view. In support of his methods he often would refer to the fact that Cato, who likewise lived for the accomplishment of a great purpose, ended all of his speeches with the familiar saying: "Carthage must be destroyed." Whatever handiwork he attempted —and he could use well his hands—was done most carefully. His great principle in all things was to work gradually. What sometimes seemed to be a digression in his speech usually was found to be a by-path that, leading through pleasanter grounds, again joined and strengthened the main course of his argument. Short cuts he avoided both in talking and in acting. He abhorred the "too much trouble" creed. His indefatigable, painstaking spirit never was daunted by too much trouble in any undertaking that promised a gain to science. And his method of work, while apparently slow, really was rapid: because when his work was done once it was finished. It did not have to be laboriously revised, for each part was proved before it was set in place. This habit of precise labor was due largely to his love for mathematics. Euclid always was his favorite book; and much study of Euclid, strengthening the natural disposition of his mind, taught him to distrust hypothesis. It was his constant habit to seek out the why and wherefore of things, and he never was content until both the cause and the proof of the cause were found.

The results of his researches, as has been already said, he was ever ready to share with all who would receive them: for he held all discoveries to be not merely for one's personal use, but for the good of all mankind. He used the most bitter invective against those physicians who refused to give the results of their observations, when of general value, to the profession at large. "Where should we have been," he was wont to ask, "had Hahnemann kept homœopathy to himself? Where should I have been?—for homœopathy saved my hand, and with my hand my life! It is a great sin for a man to keep secret a medical discovery that will benefit his fellow men." Dr. Hering had, indeed, an ardent love for the cause of homœopathy, as for homœopathy itself, such as did not exist, to a like degree, in any other breast. If the need had arisen he would have sacrificed for its success everything that he possessed. In truth, in his early years, just as he was beginning to practice as a homœopathic physician, but while he was yet dependent upon the university for support, he did make precisely this sweeping sacrifice. Among his autobiographical reminiscences is the following: "My last farthing was gone. I went to the place where my weekly stipendium was paid and asked for the allowance that was due me. I received the money, but was told that I should have no more unless I gave up dabbling in homœopathy. I resented this insult by throwing the money which the chief of the institution had just paid me, at his feet, at the same time exclaiming: 'What right have you to speak to me thus? I shall never touch another penny of this money!'" This was a bold bit of ship burning; but boldness usually wins—in this case it did certainly. The autobiography continues: "From that moment I never suffered want. When I came home I found a call to attend a patient. My practice began to flourish and I soon had enough to do. The man at whose feet I had thrown the money turned homœopath, and later offered to pay back my money, but I was too proud to receive it." Of such stout stuff as this was the Doctor made, and such was his love for the cause of homœopathy. Once, hearing a fellow physician say that he was tired, he answered: "Yes, I am tired too—of life, of everything. But as long as I live I will work for homœopathy with all my power." He believed very firmly in Hahnemann's earnestly expressed belief in the principle of "oneness." He would say: "There is an individuality in everything that the Lord has made. You cannot substitute one medicine for another. To mix medicines is a crime. Alternating is the half-way house to mixing. To make a poor prescription when much driven is excusable. But the questions which always must be kept freshly in mind are: What is your aim? What are you striving for? If a homœopathic physician once adopts the too-much-trouble creed he is lost." It certainly was not his creed. His rules of practice, golden rules, he called them, were: Learn to observe. Learn to prove. Learn to examine the sick. Learn to select a remedy. Learn how to repeat and how to change remedies. Learn how to WAIT. Learn how to profit by experience.

As the traits of character which are presented here sufficiently show, Dr. Hering was a philosopher. He looked at life from a high standpoint, and he saw life broadly. The results of discovery and of invention, the ideas of philosophers, the thoughts of poets, the works of artists, inspired him with admiration; and these, he believed, rather than the petty details of the acts of individuals and of nations, constituted the true history of the world. He believed that history, in the ordinary acceptation of the term, was governed by laws as fixed as those which govern the movements of the planets. He did not, either in great matters or in small, believe in chance. He was at one time a student of Kant, Hegel, Schopenhauer, but he was not wholly satisfied with the systems of these philosophers. "My metaphysics," he would say, "are written for shoemakers and tailors. If not intelligible to all, I'll have none of it." But what he deemed to be sound philosophy he placed above even his favorite mathematics—regarding it, possibly, as the mathematic science in a still more sublimated form. "The mathematician," he would say, "must learn to think and to ask the question 'Why?' at every step. And this is the first principle of mathematics." His concept of the order that obtained in history was peculiar. He believed that as there are governing laws in space so are there also governing laws in time. He argued: "In medicine we observe certain symptoms and expect others. From what we see and from what we infer we make a prognosis. It is so in history. We see events, and, by a process of reasoning, not prophecy, we draw from these events conclusions. History is regulated by laws. These laws bring about events. They are as sure and as harmonious as the laws which regulate the motions of the heavenly bodies. Events move in history with the same certainty that the planets move in their ellipses."

His philosophic temperament, as well as the nature of his mental processes, may be illustrated by a few pithy sentences found in his writings or treasured in memory from his speech:

Ideas rule the world.

All new ideas must be received like new-born children and cherished tenderly, for on them depends the future.

The thoughts of man develop; premature negative proof, therefore, is harmful.

We must neither accept nor reject a thing without reason.

Conclusions in science must be drawn consecutively, like links in a chain.

Houses, wards, cities, counties, states! Is not our Union built upon the Gothic plan?

Has anything ever been done in the world without being carried to extremes?

What does not advance, recedes; nothing remains fixed.

The side that hates, loses.

If every physician pondered over his work as much as does a shoemaker over his, more people would get well.

When asked how he could wait tranquilly so long while some of his theories were being proved to be true he answered, with Kepler: "The Lord had to wait a long time before people understood the harmony of His creation!"

"I was asked the other day whether it was not very trying and discouraging to meet with ungrateful patients. "Ingratitude!" said I, "why we meet it every day. Our Lord and Master met little else. God, surely, has more cause to complain of it than I have."

In his philosophy, as is seen here, was true religion; and so it was with all that pertained to him, for religion was a part of his life. He was a true Christian. The existence of a God was with him an axiom as well sustained as any in mathematics. He believed in free will, and he had a firm faith in a future existence. He argued, interrogatively: "What would this great world of the Creator be if there were no hereafter?" And his faith was great. Once he said: "I have trusted in Providence all my life; even sometimes in a way that has been called superstitious by my friends;" and this simple-hearted trust in a good God remained with him till the end. There was an entire freedom from ostentation about his religion. It was sincere, practical; and it was eminently cheerful; he did not surround the greatest joy of his life with gloom. His motto was: Love the Truth because it *is* Truth, and the Good because it *is* Good. This was the rule of life by which he lived; and, having lived by it he was waiting and ready when the time came to depart.

LITERARY LIFE.

Dr. Hering in his Study.

LITERARY LIFE.

A LONG and busy life is best understood through a knowledge of the works which have made that life useful; and there is no better way of becoming acquainted with an author than by examining and studying what he has written.

A very considerable portion of Dr. Hering's life, particularly the early morning hours, beginning at three o'clock, were devoted to literary work. His books and manuscripts were his companions by night, for his sleeping couch was placed in his library. Before it stood his writing table covered with material and necessaries: quills uncut and quill-pens in all stages of usefulness and uselessness; blue ink, used in preference on account of its readiness in drying; red and blue crayons, convenient for proof marking and for making marginal notes and interlineations; paperweights and blotters, scissors, penknives and paper-cutters, all in apparent confusion, but within easy reach. The light burning over this table had an attachment by which he could regulate it without taking the trouble to rise.

When the sleeper awoke all his materials were ready, and by curtailing sleep, which his excellent constitution seemed to allow him to do with impunity, many a small hour of the morning, when all was quiet in the house and on the street, was devoted to his literary work. This work was generally protracted until patients required his presence in the office. It was only on rare occasions such as Christmas and New Year's day, the latter his birthday, that he consented to interrupt his matutinal labor to join his family at the breakfast table. A cup of coffee or chocolate, generally prepared by Mrs. Hering, or himself, on a small gas stove, with a rusk or two, was all the breakfast that he took. The arrival of the morning paper, which he always read with interest, furnished a pleasant change of occupation and brought him in sympathy with the outside world. Nothing in it was too trivial to enlist his attention, excepting, perhaps, the fashions; and these not infrequently gave him an excuse for railing at the frailties of human nature, which he enjoyed doing, and did with all the force and freedom of which he was capable. But his chief morning pleasure, one to which he looked forward as to the rising of the sun, and one that came with almost as perfect regularity, was a daily visit from his friend Dr. Raue, whom he loved as a brother, and who came faithfully and unfailingly, through all weather, between the hours of nine and ten, for a chat with his revered old friend and teacher.

Where but a brief synopsis of an author's writings is all that space will allow, perhaps the best plan to pursue is that which gives the titles of his essays and books, arranged in chronological order, together with brief comments upon and extracts therefrom sufficiently characteristic to convey an idea of the man's views, aim and style. This I have striven to do in the following condensed review of Dr. Hering's writings. Most of the matter here reproduced had to be translated from the German, the language in which his pen was most fluent, and this I have done less with the intention of rendering the original into literal English than of catching the essence and spirit of the writer's style and so reproducing a likeness, if possible but one remove from the original.

The products of Dr. Hering's pen, principally in the form of essays, are diffused among numerous medical journals covering a period of over fifty years. The titles of these essays and the places where they may be found I have quoted, so that all who wish to peruse what he has written, may do so without much trouble by consulting the volumes in the Homœopathic Library. His later literary efforts were concentrated upon his larger medical works. A short review of these is all that space will allow. They are complete in themselves so far as they have appeared in print, and are available to practitioners; but they are links which, connected, form the chain of scientific research in which is summed up the experience of his life. In his earlier years, when cares were not so thick, nor duties so pressing, he wrote verse and light prose, fairy tales, satires and novelettes. A satirical vein runs through all of his writings, playful in the lighter products of his pen, but extremely biting and severe when in polemics he is called upon to defend the cause.

Although Medicine and the Natural Sciences were his chief love, poetry and music claimed their share of attention. Like most German students, he was passionately fond of music and the stage. Some of his leisure moments were even devoted to the composition of opera texts. Of these the principal ones were "The Water Sprite," in which the scenes are laid at the bottom of the sea, and "Der Arme Heinrich," a poetical subject which greatly pleased Spohr, who seriously thought of setting the words to music. Some of his short stories, "Die Wiedergefundene," and "Rosamunde," a novelette, were published in a series of stories, written by his elder brother Ewald and published in 1826–28 by Kollman in Leipzig under the title of "Sandsteine." These met with a ready sale, the proceeds of which helped the brothers to defray the expenses of their university course. As we read in the biographical portion of this memoir, in his early school days he wrote a composition showing that Peter the Czar was a tyrant, and so drew upon himself the stern criticism of his teacher Rudolph. It showed that "the boy was the man in miniature," who continued through life to attack fearlessly error and falsity, little caring from what source they came.

When a little more than twenty-one years old, came his engagement to write a book against Hahnemann, which was to be published by Baumgaertner in Leipzig. The book was nearly done when his conversion to homœopathy took place. He speaks of this event himself in these words:

> My services were employed to write a book against homœopathy. I first attempted to give a definition of what is similar. Next I examined the Materia Medica. Beginning with the chapter on Sensorium I found *Schwindel* under every remedy. I began to think it was all *Schwindel!* I continued my investigations. It seemed as if some mystic agency was luring me on to conviction, for there was rhyme and reason in everything.

The episode of the wounded hand occurred and put an end to this undertaking. He often said: "I am glad that my book never was printed."

As the result of his conversion he wrote an essay entitled "The Future of the Healing Art," which he sent for publication to the editor of the first homœopathic journal, *The Archives*. After the almost miraculous restoration of his hand by the infinitesimal doses of *Arsenicum*, administered by his Hahnemannian friend, he says: "The last veil that blinded my eyes to the light of the rising sun was rent and I saw the light of the new healing art dawn upon me in all its fulness." Then followed the medical examination and his thesis, "De Medicina Futura." His characteristic boldness showed itself again in this, for he stood up, a poor student, before an august body of learned medical men, the faculty of the time-honored University of Würzburg, and defended the tenets of homœopathy as taught by the fanatic Samuel Hahnemann.

From the time of his graduation in 1826, onward, but few years passed unmarked by contributions from his pen, as the following chronologically arranged statement shows. Almost with the beginning of homœopathic literature began his contributions to it; and these were extended continuously over a period of more than fifty years.

1828.—Extracts from letters from Suriname to Dr. E. Stapf. —*Archives of Homœopathic Medicine*, vol. vii.

1830.—1. Communications by letter from Parimaribo on the treatment of Leprosy with Homœopathic remedies. 2. Report of a case of fungus hæmatodes.—*Stapf's Archives*, vol. ix.

1831.—1. Some remarks on the dispute between therapeuticians and pathologists. 2. First remarks on snake poison. 3. Fragmentary observations on Hufeland's latest remarks on homœopathy and its founder. 4. The antipsoric remedies in their relation to leprosy. 5. A proving of Caladium seguinum. 6. Fragmentary remarks on the study of remedies and on diagnostics. 7. A proposed plan for a more complete repertory.— *Stapf's Archives*, vol. x.

1832.—1. What is necessary to the calling of a successful homœopathic practitioner. 2. A fragmentary proving of Selenium.—*Stapf's Archives*, vol. xii.

1833.—A Concise view of the Rise and Progress of Homœopathic Medicine. An Historical Treatise on Homœopathy delivered at the meeting of the Hahnemann Society in Philadelphia, April 18th, 1833.

This essay was written in German and translated into English by his friend Dr. Charles F. Matlack. For the motto on the title page, Dr. Hering selected the words of George Washington, "*Is there a doubt? Let experience solve it. To listen to mere speculation in such a case were criminal. Experience is the surest standard by which to test real tendency.*" The spirit of the essay may be recognized in the following parapraphs from it:

> In England and the United States little is heard of the new art. They have scarcely begun to hear of the medical reformation even now rising up before them. Some reviewers, only within a few years past, have noticed the writings for and against homœopathy. These countries have conducted themselves with the utmost quietude and discretion. In both, the physicians of which, for the most part, being governed more by experience than by theories, it has been admitted that if the system were true, it would lead to highly important consequences. Yes, certainly experience would long since have been appealed to, if alas! the almost general unacquaintance with the German language among the better classes (one of the most important languages for the arts and sciences), had not hindered that result. Soon indeed, will this defect be supplied by translations, but may we not hope that the period is not far distant when, in the United States at least, the worth of German science and of the language of Germany will be generally acknowledged? May the day soon appear in which the rich and fortunate inheritance of two thousand years of European culture, uniting the practical views of the English with the ardent zeal of the French, shall embrace also the depth and solidity of the German; so that whatever Europe may produce hereafter of greatness in science may, without difficulty, be here appreciated in this central point of the future history of man.

May our beneficent Society largely contribute to the wider prevalence and reception of the Hahnemannian doctrines; may that which single individuals can of themselves scarcely achieve, be effected by united efforts. Then in this blessed country may the miseries of disease be diminished, future generations be rescued from its leaden fetters, the bitterest human misery, disease bearing down all earthly joy, become less from year to year, and the sweetest boon on earth, health and domestic felicity, become the portion of growing thousands here as well as in Germany. In spite of all adversaries, in spite of all impediments, it will, nevertheless, succeed here sooner than in Europe; for, among a free people, who, with practised eyes, soon discern the truly useful, a treasure like this new art, must quickly be estimated in a degree commensurate with its real value; sooner here than by the kings and princes of Europe, who have other and more important cares; sooner here than in those countries where ancient institutions and proscriptive interests are supported by a vigilant police, who impede the progress of the new art by processes, penalties and bayonets. Here we are beyond such influence. The American people demand facts, and upon these we can confidently and securely rest for our support. The language of opposition may be employed, but truth is no longer obscured here by forms of speech. The victory will be ours; and in a century to come, the anniversary of our society—this first step upon the way which must lead to the public and general acknowledgment of the new doctrines —will be solemnized with grateful remembrance. So great an aim, indeed, cannot be attained without labor, but we are prepared to undertake it; we shall not arrive at it without conflict, but we stand equipped for conflict; we shall not reach it without defamation; but we will suffer ridicule and defamation with composure.

1. Fragmentary reports of symptoms. 2. A survey of the entire kingdom of drugs. 3. Preparatory attempt to serve as a guide in making future investigations (57 pages). 4. Hypothesis and Experiment. 5. Miasm and Contagion. 6. Pathogenesis and Patho-exodus, and various items of news.

7. Remarks on Psorinum. 8. On the repetition of the dose.—*Stapf's Archives*, vol. xiii.

1834.—1. What do you mean by "Similar?" 2. Fragmentary remarks on the action of several drugs on the well and sick. 3. Theridion currassavicum and Lachesis. 4. A philological note to the word "psorinum."—*Stapf's Archives*, vol. xiv.

The question "What do you mean by 'Similar'?" treated at length in the above-named essay, he had asked as early as the year 1822. He differed from the theories put forth by Hahnemann in this as well as in most other respects; and he declared his opinions candidly during the lifetime of the Master. He was the first to attack Hahnemann's doctrine of primary and secondary effects. He was the first who openly defended pathology against Hahnemann's views; and so successfully that Hahnemann sanctioned the teaching of pathology in the Allentown Institute. He was the first to propose triturations and dilutions in the decimal scale instead of in the centesimal scale used by Hahnemann. Yet, while he had little to say in favor of Hahnemann's theories, he strenuously defended Hahnemann's inductive method of reasoning and the practical rules that resulted therefrom.

1835.—Snake Poison as a Therapeutic Agent.—*Stapf's Archives*, vol. xv.

In 1831, in the same journal, as has been noted, he had

mentioned snake poison, and had predicted that experiment would raise it to the position of a valuable medical agent. This belief was founded upon the facts that its inoculation produced an effect similar to that of the most active vegetable poisons, and that its action, when taken internally, resembled that of the slow but deep acting metalloids. He now, after repeated provings and successful applications in practice during a period of five years, declared it to be a polychrest, a remedy at least equal in importance to any hitherto in use.

1835.—Domestic Physician. 1 vol. First German edition.—*Jena*.

This work, begun in a small way by Dr. Hering, and given to his friends and patients as a guide and keepsake on leaving Suriname, has passed through fourteen editions in Germany, seven in America and two in England. It has been translated into French, Spanish, Italian, Hungarian, Danish, Swedish and Russian. From its small beginning, a 32mo. volume of 290 pages containing instructions for the use of forty-five remedies, the work has grown until now, in its latest revised American edition (1883), edited by Dr. Claude R. Norton, with the assistance of Dr. Hering's daughters, Mrs. J. Foster Pope and Mrs. C. B. Knerr, and published by F. E. Boericke, of the Hahnemann Publishing House, Philadelphia, it has come to be an octavo volume of 450 pages, containing a list of sixty-six remedies, together with the symptoms of diseased conditions to which they are applicable. The purpose of this work was to popularize homœopathy, as is declared by the motto upon the title-page of the new edition: "*The greatest triumph of a science is when it becomes the common property of the people and thus contributes to the common weal.*" The purpose has been successfully accomplished. Probably there is not a village in the civilized world, the inhabitants of which have not seen or heard of this homœopathic help at home, and many of them have felt its blessings.

1836.—1. A Preface to the first American edition of Hahnemann's Organon. Allentown. 2. Homœopathic Tracts for the People: [1] The Life of S. Hahnemann. [2] Seven Characteristics of Hahnemann's Method of Cure. Skepticism. [4] Trial of Dr. Pelleteer in the County of Pukedom.

1837.—Hints by which to form a correct estimate of Hahnemann's Organon.—*Stapf's Archives*, vol. xvi.

Here again is found the free and independent spirit of the author who dared to differ with the master whom he revered and honored, and to whose practical rules he paid the highest homage, but of whose theories he did not accept a single one as given in the Organon. And this frank admission of difference of opinion on the part of a younger enthusiast in the cause, called forth encomiums from the master whose progressive mind led him to hold light theories, even his own, which were not borne out by experience. "Let Hering alone," he said, "he knows what he is about. All theories and hypotheses have no positive value, but this: that they lead to new experiments and a clearer contemplation of the results of previous ones."

3. The Effects of Snakepoison, comparatively arranged for therapeutic use, with an introduction on the study of the Homœopathic Materia Medica. 1 vol., 8vo., 115 pp. (German), Allentown.

This book, although called by the author "an initial step," marks an epoch in homœopathic literature, since it is the first attempt at classifying the pathogenetic and therapeutic effects of the virus of an important family in natural history, the ophideans, comprising Lachesis trigonocephalus, the South American Surukuku; Crotalus horridus, the North American rattlesnake; Vipera torva, the German viper; Vipera Redi, the Italian viper; and Naja tripudians, the East India cobra; according to a scientific plan. The symptoms of the poison (most extensively proven by Dr. Hering upon himself), the effects of the bite of the snake, and the results of clinical experience with their conditions or modalities, are 3,800 in number. In each instance the authority for the symptom or its origin is quoted, and in most instances counter-reference is made to symptoms bearing a similarity or relation to the one under consideration. The work is a marvel of painstaking industry, an example of the same love for work and exactness which characterized all his subsequent labors in Materia Medica. A reprint from *Stapf's Archives*, of cases cured by Lachesis, appeared in volume II (1844) of the *British Journal of Homœopathy*, and in the same volume was published a translation of the article "On the study of the Homœopathic Materia Medica."

1838.—1. The Study of Homœopathic Materia Medica.— *Stapf's Archives*, vol. xvii.

2. Jahr's Manual, translated from the German by authority of the North American Academy of the Homœopathic Healing Art, with an introduction by Dr. Constantine Hering. 1 vol., Allentown.

To this translation is appended a criticism on the original work. The translating and editing, as well as the printing of the book, was a gratuitous labor and the profits realized from the sale of it were appropriated to the support of a charitable medical institution.

1844.—An Answer to F. Freiligrath's Epistle to Audubon. A Poem. (German) Philadelphia.

Freiligrath's poem deploring the loss of the red man's liberty, warns him against the white invader and counsels him to resist both missionary and yeoman in order that his freedom may be preserved. In the answer allusion is made to the hatred existing between the various tribes of red men; to their unfitness to govern themselves or others, or to make use of the resources that lie buried in their domain; to the awe the Indian feels in the presence of any of the triumphs of civilization, in all of which he sees or divines the working or influence of the Great Spirit—the might of the ploughshare, the axe in the forest and the smoke of the forge. The conclusion arrived at is, that while the songs of the poet himself will live immortal, the savage will disappear before the march of civilization.

1845.—1. Bromine, Chlorine, Fluoric Acid and Sanguinaria. 2. What is Similar? 3. Newer Provings.—*Stapf's Archives*, vol. xx. 4. Remarks on Jenichen's High Potencies. 5. Preface to the English translation of "Chronic Diseases," (published in New York in the same year.) 6. Reminiscences of Scarlet Fever epidemics. 7. On the relationship of plants. 8. Incidental to citation-visitation. 9. A proposed plan for exchange of homœopathic preparations. 10. Pathological Anatomy viewed from its useless side.—*Allg. Hom. Zeitung*, vol. xxix.

11. Homœopathic Hackels, old and new, for friend and foe. 1 vol. 8vo. Pp. 70.—(*German*) *Jena*.

This is a collection of Essays, in German, written at various times between 1832 and 1846, on subjects pertaining to homœopathy. As the title indicates, the author here hackles and tears to pieces the arguments of foolish critics and objectors, like flax upon hatchels. The humor in these pages is, however, more playful and not so biting as in the "New Hatchels," which appeared fifteen years later. The subjects discussed in Old Hatchels are,—The Loftiness of Critique (1846); Wiseacreism (1845); Primogenitureship, or, The Mess of Pottage (1845); "What is to become of observation, when such presumptions are made? The Art of Settling the Question without Proof, a funeral discourse read before the Society of Ignoramuses in Lieberwolkandwitz; and Squirting Cucumbers.

1846.—1. Marginal Notes to the Materia Medica. 2. Fluoric acid cases. 3. What is Similar? Part Second.—*Stapf's Archives*, vol. iii. New Series. 4. A survey of our provings, arranged according to provers. An historical summary.—*Allg. Hom. Zeitung*, vol. xxxi. 5. A parody on Schiller's Song of the Bell. Pp. 45.—(*German*) *Jena*.

The parody of the "Song of the Bell" conveys some valuable hints to church and state, at the same time, it admirably preserves the rhythm and swing of the celebrated original. The parody was published under the pseudonym of "Schoolmaster of Hippelau."

In the *British Journal of Homœopathy* for this year (vol. 4), is published the anecdote, often related by Dr. Hering, of the patient who was in search of three physicians who would agree on his case.

1847.—1. The requisites to a correct estimate of Hahnemann. —*Hygea*, vol. xxii. 2. A letter to the editors "On High Dilutions."—*Brit. Jour. of Hom.*, vol. 5.

1849.—1. A note on Calcarea arsenicosa in epilepsy.—*Brit. Jour. of Hom.*, vol. vii. 2. Glonoine.—*Quart. Hom. Jour.*, vol. i. 3. Preface to the third American edition of Hahnemann's Organon.

1851.—1. Introduction to the American translation of Jahr's Symptomatology.—*Allg. Hom. Zeitung*, vol. xl. 2. Remarks on proving Arsenicum metallicum. 3. Daily cycles in Diseases and the Effects of Drugs. 4. Fragmentary contributions to Materia Medica and Therapeutics. 5. Proving of Gymnocladus Canadensis, the Chicot or Coffee tree. 6. Requisites to a correct estimation of Hahnemann, (translated from Hygea.) 7. Jatropha Curcas. 8. Myrtus Communis.—*North Am. Jour. of Hom.*, vol. i.

1852.—1. Psorinum and its chemical rescue (reprinted in North Am. Jour. Hom., vol. ii). 2. Annual recurrences.—*Allg. Hom. Zeitung*, vol. xliii. 3. American drug provings and preparatory work for constituting Materia Medica a Natural Science.—*Zeit. für. Hom. Klinik*, vol. i.

1853.—1. A reply to the "open letter" in vol. xliv. 2. A protest against falsifying history.—*Allg. Hom. Zeitung*, vol. xlvi. 3. On the periodical annual recurrence of certain phenomena (a translation of "Jæhrlich zur selben Zeit in Allg. Hom. Zeitung, vol. xliii). 4. Pathology and the Materia Medica. 5. On Materia Medica as a Natural Science. 6. Characteristic effects of Allium cepa, the common onion, with a history of the remedy.—*North Am. Jour. of Hom.*, vol. iii.

7. Suggestions for the proving of drugs on the healthy. (Adopted by the American Prover's Union and published in pamphlet form). Pp. 29.

1854.—The Voluntary System of Medical Education. A pamphlet. 20 pages. Philadelphia.

This pamphlet was an attempt to elevate the standard of medical education. In it he says:

> The rivalry of the schools in the business of doctor-making illustrates the old proverb, that "competition is the life of trade," but, let it be observed, it reduces medicine from the rank of a liberal science to that of a trade, by which the public is injured, the profession degraded, and only the traders are profited. It is not intended to say that every faculty of professors are so destitute of honor, conscience and professional pride as wantonly to sacrifice principle to interest, but it is not too much to say that too many faculties are seduced from their integrity, and that these have the power to lower the standard and compel submission in a greater or less degree from the worthier or more honorable institutions. * * * The public ought to have a more disinterested and reliable judgment in the premises. * * * At least three-fourths of the medical schools in the country are but copies of each other to all practical and important purposes. They teach nearly the same doctrines in nearly the same way; on nearly the same conditions of time and expense, and their diplomas are as nearly of the same value. Some of the professors have a higher reputation both at home and abroad than others and deserve it too, but the system under which they all work gives their pupils little or no advantage that should result from this difference of ability. Limited and crippled as these institutions are by the policy which rules them, the emulation, so natural and beneficent, which otherwise might inspirit them to noblest effort degenerates into a mere rivalry for reputation and material prosperity. They should be put under happier influences. A school must be deemed

peculiarly fortunate, that has four or five out of seven of its faculty in every way qualified for teaching acceptably and advantageously. There are not a few instances where one or more chairs are held by men tolerably well, or even very well skilled in the branches which they are appointed to teach, but very badly qualified to impart instruction. Indeed there are not many instances in which more than three or four are such as the classes would choose, if they had the liberty of making their own selections, while in an edifice not more than half a dozen squares distant, they could find the very teachers whom they would gladly prefer to those comparatively incapable men who are fastened upon them.

But even more than this: these faculties are monopolies, exclusive as well as inclusive. They at once contain and retain mischiefs which are now nearly incapable of reformation, and they shut out and keep out benefits, which would be worth more to the cause of medical education than all that they in fact secure. They shut out from the office of teacher all those able men of the profession who have not the influence of cliques and the aid of extraneous advantages to procure their election to professorships in well established colleges, or cannot find vacancies waiting to be filled, or such vacancies as they are best fitted by talents, taste and special study to fill to the best advantage. The courses of lectures given under the present system are entirely too short. During the session of four or five months six or seven branches are taught, or are attempted to be taught, by as many professors, lecturing, say, seventy hours each. The lecturers themselves invariably complain of the shortness of the time allowed. They hurry, skip and finally make a dead halt before they have nearly traversed the ground which they intended to occupy, and every succeeding winter make the same haste and the same omissions upon the same grounds of excuse. This complaint lies very justly against the system. It is every day made by its own supporters, but it is one for which the system itself admits no remedy. Out of the customary limitation to a duplicated session of four or five months (the two sessions which make up the term of public instruction are, in fact, but copies and repetitions of each other), there grows an unavoidable confusion of study, a mixture without order, relation, or natural sequence and dependency. This must be remedied. A change is demanded, not merely, however, to afford room for the subject matters of the customary programme of instruction, but to give room and verge enough besides for all those auxiliary natural sciences, and related departments of remedial practice which are now entirely shut out. Many of them are as essential to an adequate medical education as any of those which it embraces, and all are of such value that any scheme of study which excludes them must sooner or later be discarded. A Doctor of Medicine should be a man fully informed of all that experiment and observation have revealed to discoverers in every range of inquiry which promises the acquisition of a new truth, or the correction of an old error. It is a fatal objection against the systems of medical education in vogue, that they not only make no provision for such liberality and comprehensiveness of inquiry, but absolutely prevent it.

"To abate these evils and to provide the required conditions for freedom and progress in medical science," Dr. Hering, assisted by a number of influential citizens of Philadelphia and vicinity, among them Henry C. Carey, the political economist, procured an act of incorporation from the legislature of Pennsylvania, dated May 8th, 1854, for the establishment in Philadelphia of such an independent medical school. Its name was to be the The Independent Medical School of Pennsylvania, and its constitution, its powers and policy were to be based upon the Voluntary System. Its grand aim was liberty of teaching and liberty of hearing. The free intermingling of students of the several systems the founder hoped would speedily remove the bigotries which now discredit the profession, retard its progress and impair its usefulness. With these aims the proposed institution was submitted to the judgment of the public. But, as happened more than once in the life of the originator of the proposition, his plans were ahead of the times, and although he no doubt had with him the agreement of the mass of college graduates throughout the country the enterprise failed for want of practical aid. Nevertheless the doctor never faltered in his efforts to infuse a higher moral enthusiasm into college life. How far he succeeded his associates and pupils will have cause gratefully to remember.

1854.—1. The Pathologizing of Materia Medica. 2. A collocation of essentials to a good drug proving.—*Allg. Hom. Zeitung*, vol. xlvii.

During the years 1854, '55 and '56, Dr. Hering, in conjunction with Dr. Lippe, edited *The Homœopathic News*, a monthly bulletin, each number containing eight pages of printed matter arranged under the following heads: I. Important events and short reviews of new books and journals of our school. II. Practical observations. III. Original communications on prevailing diseases. IV. New and corroborating observations on the old remedies and diagnostic remarks for a comparative repertory. V. Important observations with new remedies. VI. Extracts from a collection of letters from Hahnemann, Stapf, Gross, Jenichen and others. VII. Queries and criticisms. For all this the nominal price of thirty-six cents per annum was charged, the object being to cheapen the subscription rate by making it an advertising sheet, and so to widen the circulation of homœopathic news.

1855.—For the celebration of the Centennial Anniversary of the birthday of Samuel Hahnemann, held by the friends of homœopathy in Philadelphia, at Sansom Street Hall, Dr. Hering wrote an historical introduction entitled "Hahnemann in the Cradle," from which the following is a quotation:

When the father in his delight looked upon the little boy as he lay sleeping in the cradle, could a thought of this have entered his mind? Could he have imagined that so many years after, in a far distant land and another hemisphere, reached in his day only after long, tedious and dangerous voyaging, in that small town laid out by Penn on the river Delaware, in the wilds of Pennsylvania, known to him only from the narration of missionaries, this day would be remembered? In that town, grown to be one of the great cities of the world, the birthplace of a nation's independence, a seat of intelligence, a nursery of science and a home of the arts, so great a number, impelled by gratitude, would freely gather together to do honor in solemn assembly to him who lay there in his cradle wrapt in the soft slumbers of innocence? Even the angels in their holy watch could not have forseen what was known to the Lord alone. But what was it that the father thought? It was made known to us. While he looked upon the son so much desired, this was the thought: "If that boy is permitted to grow up, I will give him lessons in thinking." As he thought and determined so he acted. An old man in Meissen who had forgotten the son when he heard of his fame, said smilingly: "Many a time have I taken a walk with his father, and always at a certain hour he would say: 'I must go home now, I have to give a lesson to Samuel, a lesson in thinking; that boy must learn to think.' And he did learn to think, and he *dared to be wise.*"

1856.—American Provings (advance notes from the work which followed a year later.)—*Zeit. für Hom. Klinik.*, vol v.

**1857.—American Drug Provings. 1 vol. 886 pp. (German).
C. T. Winter, Leipzig and Heidelberg.**

This work, one of the most important of Dr. Hering's productions, was a preliminary attempt to raise Materia Medica to the rank of a natural science. How far this attempt was successful the verdict of sincere, earnest critics has shown and will show. The collection of drugs in this first volume is varied and important. In the carefully made provings the physiological effects are brought out with a clearness and precision which establish for each of the substances tested its place in therapeutics. The *Glonoine,* so named by Dr. Hering, by chemists called nitro-glycerine, from which is prepared the powerful and destructive dynamite, although discovered some time before by a chemist named Sobrero, was nowhere obtainable and had to be made at the instigation of Dr. Hering. This was done by the Hon. Morris Davis, of Philadelphia, then chemist for the Lovering Sugar Refineries. Dr. Zumbrock, of Washington, Dr. Hering's assistant, also spent a great amount of patient labor upon its preparation, and succeeded in discovering a method by which the substance could be made, even in the hottest weather, an undertaking previously fraught with danger, on account of its ready explosiveness by contact with heat. The effects upon the provers, of whom Dr. Hering himself was foremost, were of the most painful character, some of them having symptoms strongly resembling apoplexy, the violent headache with great rush of blood to the head being painfully prominent.

The *Apium virus*, or poison of the honey bee, its derivation, nature and effects, upon the healthy as well as the sick, has received at Dr. Hering's hands the most complete and careful elaboration. It is doubtful whether in the literature of any people, any medical substance has ever received a similar amount of attention. *Oxalic* and *Benzoic acid, Millefolium, Cepa, Hippomanes,* (suggested by Rev. John Helfrich, of Pennsylvania, a skilful and enthusiastic amateur homœopath, to whom Dr. Hering was devoted in friendship), *Jatropha curcas, Xiphosura, Rumex crispus, Kalmia latifolia,* and *Aloe,* their history, introduction, proving and arrangement of symptoms, complete the volume.

A second volume was to contain studies of twelve remedies, the fruit of more than thirty years labor, including the combinations of *Calcarea* and *Phosphorus, Calcarea* and *Arsenic, Cinnabaris* and *Turpethum, Argentum, Palladium, Selenium, Tellurium, Fluorine* and *Bromine, Alumen,* one or two plants, and probably two products of the animal kingdom, the analysis of which would have been of considerable importance to science. But on account of the slow sale of the first volume, the market for this class of literature being limited, the publisher did not care to undertake the publication of a second, and the uncompleted manuscripts remained on the author's shelves, the essential portion of them waiting to be embodied in the later and larger medical work, the Guiding Symptoms of Our Materia Medica.

The "American Drug Provings" were dedicated to Dr. Hering's friend, Dr. Ernst Stapf, in Naumburg, Germany, in a letter of which a translation is subjoined, showing with what generous impulses the author was animated, and what enthusiasm he brought to his work.

Philadelphia, Aug. 28th, 1856.

DEAR FRIEND STAPF:

When Gœthe sent to Döbereiner those precious pieces of pure Platina from the Duke's collection, it having been said how useful this metal might become if better known, he gave to the delighted chemist this charge: "Examine, that good may come of it." Döbereiner felt rich as a Briton, elated as a Frenchman, happy as a German; and went to work. His investigations furnished useful contributions to the great stream of science.

When he put into the Duke's hands the igniting-machine, the purest, highest that mind of man ever invented, in which the lightest of the elements ignites a flame in the heaviest, each had reason to be satisfied with the other. Little did they dream what other flame had already been kindled through the sacrifice of the Platina ore, a flame which will continue to burn beneficially to the end of time. For thou didst think—and a great thought it was—if gold and silver in trituration can act so powerfully on the well and the sick, why not Platina?

It was this that drew thee towards the new source in the chemist's laboratory.

From his abundance he weighed thee twenty grains; and thou wert successful in reducing it to a crystalline powder. Thou didst prove on thyself and thine, on thy friend and his wife; and the new image of Platina revealed itself in lines so sharp and true as to bear examination from the keenest observer as long as there are thinking men. Thousands have already been made well by Platina, and in the same ratio as the number of physicians who gain scientific freedom through accurate thinking increases from year to year, more will be healed.

Where are the 117 grains which later were used on dogs and rabbits by Gmelin? Where the fruits of this bootless labor?

With the Platina thou didst at the same time pave the way to a new manner of preparation, that of precipitating metals in dust-form; an essential advance in the proving on the healthy as well as in the treatment of the sick. As soon as chemists had learned to make more preparations of a similar nature, and J. B. Buchner had urged their introduction, and Mayerhofer had made his excellent investigations (microscopical), this remained a permanent legacy. And still further were carried the fruits of thy thought. The first number of the Archives appeared, issued by Reclam in Leipzig. To purchase it, a poor young man parted with his last groschen. In it he found Platina; he read, and felt as did Balboa and his followers when, in the home of Platina, they reached the heights and first saw the broad ocean on the other side of the continent.

"Each metal acts, and each in its peculiar way." These words were all sufficient. Work! and Materia Medica must become a natural science. This remained the ruling idea of his life. He has since grown old, and rich in all good gifts, and greets to-day, thee, to whom he owes all this. And if these words of love do reach thee, let also hope stand by thy side: "See how the spirit-shuttles fly, and one stroke such varied combinations makes."

As Döbereiner was influenced by Goethe; thou by Döbereiner, and as thou in turn didst animate me, so may these words work good where we neither know nor can foresee. They may raise up a hero for the days that are coming, the days in which the dragon of prejudice and delusion will be slain. Therefore, in good faith as we have worked until now, let us continue to work; the time must come when the right will prevail.

Our noble art will be wedded to true science, and physicians will *be* happier and *make* happier. Our work will never go down, because it promotes the most beneficial of arts, and that by strict investigation; and because it thereby belongs to the higher, the eternal; to that which was and is and is to come.

So fare thee well.

THY CONSTANTINE HERING.

1858.—1. Baunscheidtismus; or, The Secret Discovered.—*Zeit. für Hom. Klinik.*, vol. vii.

2. A comforting elegy at the grave of despair of all medical youths in our dear country and other nice places. Printed for private distribution. Philadelphia.

This is an excellent satire in verse, containing six hundred lines, suggested by reading in a German paper an account of the forty-third convention of German naturalists and medical men held in Bonn in 1857. The closing words of Professor Strempel, the orator, which gave rise to the satire were to the effect, that there were not the least grounds for despair in the practice of medicine on the part of younger members of the profession; that although patients often got well of themselves, and nature received the credit of these cures, there was no denying those made by drugs, even in large doses; that the newer generation of doctors should turn to account the experience of the profession, and never trust to experiments made on the healthy or so-called *provings* of medicines which never could be of the slightest use in the treatment of the sick. The assembly rose *en masse* and cheered the speaker.

Dr. Hering's lines begin: "Not to write satires is hard, sighs Juvenal," and preserving the classical measure throughout, the writer deals out, in the most humorous terms, ridicule and rebuke to the Old School as well as hard knocks to those within the walls who deserve them.

1859.—1. A peal for the Jubilee, Schiller, Shakespeare, Humboldt. An Address. Philadelphia.

2. A Criticism on the British Repertory.—*Am. Hom. Rev.*, vol. i.

1860.—The Natural Boundary. Pamphlet. 8vo., pp. 27, Philadelphia.

In this pamphlet, originally a lecture delivered before the Kannegiesser Club of Philadelphia, organized for the purpose of discussing German politics in a friendly spirit, Dr. Hering defined the boundary line that equitably should exist between Germany and France. The brochure was read with considerable interest in political circles and its bold remarks, prompted by love and loyalty to the fatherland, were greatly commended by those on the German side. He defined the natural boundary of a country to be its natural landmarks, such as the sea, mountain ranges and water-sheds. The German Rhine stream was not to be the dividing line between two countries so different in character. The Germans must have what belonged to them centuries ago, portions of the land on the left bank of the stream, Alsace and Lorraine. In illustration of this he made very ingenious use of "Red Riding Hood," the favorite French nursery tale, but gave it the German ending.

Not Red Riding Hood (Alsace) alone must come out of the wolf again, but also the old grandmother (Lorraine), who for long centuries has been sleeping there. (Strange to say the grandmother does not figure in the

French version of the fairy tale; in the German she plays an important part.) As all know the wolf had gobbled up the grandmother; to carry out our simile, in the hurly-burly of time, he had appropriated the Rhone district. He next cast his eye upon charming Red Riding-Hood, flattered her and fawned upon her, tried his old tricks, went to bed and put on the Richelieu cap. Red Riding-Hood had gathered flowers in the woods; the blessed blue flower which opens heaven and its wonders; the red flower which opens the poet's mind to all that happens on earth; the yellow flower to which are subject all treasures in and upon the earth, and she came to offer her flowers to grandmother. O, thou home of poetry since time immemorial, thou land of Burgundy, dost thou not find pleasure in the flowers that now blossom on the Rhine?

There lay the wolf in bed. "What big eyes you have!" "That I can better see you!" "What a big mouth you have!" "That I may better eat you." No sooner said than done; Red Riding-Hood is gobbled up. Here the nursery tale ends as told by the French. Grandmother is eaten up, Le Petit Chaperon-rouge too, and the wolf is master of the situation. He thinks he has a right to both, the rapacious creature who figures so largely in French nursery tales and sayings. (There is, however, a young hunter in the German version of the tale, who comes to the rescue, shoots the wolf through the head, cuts him open with his hunting knife and liberates Red Riding-Hood.) Alsace, our beloved Alsace, with its cathedral in Strasburg, and all the true glory of our Goethe, the young hunter, meet and embrace. Thus far my grandmother had told me the story without mentioning Alsace, for I was but six years old. I wanted to know what had become of the grandmother. Where was she? This pleased the old lady and she answered, "that is what Red Riding-Hood asked the young hunter when they were so happy, and he looked into the wolf again, and there found grandmother fast asleep. They helped her out, she rubbed her eyes and said, 'how long I have been asleep this morning!' and bustled off to bake some cakes." The end, of course, pleased me, the six year old, best; but I know that I was then a true and thorough German without being aware of it. And now, past sixty, I am still a German, with this difference, that I am *thoroughly* aware of it. And I am aware of more than this. I know that if we ever regain Alsace, Lorraine the grandmother, must not be forgotten.

Since the great struggle between the Powers of 1870 and 1871, Alsace and Lorraine once more belong to Germany, and it is easy to imagine what joy filled the heart of the author of "The Natural Boundary" at this consummation of his intense desire. The pamphlet written ten years before seemed almost prophetic.

New Hatchels. 1 vol. (German) Leipzig. A. Wienbrack.

Like its predecessor, this volume is a collection of satirical essays. Under their several titles, a commentary, with extracts, is appended.

No. 1.—Homœopathic College- and other Chairs. This is a reply to three columns in the *German Klinik*, headed "A Homœopathic Chair," by Dr. Alexander Göschen, addressed to the Prussian Government, with the intention of rendering unsuccessful an appeal for the founding of a homœopathic hospital. The issue joined is theoretical rather than practical, for Dr. Hering was ever opposed to courting favor from corporation authorities, and would rather have seen his cause slighted than introduced by force, as was near happening when Napoleon read Hahnemann's Organon before his march to Russia, and threatened to introduce the new treatment into the army on his return. On hearing of this Dr. Hering said he was twice as glad of his overthrow. Restraint upon the arts and sciences was as odious to him as the loss of personal liberty.

Dr. Göschen makes free use of the old and threadbare phrases, "homœopathy is dead," "homœopathy is dying," "homœopathy is losing ground," to which Dr. Hering replies:

Were it not much wiser if such were really the case not to interfere with the granting of an appeal for a hospital in which, according to the logic of the learned doctor who writes for the *Klinik*, not the least good could be done, and hence must, on account of its own masterly inefficiency, end in a total smash-up? These phrases I have often heard in many lands and in different places. The first time they fell on my ear is exactly as many years ago as Moses saw fit to keep the Jews wandering through the wilderness, with this difference, that the Jews finally entered the promised land, but the doctors still remain outside. I was at that time employed in writing against homœopathy, it was in the winter of 1821, and when I declared my intention to make the experiments, I was warned by the apothecary in Leipzig, in whose good graces I stood and who had given me many a handsome specimen for my pharmacological collection, of the danger a young man exposed himself to under such circumstances, the risk of falling into the trap, the almost inevitable chance of ending in self delusion. At these well meant admonitions I probably turned up my nose, but when, after carefully examining into the matter I found there was something in it, something that could not be refuted, my book remained unpublished, and with the renewed violent outbreak against Hahnemann which occurred at the time, I had much to suffer, even the pangs of hunger. I was warned by kind friends to desist from making sacrifices to a dead cause. That was the *first* news I had of the death of homœopathy.

In despite of all homœopathy was yet alive a year later, although I had come near dying myself, that horrible death to which so many young physicians have fallen victim. I was called upon to make a post mortem in the case of a suicide whose body had been taken from the grave, because others were afraid to undertake the job. Through working too long among the poisoned entrails, a cut on my finger which had scabbed over became denuded, partly through washing my hands in hot water and soap, and in a few days my finger had begun to mortify. I was enabled to study the disease against which leeches, calomel and hell-stone proved powerless. Amputation I declined, because the loss of my first finger would have seriously embarrassed me in the practice of my profession. So deeply incredulous was I at the time, of the action of remedies applied internally, and especially in small doses for external diseases, that it was with difficulty a pupil of Hahnemann persuaded me to take the ridiculously minute doses of *Arsenicum*. When a sense of recovery from this terrible affliction began to pervade me, there vanished the last obstacles that interposed between my eyes and the rising sun of the new healing art. The finger is still my own; it is the one with which I pen these lines. To Hahnemann who restored it was given the hand, even more, the man, body and soul; his teachings had not only been the means of saving my life, but new life filled my very soul. And they say to me, the living, "homœopathy is dead!" So time and time again, the dead have buried their dead, and the world moves on.

We do not hold in contempt your teachings, which we accept as far as they accord with truth, nor do we disdain your opposition, for we recognize the historical necessity of antagonism in a province in which probabilities must be weighed. We admit that the newness and strangeness in the teachings of Hahnemann must astonish investigators as they have astonished us. We are prepared to answer all objections made in a proper spirit, and will do so cheerfully. But we do hold in contempt all efforts to slander and undermine our cause. We regard our cause in the light of an historical event destined to benefit humanity, and we carry within us the assurance that victory will be ours.

No. 2.—Doppelmops (snuff) in homœopathy. This satire, put in the form of a letter, from school-master Sneezeback, in Wartewitz, to Dr. Hering, and an answer from the same to school-master Sneezeback, was occasioned by an attempt on the part of a bungler in the homœopathic ranks to introduce mixed prescriptions. Schoolmaster Sneezeback has caught the mania to dabble in homœopathic medicines. He sends for a box of the highest potencies, which he obtains through the wife of the magistrate, whose husband, however, is not favorable to the cause, and surreptitiously tampers with the medicines as they pass through the custom house.

Imagine Sneezeback's consternation when, on opening the box, he finds a chaos of broken glass, pellets and corks. Through every curl in the paper shavings are visible the sharp projecting, yet gently curving glass splinters, looking for all the world like the poison fangs of a young brood of rattlesnakes. In what idiotic bewilderment lie the smooth corks, their tops bearing the imprint of abbreviated names and numbers prefiguring lofty things. And alas, the globules! Where are they? Scattered like Napoleon's army when routed by the icy winds of the north and Moscow's flames. Never had he seen such a lot of priceless, forty-day acting, high, most highly charged pellets rolling in such utter and hopeless confusion among the litter of paper and glass in the bottom of the box! Oh, schoolmaster, sobbed the magistrate's wife, how rough was the coach-box in which came this precious parcel; how uneven are still the ways of our dear fatherland! Sneezeback took comfort to his soul by "saving the pieces," which he carried home, sifted the globules from the paper and broken glass, put all the globules together into a jar with dilute alcohol, labelled the bottle "Universalinum," and the greatest idea of the century was complete. Here was a ready remedy for every ill. Good bye to books and hard study, in future the practice of medicine is easy!

No. 3.—A proposal for the entire annihilation of the so-called homœopathy by a scientific method.

Under the adopted name of Dr. Wisent, the sobriquet of his student days, the author has here written over fifty pages of as interesting matter as ever entered into the composition of a hoax. The proposition to kill homœopathy in a highly respectable manner, is put into the mouth of Professor Wunderlich, the celebrated medical practitioner and historian in the old school. To him also is satirically dedicated the second edition of this pamphlet. Perhaps some idea of the admirable irony which pervades the whole composition may be formed from reading the following brief extracts. Without any regard to the high and influential position of his opponent, the doctor applies the lash without mercy.

Says the allopathic professor: It is in vain that the students of medicine in all German universities are warned against, and influenced to abhor, this monstrosity (homœopathy). The dangerous period arrives when these young doctors enter practice. It is then that they are misled by acquaintances and friends, or seduced by the prospect of gain; and too often after trying the dangerous method in secret they later become open professors of it; and what is most remarkable is that these deluded victims become enthusiasts in defence of what formerly, in the light of reason, appeared absurd to them.

The articles of confession divulging the weak points in the old faith, which precede the proposition to kill, are six in number.

1. In the first place we are too hotheaded in our written replies as well as in our personal remarks. It is a fault, but it is poor strategem. We have been tried to the extreme verge of endurance, but this does not excuse our want of etiquette in the eyes of the public. I would counsel,

either that we entirely ignore our opponent's doings, their writings as well as all they say and do, or that we confront them with cool and dignified selfpossession, in literature as well as in private life. Not a year passes but we hear of new steps of progress made by our opponents; each month brings us news of influential people having placed themselves under their treatment. We now and then hear of their failures to save a patient, but more often we hear of imaginative people who are credulous enough to believe that they have gotten well under that treatment. I would therefore strongly counsel that we refrain from crowing over every bad failure our opponents make; it only incites them to redoubled exertions, and we cannot expect to awaken enthusiasm *against* them, but they understand how to arouse it in their behalf. It would be better to throw from us all such useless weapons.

2. It is not a good plan to underrate the strength of an enemy. Many a lost battle recorded in history will serve as a warning example to all who would disregard this admonition. We cannot close our eyes to the fact that men of influence, mind and intellectual attainments, have gone over to the other side. Persons who have been inveigled will not thank you for trying to open their eyes; besides, in a field where facts may be so differently interpreted, it were folly to attempt aught else than the expression of an opinion.

3. It is not safe to challenge a comparison of work done in hospitals, clinics and the like.

4. It does not pay to ridicule the enemy. It is a game at which two can play; besides, attempts of the kind such as the well known allusions to sugar powders, bottle washing, etc., always fall flat, and often have the reverse effect of what was intended. Our opponents appeal to experience and tell us to make the experiments, which is, of course, altogether out of the question for a *regular* physician to do.

5. It is a mistake to attribute cures made by homœopaths to faith, nature or diet. Our patients will naturally clamor to be cured in a like easy manner. It is likewise futile to endeavor to instruct our patients and talk them into a belief that homœopathy is all moonshine and devoid of merit. It has been my sad experience that after such well meant instruction, some

of my best families have taken the first opportunity to try secretly the new method, and became converts. People have a strong leaning to a belief in wonders and so-called miracles, and it is useless to try to explain away anything of the kind, particularly when they have made trial and obtained relief.

6. Finally, it is an unpardonable and fatal mistake if we resort to untruths or become guilty of injustice, as I blush to own has often happened, in our mode of warfare against the new school. The fruits have been bad. With all due respect to a high code of morals, I am not at all disposed to moralize or preach, I will simply call attention to the advice given by a French woman of the world to her nephew. "Dear nephew," she said, "never tell a lie!" When the nephew received this advice, with a somewhat surprised air she continued, "I will tell you why. Because none but fools and blockheads will believe you!" A good cause will never be helped by an untruth. It pains me to meet again and again with such unjust assertions as these: "Hahnemann was a charlatan," "homœopaths conceal the most deadly poisons in their small doses," "homœopaths are no surgeons," "their standard of medical education is not up to the mark." All such assertions serve but to place us in a contemptible position, and fail to have the desired effect of annihilating homœopathy.

Arrived at this point of self-abnegation and high standard of medical ethics, the professor offers a series of resolutions, which if carried out, he believes will be calculated to give homœopathy the death blow: " Resolved, That we forbear hostilities against homœopaths in general as well as individually, as nugatory in effect and discreditable to ourselves; that in the light of enemies we ignore their existence in word, social intercourse and literature. By this course we hope to quell their opposition, and should they persist in persecuting us, it will be the means of turning the tide of public sympathy in our favor; it is by no means intended that we should hold ourselves aloof from all means of becoming better acquainted with their doctrines; on the contrary we should not miss an opportunity of learning from them; we need not scruple that by this means we raise them into undue prominence.

Resolved, That we no longer experiment on the sick, but try the effect of our drugs on the healthy; that we pay more attention to what are called trifles; in short, that we learn to individualize as closely as our opponents do. We are aware of the importance of experiments hitherto made on animals, but realize that provings made upon ourselves and such friends as are willing to assist science, are of greater importance.

Resolved finally, That we exercise the utmost justice in giving credit where it is due; let us acknowledge the good Hahnemann and his school have done; the modifying influence it has exerted on our practice; the almost total abandonment of blood-letting; the reduction in size and severity of blisters; the diminution of the quantities of medicine heretofore given; the finer physiological effects of drugs of which we have become convinced through the experiments on the healthy; the greater acuteness with which we observe and investigate diseases; the more minute attenttention paid to the injurious influence on the health of stimulants and other agencies formerly considered inert, now forbidden as disturbing elements in the treatment of a case; the addition of new remedies to the Materia Medica, as for example, Nux vomica, Arnica, Pulsatilla, etc. As all this has exerted a powerful influence to remodel our practice, let us then give honor where honor is due; let us above all things be scrupulously just, and we shall surely triumph over our opponents, who, perhaps, in less than a decade will be spoken of as having existed and fulfilled their mission; homœopathy will have experienced total annihilation.

No. 4.—Anacardium as Anticriticum.

Hatchel No. 1, against Goschen & Co., being thought a little too severe, drew upon the author the censure of one of the homœopathic periodicals, and in this, No. 4, in his usual lively vein, he takes occasion to criticise the critic. *Anacardium*, a drug which has among its provings the symptom "all things taste to him like herring-brine" is recommended. It might also benefit the critic's "weak memory" in regard to the effects of high potencies, which he often fails to remember. The Anacardium symptoms of the "popular Polonius" are analyzed at greater length; let us hope that he took the remedy and was cured of hyper-criticism.

With this, the fourth essay, the author of "Homœopathic Hatchels" makes his bow to the public, and closes his short series of satires with the following remarks:

* * * I am nothing more than a pennon bearer in the bull fight; I throw my banderillas (little harpoons with rustling ribbons and explosive squibs) into the bull's neck when he snorts in the arena, or has grown indifferent to the picadores; but I withdraw into the farthest corner when the matadors enter. I see the principles of Grauvogl excite the bull to rage and frenzy, and in his maddening attack receive into his heart the piercing sword of philosophy; I see him fall; the matador, quick as lightning, has withdrawn his sword, and proudly waving it aloft, he marches triumphantly through the arena, and then forgetting all prevention-of-cruelty disapproval, I shout for joy with the people because of the victory achieved.

1. Cases of Diphtheria.—*Am. Hom. Review*, vol. ii.
2. Preface to the Fourth American edition of Hahnemann's Organon.

1861.—1. Critical Remarks on the Scientific Communications on Snake-poison.—*Allg. Hom. Zeitung*, vol. lxiii.

2. Where is the Proof to these Symptoms? A Reply to Dr. Hoppe.—*Hom. Vierteljahrschrift*, vol. xii.

1862.—1. Gelseminum nitidum, an important new polychrest. —*Allg. Hom. Zeitung*, vols. lxiv and lxv. 2. The controversy is ended; to what purpose now the Shiboleth, an unintelligible **one at that?**—*Hom. Vierteljahrschrift*, vol. xiii. 3. Digitalis according to the Monography of Bæhr and Black.—*Am. Hom. Review*, vol. iii.

1863.—1. A warning against the Parisian "Lachesis." 2. Anecdotes from life. 3. A review of Kleinert's "Sources of Physiological Drug Provings." 4. A Historical Remark on Euphrasia. 5. Conciliatory Criticism upon the Parisian Lachesis.—*Allg. Hom. Zeitung*, vol. lxvii. 6. Proving of Lithium carbonicum. 7. Chessmoves; a reply to the "Studies" of Dr. Roth in Paris.—*Hom. Vierteljahrschrift*, vol. xiv. 8. Provings of Lithium carbonicum.—*Am. Hom. Review*, vol. iv.

9. Moss and Mosquitos. A popular science discourse. Pamphlet, 8vo., pp. 8. Philadelphia.

In this short paper the author puts in a plea for the much disliked and abused mosquito, claiming for that little insect useful services rendered for which mortals cannot be too grateful. He very carefully studied the habits of the mosquito and discovered that its larvæ purify swamps and stagnant pools from the matter which renders noxious the atmosphere and breeds malaria.

By observation he estimated that a single active larvæ is able to purify half a pint of dirty water in an hour.

* * * Giving the little worker eight hours out of the twenty-four in which to rest he would still accomplish the purification of a gallon per day, or in his short life of about three weeks duration, a total of twenty-one gallons. There are millions of mosquitos. Each mosquito lays about three hundred eggs, from which come three hundred more larvæ, and as she repeats this effort half a dozen times in a season, she is capable, with her active family, of purifying six trillion gallons of water in a year. Is she not entitled to our respect? In future let us not begrudge her the wee drop of blood in return for which she renders us such valuable service.

In a study of mosses is found a further illustration of the great utility of small things.

* * The mosses, joining their leaflets, cover large tracts of hillside, and with their tiny hands catch the torrents which pour from the clouds, break their force, and gradually, little by little, give the water to the fountains, the rivulets and the streams. Where the mosses are not, the sudden and violent showers of rain pour precipitously down the hillside, carry with them the good soil, choke with mud the valleys, fill with sand the beds of brooks, produce freshets and destroy the work of human hands. Moss protects the forests, and the forests maintain the world.

In the year 1863–'64, Dr. Hering wrote a series of short German stories or novellettes which were published in Sondershausen by Fr. Aug. Eupel, under the title of "Flugblaetter," Flying Leaves. As the title would indicate these publications were written in a popular style, their purpose being to acquaint the laity with homœopathy in a pleasant and readable form. It was always his aim to instruct the people, and when he wrote for them his style was at its best; he then gave utterance to his best thoughts, in language both plain and forcible, as may be seen in his popular work on domestic medicine, particularly in the German edition.

1864.—1. Langhammer and no end. 2. A Request for information from Dr. Eidherr. 3. The morbid fear of Hydrophobia (reproduced in *Am. Hom. Review*, vol. v.).—*Allg. Hom. Zeitung*, vol. lxviii. 4. Tellurium against trichinæ. 5. A proposed complete Materia Medica (reproduced in *Am. Hom. Review*, vol. v.). 6. The superficial and the vital in our Materia Medica.—*Ibid*, vol. lxix. 7. Introduction to the course of lectures on Therapeutics at the Homœopathic College, Philadelphia (delivered October 13th). 8. A few wellmeant words to beginners on our Materia Medica.—*Ibid*, vol. lxxi. 9. Provings of Tellurium. 10. A proposal to publish a standard work on Materia Medica.—*Am. Hom. Review*, vol. v.

1865.—1. An American protest against Lutze's publication of Hahnemann's Organon. 2. The new Materia Medica. 3. A golden wedding in Philadelphia. 4. Sifting the drug symptoms (reproduced in *Am. Hom. Review*, vol. vi, and in the *Brit. Jour. of Hom.*, vol. xxiv). 5. An example of pathological presumption. 6. An essay on taste and smell.—*Allg. Hom. Zeitung*, vol. lxxi. 7. Hahnemann's three rules concerning the rank of symptoms. 8. The rules of sides. 9. Rule and rules again.—*Hahnemann Monthly*, vol i. 10. Our Materia Medica.—*Am. Hom. Review*, vol. vi.

1866.—1. Provings of Cistus canadensis. 2. Gross's differential diagnosis of remedies, with specimen pages from his work. 3. The importance of complete collections of symptoms. —*Allg. Hom. Zeitung*. vol. lxxii. 4. Kobalt; an American proving. 5. The so-called cholera on board of English ships. 6. Wilful misrepresentations. 7. Our success.—*Ibid*, vol. lxxiii. 8. Remarks on Badiaga.—*Hahnemann Monthly*, vol. ii.

It was about 1866 or 1867 that Dr. Hering first issued his "Characteristics" or "Materia Medica Cards," several editions of which have appeared since then. This system for memorizing the chief symptoms of our remedies, invented by a student, now Dr. D. G. Tucker, of Rhode Island, has simplified and made convenient the study of Materia Medica to many a student; even older practitioners have joined in the instructive pastime.

1867.—Gross' Comparative Materia Medica. 1 vol., royal octavo. 520 pp. F. E. Boericke, Philadelphia.

The manuscript for this work, the fruit of many years patient labor on the part of Dr. R. H. Gross, a German homœopathic physician, was sent to Dr. Hering, who undertook as a labor of love, to complete, translate and edit the same in this country. After having the whole of the manuscript copied into more legible German by his scribe, Dr. Hering with the assistance of his daughter Odelia, now Mrs. J. Foster Pope, devoted an entire year to the translation and revision of the same. The reading of the proofs, eight of which had to pass under the yes of the reader in order to insure the greatest possible accuracy, was an arduous task, particularly since "the setting in type of the manuscript offered such uncommon difficulties that it required great skill, experience and ingenuity to overcome them." The latter named part of the work was very creditably performed under the superindence of Mr. John H. Schwacke foreman of the book department in the printing establishment of King & Baird. The work was not only a stepping stone, on the part of the publishers, whose edition of the work was universally admired and commended, to the publication of other large works, but it also proved to be a transition to more complete works on Materia Medica which have since followed. The book contained about five hundred comparisons of one hundred of our most frequently used medicines, and the earnest student and careful practitioner have now a better chance than they ever had before to obtain a differential knowledge of them. The book is of the greatest value in all cases where the practitioner is not perfectly certain of his choice between two or three highly similar remedies; a single glance at the columns of related and opposite symptoms will often decide the most important questions and save much time and trouble in arriving at a choice of the prescription.

1. **Midwifery in America.**—*Allg. Hom. Zeitung*, vol. lxxv.
2. **Characteristics.**—*Hahn. Monthly*, vol. iii.

In the year 1867, Dr. Hering was elected Dean of the Hahnemann College and lecturer in that institution on the Institutes of Medicine and Materia Medica. In the following September he delivered the introductory lecture to the course. With what vigor and energy he came to his work is shown in the following extract from the closing portion of his address, where he alluded to the year 1876, in which was to occur the fiftieth anniversary of his graduation in medicine and his seventy-sixth birthday.

* * After Napoleon had disturbed the peace of Europe, and was finally beaten in the battle of Leipzig by the allied powers, and banished by them to the Island of Elba, he returned again with a large army. The allies had once more to march from the North to the South. Blücher was placed at the head as main commander of the Prussian army, and marched from the North towards Belgium. Great objections were raised on account of his age. "He is old now and infirm and full of queer notions," the objectors said. He was attacked near Ligny before he was ready and was beaten; his horse fell, he was thrown under it, and was carried away for dead. Of course in a day he rallied again, sat on the back of another horse, and was smoking his pipe lustily.

Napoleon now turned his whole power against Wellington who was before Waterloo. The Iron Duke stood it manfully and not yielding an inch all day, kept his position firm. But as the sun turned towards the West and sank deeper in the horizon, the Duke wrote with a lead pencil the order to his generals to be ready to retire during the night and retreat to another position. There was a little cloud seen in the far East on the horizon. The cloud increased. It was an army coming nearer like a hailstorm, and the cloud opened, and cannon balls burst from its depths like hail into the right wing of the French army and rolled it up. The battle was won. Who was the commander of that army? Who rolled up Napoleon's old guards with his young volunteers? It was Blücher, the old man of seventy-six.

1868.—The Last Events of 1867, or the Telemicroscope of Gottlieb Juntz, and the Organopathy of Wm. Sharp, M.D., F.R.S. Dedicated to the young men of this country, our hope, our pride. Not written for incurables, either in the New or the Old World. (Pamphlet, 22 pp.) Philadelphia.

This little work is of a polemical character, and it was of it that a friend said to the author, "you have not only killed your opponent dead, but you have opened his skull and shown to the world that there are no brains in it." The pamphlet is written in the humorous satirical vein, but how much the writer was in earnest is shown by its closing words.

<small>Kepler said: "If the Lord had patience to wait so many thousand years until the harmony of the universe was understood by some of his own images, made in his own likeness, shall we, the poor creatures, 'men of like passions,' not have the patience with our fellow-men to wait a few years? Let us wait! Truth from heaven will never perish."</small>

1. **Spongia in heart affections, from lectures on Materia Medica.**—*Allg. Hom. Zeitung*, vol. lxxvi. 2. **Skirmishes on our Eastern coast.** 3. The lectures on Hausmann's book in Philadelphia. 4. **Proving of Tetradymit.**—*Ibid*, vol. lxxvii. 5. **Homœopathy in Iceland.**—*Ibid*, vol. lxxviii.

1869.—Heaven for Homœopathy. An Historical Document. Pamphlet. 5 pp. Philadelphia.

This curious piece of antiquity is taken from a work entitled *Acta Sanctorum*, published by the Roman Catholic church in the year 1658, the manuscript of which had been kept in Rome since A.D. 787, the time when it was written. The portion of the manuscript having a bearing on the law of similars treats of the case of Theodorus, "who was suffering from a disease which he had contracted by eating noxious food given to him by wicked men," and was cured by the saints " who, being powerful through a heavenly decree, applied a means of cure wonderful and evidently divine, *not curing contrary with contraries, as mortal physicians are wont to do, but like things by the use of like.*" The translation from the *Acta Sanctorum* was made by the doctor's friend and patient, Prof. Geo. Allen, LL.D., professor of Greek in the University of Pennsylvania. The pamphlet was reprinted in the *Hahnemann Monthly*, Vol. 5.

Annual Meeting of Homœopathic Physicians.—*Allg. Hom. Zeitung*, vol. lxxix.

1870.—Houatt's Provings and their self-styled Critics.—*Hahnemann Monthly*, vol. vi.

1871.—American Votes on the Question: German or Roman Type? Collected by Dr. Constantine Hering in Philadelphia, with a few words in conclusion by F. I. Frommann, in Jena. Pamphlet, 16 pp. German. Jena.

Dr. Hering being of the opinion that Latin or Roman letters do not facilitate the reading of German books to American and English students, that on the contrary, they render it more difficult, published this pamphlet, and in support of his argument he included in his work letters, substantiating his views, from the following eminent philologists, professors, doctors of medicine and men of letters: Prof. O. Seidensticker, University of Pennsylvania; Prof. Oelschlaeger, compiler of Oelschlaegers'

German-English dictionary; Prof. E. R. Schmidt, historian; Prof. Angela, teacher of the German language in the Philadelphia High School; Prof. J. E. Hilgard, of the United States Coast Survey; Dr. I C. Hilgard; Dr. Chas. G. Raue, professor in the Hahnemann College, in Philadelphia; Mr. R. Koradi, of the firm of Schaefer & Koradi, and Fr. Frommann, the head of the German Publishing House, in Jena. This belief concerning the relative merits of German and English type is shared by many readers of German, who will unhesitatingly say that it is easier for them to read German in its proper than in Roman type. In the choice of German text, Dr. Hering's taste was governed in a large measure by his love for the Gothic in art, but he was also influenced by his patriotism, which made it painful for him to look upon his mother tongue in a foreign dress. His opinions in regard to a preference in type, were likewise confirmed in a practical way, by the results obtained by his friend, Professor Frederick Knorr, teacher of German, who is affectionately remembered by his numerous pupils in Philadelphia. His plan was to teach his pupils first to read and write German script, afterwards the printed text. In this way they learned to write German letters, besides becoming familiar with the works of the most diffcult of the German authors. Dr. Hering never missed an opportunity, either directly or indirectly, to influence the minds of his patients in a way to improve and enrich them with useful knowledge, believing that a fresh interest awakened in any useful subject was a strong aid to getting well.

1. The ant as a medicine. 2. Critical hodge-podge.—*Allg. Hom. Zeitung*, vol. lxxxii. 3. Our invitation to the International Congress. 4. Sulphur in Cholera.—*Ibid*, vol. lxxxiii. 5. Formica, the ant. 6. Calcarea phosphorica, a resume of provings and cures.—*North. Am. Jour. Hom.*, vol. xx.

7. Formica as a remedy. 8. History of the Provings of Calcarea phosphorica. 9. Provings of Lobelia cœrulea.—*Hahn. Monthly*, vol. vi. 10. The Great Desideratum.—*Ibid*, vol. vii.

1872.—1. Virchow's Verdict.—*Allg. Hom. Zeitung*, vol. lxxxiv. 2. Seven Notes on Hahnemann and his "Absurdities." 3. A Protest. 4. Silicea after Vaccination. 5. Critical Remarks on Dysentery.—*Hahn. Monthly*, vol. vii. 6. Disease Germs.—*Ibid*, vol. viii.

1873.—Introductory of X. Y. on taking the chair as Professor of Homœopathy at the University of Strasburg in the year * * *. Pamphlet, 14 pp. International Hom. Press, Leipzig, German.

This is a lecture on Paracelsus and Hahnemann, in which the lecturer addresses an imaginary class of medical students of the old school, giving expression to some hitherto little known historical facts, in the endeavor to excite an interest in homœopathic principles and experiments.

1. How to treat prevailing diseases.—*North Am. Jour. Hom.*, vol. xxi. 2. Offensive odors from the mouth and their treatment.—*Hahn. Monthly*, vol. ix.

Complete Materia Medica. 1 volume. Boericke & Tafel. Philadelphia, 1873.

The collection of sixteen monographs printed seriatim in the *American Journal of Homœopathic Materia Medica* was republished in the form of an octavo volume of 700 pages, including a Pathological Index, by Boericke & Tafel, Philadelphia, in 1873. The volume includes the complete symptoms, pathogenetic and clinical, of *Alum, Carburetum sulphuris, Coca, Cuprum, Eupatorium perfoliatum, Eupatorium purpureum, Formica, Mercurius iodatus rubrum, Natrum sulphuricum, Nux moschata, Osmium, Phytolacca decandra, Sarsaparilla, Spongia tosta, Stramonium* and *Theridion curassavicum*.

Of these, *Stramonium* and *Nux moschata* are specimens of complete and indefatigable research. In the case of *Nux moschata* nearly 200 authorities have been quoted, their observations extending over a space of more than eight centuries. It forms the most complete history of any drug in any Materia Medica. On account of the full, comprehensive and comparative arrangement of the drug effects entering into the composition of this volume of Complete Materia Medica it is in many respects the most instructive ever issued. It is the result of gigantic labor, and yet forms only a very small portion of the work the author intended to do and would have done, could another lifetime have been granted him in which to complete what he had begun.

1874.—1. Observations on Solar and Lunar Influences and their relation to our Materia Medica. 2. Correspondence.—*Hahn. Monthly*, vol. ix.

1875.—Mathematical certainty.—*North Am. Jour. Hom.*, vol. xxiv.

Analytical Therapeutics, vol. 1, 8vo., 352 pp. Philadelphia.

This first volume of the "Analytical Therapeutics" was published under Dr. Hering's personal supervision, and was dedicated to his dear old friend, Dr. Jacob Jeanes, "the true Hahnemannian, the father of many new ideas, the faithful prover, who freely bestowed on all the fruit of his researches." The typographical arrangement and style of printing, executed by the author's son, Walter E. Hering, is a model of excellence. Dr. Hering had the work in anticipation for nearly thirty years, and next to the Materia Medica it is his most important production. When completed, it will comprise about six volumes, containing, condensed into the smallest available compass, the chief points of physiological experiment and homœopathic practice. The first volume contains the mental effects as they have been observed in connection with bodily symptoms. Dr. Hering well realized, and often declared, that a knowledge of the *combination* of symptoms is what physicians most stand in need of. In practice he never made use of the whole range of symptoms in any remedy, but always only of particular combinations of them. Every remedy contains the indications of a vast variety of diseases. In this analytical work, therefore, it was his intention to give to the busy practitioner in a *comparable* form, "the manner in which each drug acts upon and influences each organ and part of the body, as regards the nature, kind and degree of action." While in the Materia Medica he constantly aimed to perfect and complete the form of each remedy by synthesis, in this work he proceeds by analysis to give a *digest* of the most essential results of our provings as well as of our clinical experience.

A revised edition of this first volume, edited by Dr. Hering's literary executors, with a more complete index prepared by Dr. L. J. Knerr, has been published under the auspices of the American Homœopathic Publishing Society (Philadelphia, J. M. Stoddard & Co., 1881), under the title "Symptoms of the Mind." The material for the remaining volumes of this great work was left in available shape at Dr. Hering's death, and may be published after the completion of the Materia Medica.

1876.—On Primary and Secondary Symptoms.—*North Am. Jour. Hom.*, vol. xxv.

1877.—1. Our Nosodes, part I. 2. The Desiderata of our school. 3. Terebinthinæ oleum, recommended for the prevention and treatment of malarial and intermittent fevers.—*North Am. Jour. Hom.*, vol. xxvi.

The Condensed Materia Medica. 1 vol., 8vo, 870 pp. Compiled with the assistance of Drs. Farrington and Korndoerfer. Dedicated by the author to Dr. Chas. G. Raue, his former pupil and assistant and for seven years his colleague as professor in the Hahnemann College of Philadelphia. Philadelphia, Globe Printing House of Walter E. Hering. Publishers, Boericke & Tafel.

In 1879 the author, assisted by Drs. Raue, Mohr and Knerr, issued a more condensed, revised, enlarged and improved edition of his Condensed Materia Medica, likewise enriched by contributions from friends in the profession. Printer and publishers the same.

It was Dr. Hering's object to give in this work the chief characteristics of the principal remedies in use, for he said: "The proper mode of studying the whole Materia Medica consists in making one's self completely master of a few medicines, and afterwards of those most nearly connected with them." In another place he said: "And yet the homœopathic physician who knows little more than the characteristics of a few polychrest medicines is like a weak chess-player, who only knows one or two methods of giving checkmate which he has learned from studying the fag-ends of games played by master players, together with some few other modes which he has himself discovered."

As a text book for students the "Condensed Materia Medica" has its place, but the careful practitioner will far more often have recourse for guidance to the more ample and more profound "Guiding Symptoms," or "Analytical Therapeutics."

1878.—1. Our Nosodes, part II. 2. Palladium.—*North Am. Jour. Hom.*, vol. xxvii. 3. Hahnemann's three rules concerning the rank of symptoms. 4. The rules of sides.—*Am. Hom.*, vol. ii.

1879.—1. Origin of the theory of primary and secondary symptoms.—*North Am. Jour. Hom.*, vol. xxvii. 2. A way to become rulers of the medical world. 3. Correspondence on topics of the time.—*Med. Counsellor*, vol. i.

Guiding Symptoms. Vol. I, 8vo, pp. 506, and in 1880 Vol. II, 8vo., 506 pp. Philadelphia. Globe Printing House of Walter E. Hering. Published by the American Homœopathic Publishing Society. J. M. Stoddart & Co., Agents.

On this extensive medical work was bestowed the best labor of Dr. Hering's life. In a letter to the *British Journal of Homœopathy* on the subject of high dilutions, he says: "All my labors, all my meditations and researches for more than twenty years past (this was in 1847), have been expressly directed to obtain and to arrange with scientific precision those peculiar characteristic symptoms which in practice will determine us in our choice of the remedy."

For more than fifty years, therefore, he was engaged in preparing the material for this work. All the provings made by himself, his pupils and friends; all the carefully prepared provings of others in the profession; the toxicological reports of trustworthy men in the old school; all his own clinical observations, as well as those culled from books and journals, were collected by him, and, after being subjected to a most critical examination, were placed in his collection, which year by year, assumed larger proportions. From this voluminous material, however, only the best was to be taken for this book, only "the peculiar characteristic symptoms arranged with scientific precision," and only the symptoms of those remedies that had been tested in practice.

As a basis, the well known scheme of Hahnemann is taken. But this is much improved upon by additions of new chapters, which give the work more practical value. "Groups of symptoms as they appeared in the provings, or as they were cured at the bedside, remain as far as possible undetached, but single divisions of the symptom-group are quoted wherever it is likely that they may be looked for."

The admission of purely clinical symptoms is a feature of the book which the author vindicates upon the plea that "clinical symptoms must be noted as well as those obtained from provings, since a drug cures many things which it cannot produce, although, as we must suppose, it should have the power to do so, for provings on the healthy are confined to a narrower limit, while diseases have a wider range of symptoms; that is, symptoms on a larger scale. Produced symptoms, however, are far more positive and reliable; more sharply defined; more characteristic."

Some of his ideas of the manner in which the remedies in the Materia Medica should be studied we have in the following quotation:

"A mere acquaintance with the principal symptoms cannot be called studying the remedies, although we might make it the basis of our study. The study of Materia Medica must be regarded and dealt with in exactly the same manner as that of other natural sciences; in their present state all the relationship existing among the various classes and orders may be seen at a glance, and the study of them is thereby greatly simplified." It was his intention to bring Materia Medica to such a pitch of perfection. He well understood the laborious path he was treading, but he followed it patiently and perseveringly, for he saw light in the distance. In one of his essays he says:

As the progress of invention facilitates commerce and travel more and more, so the progress of science always lightens the task of learning what has been discovered, and the same will be the case as regards the Materia Medica. Until that time comes we must study the remedies as we find them; the time is, we hope, not far distant when we shall be able to talk about the objects of our science in the same manner as natural historians do of theirs; when, like them, we may be able to give complete descriptions of these objects, without touching upon the unimportant matter; the time, we hope, is at hand when we shall know what is and what is not important in our Materia Medica.

That he had cause to feel proud of the attainments of our school, we see in a quotation from his article, "Mathematical Certainty," published in the *New York Quarterly*, in 1875, five years before his death. He wrote: "The progress we have made in our Materia Medica towards a natural science is much greater than has ever been the case with any other natural science in the same time. They all have ages behind them—we have our centennial before us in 1890." And the additional words: "Let every man do his duty." This is what he tried to do from the beginning when the determination to build up our Materia Medica became a settled purpose in his mind, and nothing could make him swerve from it; nothing daunt his will: he even staked existence for its fulfilment.

He spent his life in research for our benefit. He prepared the harvest for us to reap. He had even begun to cut the ripened grain, and in the first and second volumes, finished by himself, shows us how to bind up the sheaves. At the beginning of the third, the hand that had worked so long and untiringly fell nerveless, even before the ink had fully dried on the page last written.

The third volume of the work has since been finished, and the fourth nearly so. To carry the work to completion, strictly in accordance with the plan of the architect, is the intention of the workmen employed upon it. The work of arranging and placing the material is laborious, but finds encouragement and reward in the prospective pleasure of seeing the building when completed an ornament to medical science, and of use to countless suffering individuals.

1880.—During this year, the last of his life, Dr. Hering's time, so far as literary occupation was concerned, was devoted almost exclusively to vigorous work upon his "Guiding Symptoms"—to reading and revising the proofs of the volume then going through the press, and to preparing further instalments of the voluminous manuscript for the printer.

Being thus closely employed, his usual flow of contributions to the professional journals ceased. One single paper only over his signature was published during the year: a letter to the editor of *The Medical Counsellor*, Dr. J. P. Mills, narrating the wonderful effects of *Staphisagria* after an operation for lithotomy, performed in the year 1836 by the celebrated old school surgeon, Dr. George McClellan, then Professor of Surgery in Jefferson Medical College. This account of one of the earliest of the triumphs of homœopathy in this country, was the last product of Dr. Hering's pen that appeared in print while he was yet alive.

Few men, even in a literary life-time of half a century, have added to the world's store of knowledge to the extent that Dr. Hering did; and still fewer have been the men who, doing so prodigous an amount of hard work, have done it so uniformly well. The motive that animated him, the power that upheld him in his long labor, the purpose for which he lived, he himself, indirectly, but most truly, has set forth. His character as a man cannot be more fitly described, nor can this account of his literary life be ended more aptly, than by quoting these his noble words, written in the year 1855, after his organization of the Provers Union, to encourage among its members the proving of poisonous drugs. His words are:

"*Let every true Christian follow in the footsteps of the Great Captain of his salvation and 'lay down his life for the brethren'; that is, let every true homœopathic physician experiment on himself as a healthy subject, instead of his patient ' as a diseased one, let him offer himself a sacrifice, give a free-will offering of his own suffering, pour out a part of his own life, to win the guerdon of the divine gift of a more infallible and increasing ability to heal the sick.*"

INDEX.

Abbreviations:—*A. H. Z.*, Allgemeine Homœopathische Zeitung; *Am. Hom.*, American Homœopath; *Am. Hom. Rev.*, American Homœopathic Review; *Brit. Jour. of Hom.*, British Journal of Homœopathy; *Cor. Blatt*, Correspondenz-Blatt; *H. M.*, Hahnemannian Monthly; *Hom. Clin.*, Journal of Homœopathic Clinics (part of American Journal of Homœopathic Materia Medica); *Hom. News*, Homœopathic News; *Hom. Viertjschft.*, Homœopathische Vierteljahresschrift; *Int. Hom. Press*, Internationale Homœopathische Presse; *Med. Couns.*, Medical Counsellor; *N. A. J. of H.*, North American Journal of Homœopathy; *Quar. Hom. Jour.*, Quarterly Homœopathic Journal; *St. Ar.*, Stapf's Archives; *Zeit. für Hom. Kl.*, Zeitschrift für Homœopatische Klinik.

A Collocation of Essentials to a good Drug Proving. 1854. A. H. Z., v. 47.
A Comforting Elegy at the Grave of Despair of all Medical Youths in our dear Country and other Nice Places. Philadelphia, 1858.
A Concise View of the Rise and Progress of Homœqpathic Medicine; historical treatise. Philadelphia, 1833.
A Criticism on the British Repertory. 1859. Am. Hom. Rev., v. 1.
A Few Well-meant Words to Beginners, on our Materia Medica. 1864. A. H. Z., v. 71.
A Golden Wedding in Philadelphia. 1865. A. H. Z., v. 71.
A Historical Remark on Euphrasia. 1863. A. H. Z., v. 67.
Allium cepa. 1853. N. A. J. of H., v. 3.
American Drug Provings. Leipzig, 1857.
American Drug Provings and Preparatory Work for Constituting Materia Medica a Natural Science. 1852. Zeit. für Hom. Kl., v. 1.
American Provings, advance notes. 1856. Zeit. für Hom. Kl., v. 5.
American Votes on the Question: German or Roman Type? Jena. 1871.
Anacardium as Anticriticum; No. 4 of New Hatchels. Leipzig, 1860.

Analytical Therapeutics. 1 vol. Philadelphia, 1875.
An American Protest Against Lutze's Publication of Hahnemann's Organon. 1865. A. H. Z., v. 71.
An Answer to F. Freiligrath's Epistle to Audubon. Poem. Philadelphia, 1844.
Anecdotes from Life. 1863. A. H. Z., v. 67.
Anecdote of a Patient in Search of Three Physicians to Agree in His Case. Brit. Jour. of Hom., v. 4.
An Essay on Taste and Smell. 1865. A. H. Z., v. 71.
An Example of Pathological Presumption. 1865. A. H. Z., v. 71.
Annual Meeting of Homœopathic Physicians. 1869. A. H. Z., v. 79.
Annual Recurrences. 1852. A. H. Z., v. 43. 1853. N. A. J. of H., v. 3.
Antipsoric Remedies in Relation to Leprosy. 1831. St. Ar., v. 10.
A Peal for the Jubilee, Schiller, Shakspeare, Humboldt. Philadelphia, 1859.
A Proposal for the Entire Annihilation of the So-called Homœopathy by a Scientific Method; No. 3 of New Hatchels. Leipzig, 1860.
A Proposed Complete Materia Medica, a standard work. 1864. A. H. Z., v. 69; and Am. Hom. Rev., v. 5.
A Proposed Plan for Exchange of Homœopatic Preparations. 1845. A. H. Z., v. 29.
A Protest. 1872. H. M., v. 7.
A Protest Against Falsifying History. 1853. A. H. Z., v. 46.
A Reply to the "Open Letter" in vol. 44. 1853. A. H. Z., v. 46.
Arnica, in Intermittent. 1868. Hom. Clin., v. 2., p. 210.
Arsenicum Metallicum, Remarks on Proving. 1851. N. A. J. of H., v. 1.
A Request for Information from Dr. Eidherr. 1864. A. H. Z., v. 68.
A Review of Kleinert's "Sources of Physiological Drug Provings." 1863. A. H. Z., v. 67.
Arum triphyllum in Scarlatina. 1868. v. 2, p. 273.
A Survey of our Provings, arranged according to provers; an historical summary. 1845. A. H. Z, v. 31.
A Survey of the entire Kingdom of Drugs. 1833. St. Ar., v. 13.
A Warning Against the Parisian "Lachesis." 1863. A. H. Z., v. 67.
A Way to Become Rulers of the Medical World. 1879. Med. Couns., v. 1.
Badiaga, Remarks on. 1866. H. M., v. 2.
Baunscheidtismus; or, The Secret Discovered. 1858. Zeit. für Hom. Kl. v. 7.
British Repertory, A Criticism on the. 1859. Am. Hom. Rev., v. 1.
Bromine. 1845. St. Ar., v. 20.
Caladium Seguinum, A Proving. 1831. St. Ar., v. 10.

Calcarea arsenicosa in Epilepsy, a note. 1849. Brit. J. of H., v. 7.
Calcarea ostrearum., Case 168. 1868. Hom. Clin., v. 2, p. 184.
Calcarea phosphorica, a resumé of provings and cures. 1871. N. A. J. of H., v. 20. History of Provings, H. M., v. 6.
Carbo vegetabilis, Note to Case 244, by Goullon. 1869. Hom. Clin., v. 3., p. 10.
Caries of Teeth, Therapeutic Hints. 1868. Hom. Clin., v. 2., p. 186.
Cepa and Euphrasia, Comparison. 1869. Hom. Clin., v. 3., p. 84.
Characteristics. 1867. H. M., v. 3.
Characteristics, or Memory Cards. Philadelphia, 1866–67.
Characteristics and Therapeutic Hints. 1867. Hom. Clin., v. 1. 1868. v. 2.
Chessmoves, A Reply to Roth's "Studies." 1863. Hom. Viertjschft., v. 13.
Chlorine. 1845. St. Ar., v. 20.
Cholera, So-called, on Board of English Ships. 1866. A. H. Z., v. 73.
Cholera, Sulphur in. 1871. A. H. Z., v. 83.
"Chronic Diseases," Preface to. 1845. A. H. Z., v. 29.
Cistus Canadensis, Provings. 1866. A. H. Z., v. 72.
Citation-Visitation, Incidental to. 1845. A. H. Z., v. 29.
Coca, Practical Remarks. 1869. Hom. Clin., v. 3, p. 142.
Collections of Symptoms, The Importance of complete. 1866. A. H. Z., v. 72.
Complementary Relations. 1868. Hom. Clin., v. 2, p. 210.
Complete Materia Medica. 1 vol. Philadelphia, 1873.
Conciliatory Criticism upon the Parisian Lachesis. 1863. A. H. Z., v. 67.
Conium, Case 62. 1867. Hom. Clin., v. 1, p. 68.
Contagion and Miasm. 1833. St. Ar., v. 13.
Correspondence. 1874. H. M., v. 9.
Correspondence on Topics of the Time. 1879. Med. Couns., v. 1.
Cough, Chronic, Case 265, Boenninghausen. 1868. Hom. Clin., v. 2, p. 271; translation.
Critical Hodge-Podge. 1871. A. H. Z., v. 82.
Critical Remarks on Dysentery. 1872. H. M., v. 7.
Critical Remarks on the Scientific Communications on Snake Poison. 1861. A. H. Z., v. 63.
Criticism on Case 9, Porrigo Decalvans. 1867. Hom. Clin., v. 1, p. 14; on Cases 16 and 17, p. 19.
Cycles, Daily, in Diseases and Drug Effects. 1851. N. A. J. of H., v. 1.
Desideratum, the Great. 1871. H. M., v. 7.
Diagnostics and Remedies, the Study of. 1831. St. Ar., v. 10.
Diarrhœa, Chronic, Case 121. 1867. Hom. Clin., v. 1, p. 123.

Digitalis According to Baehr and Black's Monography. 1862. Am. Hom. Rev., v. 3.
Digitalis in Menorrhagia. 1860. Hom. Clin., v, 3, p. 50.
Diphtheria Cases. 1860. Am. Hom. Rev., v. 2.
Disease Germs. 1872. H. M., v. 8.
Domestic Physician. 1835. First German edition, Jena, Fr. Fromman. English editions, Philadelphia, Boericke & Tafel.
Doppelmops in Homœopathy, No. 2, New Hatchels. Leipzig, 1860.
Dose, Repetition of. 1833. St. Ar., v. 13.
Drugs, a Survey of the Entire Kingdom. 1833. St. Ar., v. 13.
Drug Proving, a Collocation of Essentials thereto. 1854. A. H. Z., v. 47.
Drugs, Several, their Action on the Well and Sick. 1834. St. Ar., v. 14.
Drug Symptoms, Sifting the. 1865. A. H. Z., v. 71; Am. Hom. Rev., v. 6; Brit. Jour. of Hom., v. 24.
Dysentery, Critical Remarks on. 1872. H. M., v. 7.
Eidherr, a Request for Information from. 1864. A. H. Z., v. 68.
Elegy. Satire. Philadelphia, 1858.
Epilepsy, Calc. arsen. as a Remedy. 1849. Brit. Jour. of Hom., v. 7.
Essentials to a Good Drug Proving. 1854. A. H. Z., v. 47.
Euphrasia and Cepa, Comparison. 1869. Hom. Clin., v. 3, p. 84.
Experiment and Hypothesis. 1833. St. Ar., v. 13.
Extracts from Letters from Surinam. 1828. St. Ar., v. 7.
Falsifying History, a Protest Against. 1853. A. H. Z, v. 46.
Ferrum and Rhus rad. in Cough. 1869. Hom. Clin., v. 3, p. 84.
"**Flugblætter**" (Flying Leaves), Novelettes. Sondershausen, 1864.
Fluoric Acid. 1845. St. Ar., v. 20.
Fluoric Acid Cases. 1845. St. Ar., v. 3. New series.
Formica as a Remedy. 1871. H. M., v. 6; A. H. Z., v. 82.
Formica, the Ant. 1871. N. A. J. of H., v. 20.
Fragmentary Contributions to Materia Medica and Therapeutics. 1851. N. A. J. of H., v. 1.
Fragmentary Remarks on the Action of Several Drugs on the Well and Sick. 1834. St. Ar., v. 14.
Fragmentary Remarks on Study of Remedies and Diagnostics. 1831. St. Ar., v. 10.
Fragmentary Reports of Symptoms. 1833. St. Ar., v. 13.
Fungus Hæmatodes. 1830. St. Ar., v. 9.
Future Investigations, a Guide to. 1833. St. Ar., v. 13.
Gelsemium nitidum. 1862. A. H. Z., v. 64 and 65.
Germs, Disease. 1872. H. M., v. 8.

Glonoine. 1849. Quar. Hom. Jour., v. 1.
Golden Wedding in Philadelphia. 1865. A. H. Z., v. 71.
Gross's Comparative Materia Medica. Philadelphia, 1867.
Gross's Differential Diagnosis of Remedies. 1866. A. H. Z., v. 72.
Guide to future Investigations. 1833. St. Ar., v. 13.
Gymnocladus Canadensis, Proving. 1851. N. A. J. of H., v. 1.
Hahnemann's Analysis of Stapf's Case, Translation with Comment. 1868. Hom. Clin., v. 2, p. 150.
Hahnemann and his Absurdities, Seven Notes on. H. M., v. 7.
Hahnemann's Letter to Stapf on Fevers; translation. 1868. Hom. Clin., v. 2, p. 187.
Hahnemann in the Cradle. Philadelphia, 1855.
Hahnemann, The Requisites to a Correct Estimate of. 1847. Hygea, v. 22. 1851. N. A. J. of H., v. 1.
Hahnemann's Three Rules Concerning the Rank of Symptoms. 1865. H. M., v. 1. 1878. Am. Hom. Rev., v. 2.
Hausmann's Book, The Lectures on. 1868. A. H. Z., v. 77. Announcement, 1867, Hom. Clin., v. 1, p. 83.
Headache after Diarrhœa, Case 440. 1869. Hom. Clin., v. 3, p. 114.
Heart Affections, Spongia in. 1868. A. H. Z., v. 76. 1867. Hom. Clin., v. 1, p. 133.
Heaven for Homœopathy. Philadelphia, 1869. H. M., v. 5.
Hepar in Suppuration, Remark. 1869. Hom. Clin., v. 3, p. 21.
Hepatic Enlargement, Case 307. 1869. Hom. Clin., v. 3, p. 29.
High Dilutions, a Letter. 1847. Brit. Jour. of Hom, v. 5.
High Potencies of Jenichen, Remarks on. 1845. A. H. Z., v. 29.
Hints by which to Form a Correct Estimate of Hahnemann's Organon. 1837. St. Ar., vol. 16.
Homœopathic College and other Chairs, No. 1 of New Hatchels. Leipzig, 1860.
Homœopathic Hackels. Jena. 1846.
Homœopathy in Iceland. 1868. A. H. Z., v. 78.
Homœopathic Physicians, Annual Meeting. 1869. A. H. Z., v. 79.
Homœopathic Practitioner, What is Necessary to the Calling. 1832. St. Ar., v. 11.
Homœopathic Preparations, A Proposed Plan for Exchange of. 1845. A. H. Z., v. 29.
Homœopathic Tracts for the People. Allentown, 1836.
Hoppe, A Reply to "Where is the Proof?" 1861. Hom. Viertjschft., v. 12.
Houatt's Provings and their Self-styled Critics. 1870. H. M., v. 6.
How to Treat Prevailing Diseases. 1873. N. A. J. of H., v. 21.

Hufeland's Latest Remarks on Homœopathy and its Founder, Fragmentary Observations. 1831. St. Ar., v. 10.
Hydrophobia, The Morbid Fear of. 1864. A. H. Z., v. 68. Am. Hom. Rev., v. 5.
Hypothesis and Experiment. 1833. St. Ar., v. 13.
Iceland, Homœopathy in. 1868. A. H. Z., v. 78.
Influenza, Epidemic. 1868. Hom. Clin., v. 2, p. 248.
Incidental to Citation Visitation. 1845. A. H. Z., v. 29.
Intermittent, **Arnica** in. 1868. Hom. Clin., v. 2, p. 210.
Intermittent Fevers, Terebinthinæ oleum, a remedy and preventive. 1877. N. A. J. of H., v. 26.
International Congress, Our Invitation to the. 1871. A. H. Z., v. 83.
Introduction to the American Translation of Jahr's Symptomatology. 1851. A. H. Z., v. 40.
Introduction to Jahr's Manual. Allentown, 1838.
Introductory of X. Y, on Taking the Chair as Professor of Homœopathy at the University of Strasburg. Int. Hom. Press. Leipzig, 1873.
Jatropha Curcas. 1851. N. A. J. of H., v. 1.
Jenichen's Potencies, Remarks on. 1845. A. H. Z., v. 29.
Kleinert's Sources of Drug Provings, a review. 1863. A. H. Z., v. 67.
Kobalt, An American Proving. 1866. A. H. Z., v. 73.
Lachesis, A Conciliatory Criticism upon the Parisian. 1863. A. H. Z., v. 67.
Lachesis and Theridion. 1834. St. Ar., v. 14.
Lachesis, A Warning Against the Parisian. 1863. A. H. Z., v. 67.
Langhammer and No End. 1864. A. H. Z., v. 68.
Lecture Introductory to Course on Therapeutics. 1864. A. H. Z., v. 71.
Leprosy, Homœopathic Treatment of. 1830. St. Ar., v. 9.
Leprosy, the Relation of Antipsorics. 1831. St. Ar., v. 10.
Lithium carbonicum, Provings. 1863. Hom. Viertjschft., v. 14. Am. Hom. Rev., v. 4.
Lobelia cœrulea, Provings. 1871. H. M., v. 6.
Malarial Fevers, Terebinthinæ oleum as a Remedy and Preventive in. 1877. N. A. J. of H., v. 26.
Marginal Notes to the Materia Medica. 1845. St. Ar., v. 3. New series.
Materia Medica, a Natural Science. Preparatory work. 1852. Zeit. für Hom. Kl., v. 1.
Materia Medica, Marginal Notes to. 1845. St. Ar., v. 3. New Series.
Materia Medica, As a Natural Science. 1853. N. A. J. of H., v. 3.
Materia Medica, The New. 1865. A. H. Z., v. 71.

Materia Medica, Our. 1865. Am. Hom. Rev., v. 6.
Materia Medica and Pathology. 1853. N. A. J. of H., v. 3.
Materia Medica, Review. 1867. Hom. Clin., v. 1, p. 11; Remarks, v. 1, p. 34.
Materia Medica, the Pathologizing of. 1854. A. H. Z., v. 47.
Materia Medica, a Proposed Complete. 1864. A. H. Z., v. 69. Am. Hom. Rev., v. 5.
Materia Medica, The Superficial and the Vital in Our. 1864. A. H. Z., v. 69.
Materia Medica, a Few Well-meant Words to Beginners. 1864. A. H. Z., v. 71.
Materia Medica and Therapeutics, Fragmentary Contributions to. 1851. N. A. J. of H., v. 1.
Mathematical Certainty. 1875. N. A. J. of H., v. 24.
Menorrhagia, Digitalis in. 1869. Hom. Clin., v. 3, p. 59.
Miasm and Contagion. 1833. St. Ar., v. 13.
Midwifery in America. 1867. A. H. Z., v. 75.
Misrepresentations, Wilful. 1866. A. H. Z., v. 73.
Moss and Mosquitoes. Philadelphia, 1863.
Myrtus Communis. 1851. N. A. J. of H., v. 1.
Newer Provings. 1845. St. Ar., v. 20.
New Hatchels. Leipzig, 1860.
Nosodes. Part I, 1877, N. A. J. of H., v. 26; Part II, 1878, v. 27.
Observations on Solar and Lunar Influences and their Relation to our Materia Medica. 1874. H. M., v. 9.
Obstetrics (Midwifery) in America. 1867. A. H. Z., v. 75.
Offensive Odors from the Mouth and their Treatment. 1873. H. M., v. 9.
On the Relationship of Plants. 1845. A. H. Z., v. 29.
On the Repetition of the Dose. 1833. St. Ar., v. 13.
Organon, Preface to the First American Edition. Allentown, 1836.
Organon, Preface to the Third American Edition. Philadelphia, 1849.
Organon, Preface to the Fourth American Edition. Philadelphia, 1860.
Organon, Hints by which to Form a Correct Estimate. 1837. St. Ar., v. 16.
Organon, a Protest Against Lutze's Publication. 1865. A. H. Z., v. 71.
Organopathy; or, The Last Events of 1867. Philadelphia, 1868.
Origin of the Theory of Primary and Secondary Symptoms. 1879. N. A. J. of H., v. 27.
Our Invitation to the International Congress. 1871. A. H. Z., v. 83.
Our Materia Medica. 1865. Am. Hom. Rev., v. 6.
Our Nosodes. Part I, 1877, N. A. J. of H., v. 26; Part II, 1878, v. 27.
Our Success. 1866. A. H. Z., v. 73.

Palladium. 1878. N. A. J. of II., v. 27.
Pathogenesis and Patho-exodus. 1833. St. Ar., v. 13.
Pathological Anatomy Viewed from its Useless Side. 1845. A. H. Z., v. 29.
Pathology and the Materia Medica. 1853. N. A. J. of II., v. 3.
Pathological Presumption, an Example of. 1865. A. II. Z., v. 71.
Pathologists and Therapeuticians, Remarks on their Dispute. 1831. St. Ar., v. 10.
Potencies of Jenichen, Remarks on. 1845. A. H. Z., v. 29.
Practical Remarks. 1867-69. Hom. Clin., v. 1, 2, 3 and 4.
Practitioner, Successful Homœopathic; What is Necessary to the Calling. 1832. St. Ar., v. 11.
Preface to the First American Edition of Hahnemann's Organon. Allentown, 1836.
Preface to the Third American Edition of Hahnemann's Organon. Philadelphia, 1849.
Preface to the Fourth American Edition of Hahnemann's Organon. Philadelphia, 1860.
Preface to English Translation of "Chronic Diseases." 1845. A. H. Z., v. 29.
Preparatory Attempt as a Guide to Future Investigation. 1833. St. Ar., v. 13.
Prevailing Diseases, How to Treat. 1873. N. A. J. of H., v. 21.
Primary and Secondary Symptoms. 1876. N. A. J. of II., v. 25.
Primary and Secondary Symptoms, Origin of the Theory of. 1870. N. A. J. of H., v. 27.
Provings of Lithium carbonicum. 1863. Hom. Viertjschft, v. 14; Am. Hom. Rev., v. 4.
Provings, Newer. 1845. St Ar., v. 20.
Provings, a Survey Arranged According to Provers. 1845. A. H. Z., v. 31.
Psorinum and its Chemical Rescue. 1852. A. H. Z., v. 43; N. A. J. of H., v. 2.
Psorinum, Remarks. 1833. St. Ar., v. 13.
Rank of Symptoms, Hahnemann's Three Rules. 1865. H. M., v. 1. 1878. Am. Hom., v. 2.
Relations, Complementary. 1867. Hom. Clin., v. 2, p. 210.
Relationship of Plants. 1845. A. H. Z., v. 29.
Remarks on Badiaga. 1866. H. M., v. 2.
Remarks on Jenichen's High Potencies. 1845. A. H. Z., v. 29.
Remarks, Practical. 1867. Hom. Clin., v. 1, p. 117.
Remedies and Diagnostics, the Study of. 1831. St. Ar., v. 10.
Reminiscences of Scarlet Fever Epidemics. 1845. A. H. Z., v. 29.

Repertory, a Plea for a More Complete One. 1831. St. Ar., v. 10.
Requisites to a Correct Estimate of Hahnemann. 1851. N. A. J. of H., v. 1.
Rhododendron and Rhus, Diagnostic Remarks. 1868. Hom. Clin., v. 2, p. 247.
Rhus rad. and Ferrum in Cough. 1869. Hom. Clin., v. 3, p. 84; Hom. Viertjschft., v. 14.
Roth's Studies, a Reply. 1863. Hom. Viertjschft., v. 14.
Rules, Hahnemann's, Concerning Rank of Symptoms. 1865. H. M., v. 1. 1878. Am. Hom., v. 2.
Rule and Rules Again. 1865. H. M., v. 1.
Rules of Sides. 1865. H. M., v. 1. 1878. Am. Hom., v. 2.
Sanguinaria. 1845. St. Ar., v. 20.
Scarlatina, Comments on Case 227. 1868. Hom. Clin., v. 2, p. 238.
Scarlatina, Comments on Case 293. 1869. Hom. Clin, v. 3, p. 19.
Scarlatina, Arum triphyllum Cases. 1868. Hom. Clin., v. 2, p. 273.
Scarlet Fever Epidemics, Reminiscences. 1845. A. H. Z., v. 29.
Scirrhus of Tongue, Cases. 1868. Hom. Clin., v. 2, p. 239.
Selenium, Fragmentary Proving. 1832. St. Ar., v. 12.
Seven Characteristics of Hahnemann's Method of Cure. Tract. Allentown, 1836.
Seven Notes on Hahnemann and His "Absurdities." 1872. H. M., v. 7.
Shibboleth, to What Purpose. 1862. Hom. Viertjschft., v. 13.
Sides, The Rules of. 1865. H. M., v. 1. 1878. Am. Hom., v. 2.
Sifting the Drug Symptoms. 1865. A. H. Z., v. 71. Am. Hom. Rev. v. 6. Brit. Jour. of Hom., v. 24.
Silicea after Vaccination. 1872. H. M., v. 7.
"Similar," What Do You Mean By It. 1834. St. Ar., v. 14.
Similar, What is. 1845. St. Ar., v. 20.
Skepticism. Tract. Allentown, 1836.
Skirmishes on our Eastern Coast. 1868. A. H. Z., v. 77.
Smell and Taste. An essay. 1865. A. H. Z., v. 71.
Snake Poison, Critical Remarks. 1861. A. H. Z., v. 63.
Snake Poison, First Remarks. 1831. St. Ar., v. 10.
Snake Poison as a Therapeutic Agent. 1834. St. Ar., v. 14.
Snake Poison, The Effects of. Allentown, 1837.
Solar and Lunar Influences, Their Relation to our Materia Medica. 1874. H. M., v. 9.
Song of the Bell. A parody. Jena. 1845.
Sore Throat, Case 120. 1867. Hom. Clin., v. 1, p. 122.
Spongia in Heart Affections. 1868. A. H. Z., v. 76. 1867. Hom. Clin., v. 1, p. 133.

Staphisagria after the Operation of Lithotomy. Correspondence 1880. Med. Couns , v. 2.
Success, Our. 1866. A. H. Z., v. 73.
Suggestions for the Proving of Drugs on the Healthy. Philadelphia, 1853.
Sulphur in Cholera. 1871. A. H. Z , v. 83.
Sulphur in Gastritis. 1869. Hom. Clin., v. 3, p. 115.
Sulphur in Headache after Diarrhœa. 1869. Hom. Clin., v. 3, p. 114.
Symptoms, Fragmentary Reports of. 1833. St. Ar., v. 13.
Symptoms, The Importance of Complete Collections of. 1866. A. H. Z , v. 72.
Taste and Smell. An essay. 1865. A. H. Z , v. 71.
Teeth, Caries of, Therapeutic Hints. 1868. Hom. Clin., v. 2, p, 186.
Tellurium Against Trichinœ. 1864. A. H, Z., v. 49.
Tellurium, Provings. 1864. Am. Hom. Rev., v. 5.
Terebinthinœ oleum, Recommended for the Treatment of Malarial and Intermittent Fevers. 1877. N. A. J. of H., v. 26.
Tetradymit, Proving. 1868. A. H. Z., v. 77.
The Ant as a Medicine. 1871. A. H. Z., v. 82. H. M., v. 6.
Therapeuticians and Pathologists; Remarks on their dispute. 1831. St. Ar., v. 10.
The Condensed Materia Medica. Philadelphia, 1877. Second Edition. 1879.
The Controversy Ended, To What Purpose the Shibboleth? 1862. Hom. Viertjschft., v. 13.
The Desiderata of our School. 1877. N. A. J. of H., v. 26.
The Effects of Snake Poison. Allentown, 1837.
The Great Desideratum. 1871. H M., v. 7.
The Guiding Symptoms of our Materia Medica. Philadelphia, 1879.
The Homœopathic News. Philadelphia, 1854, '55 and '56.
The Importance of Complete Collections of Symptoms. 1866. A. H. Z,. v. 72.
The Last Events of 1867, or the Organopathy of Wm. Sharp. Philadelphia, 1868.
The Lectures on Hausmann's Book. 1868. A. H. Z., v. 77. Announcement, 1867. Hom. Clin , v. 1, p. 83.
The Life of S. Hahnemann. Tract. Allentown, 1836.
The Morbid Fear of Hydrophobia. 1864. A. H. Z., v. 68. Am. Hom. Rev., v. 5.
The Natural Boundary. Philadelphia, 1860.

The New Materia Medica. 1865. A. H. Z., v. 71.
The Pathologizing of Materia Medica. 1854. A. H. Z., v. 47.
Therapeutic Hints and Characteristics. 1867-69. Hom. Clin., v. 1, 2, 3 and 4.
The Requisites to a Correct Estimate of Hahnemann. 1847. Hygea, v. 22.
Theridion Currassavicum and Lachesis. 1834. St. Ar., v. 14.
The Rules of Sides. 1865. H. M., v. 1. 1878. Am. Hom. v. 2.
The So-called Cholera on Board of English Ships. 1866. A. H. Z , v 73.
The Study of Homœopathic Materia Medica. 1838. St. Ar., v 17.
The Superficial and the Vital in our Materia Medica. 1864. A. H Z, v. 69.
The Voluntary System of Medical Education. Philadelphia, 1854.
Throat Affections, Therapentic Hints 1868. Hom. Clin , v. 2, p. 175.
Trial of Dr. Pelleteer. Tract. Allentown, 1836.
Trichiasis, Suggestions 1869 Hom. Clin., v. 3, p 132.
Trichinœ, Tellurium Against 1864. A. H. Z, v. 69.
Vaccination, Silicea After. 1872. H. M, v. 7.
Virchow's Verdict. 1872. A. H. Z, v. 84.
What Do You Mean by "Similar." 1834. St. Ar, v. 14.
What is Necessary to the Calling of a Successful Homœopathic Practitioner. 1832 St. Ar., v. 11.
What is Similar? Part I 1845 St. Ar., v. 20. Part II. 1845. St. Ar., v. 3 New Series.
Where is the Proof to these Symptoms? A Reply to Hoppe. 1861. Hom. Viertjschft, v. 12
Whitlow, Case 103. 1867. Hom Clin, v. 1, p 102.
Wilful Misrepresentations. 1866. A. H. Z, v. 73.
Zincum, Hepatic Enlargement, Case 307. 1869. Hom. Clin, v. 3, p. 29.

IN MEMORIAM.

IN MEMORIAM.

MEETING OF PHILADELPHIA PHYSICIANS.

AT a meeting of the homœopathic physicians of Philadelphia, held at the Hahnemann Medical College, 1105 Filbert street, on Sunday afternoon, July 25th, 1880, at five o'clock, to take action on the sudden demise of Dr. Constantine Hering, Dr. John K. Lee was called to the chair, and on motion, Dr. H. N. Guernsey was appointed secretary.

The chairman, having called the meeting to order, requested Dr. Lippe to state the object of the meeting. Dr. Lippe then spoke as follows:

Mr. Chairman, and Fellow-Members of the Profession:—

The sad event that has called us together on this occasion is the unexpected and sudden death of our old and venerable colleague, Constantine Hering. Before I offer for your kind consideration and approval, a series of resolutions drawn up for this occasion, permit me to express my sentiments, and no doubt the sentiments of all those who have known our departed colleague best. Dr. Constantine Hering deservedly and undisputably was considered the father of the homœopathic school of medicine in the United States. It is now almost half a century since he came here, attracted by the institutions of the Republic, and here he remained to enjoy for himself and to see his chosen school of medicine enjoy the fruits of a Republican form of government. Even at that early day the name of Constantine Hering was well known all the world over, his contributions to homœopathic literature beginning in the "Archives," secured him an honorable place among the foremost standard-bearers of the law of cure. Fifty years have passed by since this scientist made his first observations on the sick-making properties of the poison of Lachesis trigonocephalus, and this observation and the deductions drawn from them as to its health-restoring properties, would alone have made him what he was—a shining light among medical men. The beginning of a great work was then made, and soon we find him giving us the first works on Homœopathy in the English language, while engaged in teaching the new healing art at Allentown in this State. Later we find him publishing his "Domestic Physician" as a text-book for those who could not avail themselves of the assistance of the then few homœopathic practitioners, a work which was translated into almost all languages; we find him a large contributor to the homœopathic journals, and especially defending the teachings of Hahnemann, protesting against multiplying departures from the methods of the Master. Notwithstanding his increasing professional duties, we find him continually adding to the Homœopathic Materia Medica; his numerous monographs on old and new remedies being an heirloom to posterity, so that this worker shall never be forgotten. We find him teaching the principles and practices of the new school in private and in public. The caller on him who earnestly desired to learn, found him ever ready to give the wished-for information; we find his enthusiasm not diminished as he became older, his fidelity to our principles was as firm as were the enthusiastic hopes he entertained for the perpetuation of our school of medicine. Always ready to advance the true interests of Homœopathy, he took especial pleasure in guiding the younger members of the profession, by explaining to them the great results obtainable for the cure of the sick by following strictly, honestly and persistently the rules and directions to be found in the methods of Hahnemann.

As an individual who has known our departed colleague for more than forty years, who profited by his kind instructions and example, who with him, as one of the early pioneers, saw the almost miraculous growth of our school of medicine, I can only faintly express the grief felt when so noble and so self-sacrificing a member of our school is removed from among us. His works will live after him; coming generations will profit by them, and like the present will honor his memory.

Dr. Lippe then offered the following preamble and resolutions:

Whereas, It has pleased an overruling and all-wise Providence to remove from among us our highly esteemed colleague and co-laborer, Dr. Constantine Hering; and

Whereas, We deeply feel the great loss of one who was endeared to us as the father of our school in this country; of one, who for almost half a century, so earnestly, so honestly, so unostentatiously and so unselfishly devoted himself, aided by an unusually large store of knowledge and by a ripe scholarship, to propagate, advance and develop the true healing art; of one who added such treasures to our literature; of one so universally known and honored; therefore,

Resolved, By the homœopathic physicians

of this city, in which he resided so long, that in the death of Constantine Hering, M. D., we, as well as the medical profession throughout the world, have suffered a great loss.

Resolved, That the homoeopathic physicians of this city will attend his funeral, on July 28th, at 11 A. M., from his late residence, in a body.

Resolved, That a copy of this preamble and resolutions be transmitted to the family of our departed friend and colleague.

Before putting the question on these resolutions, the chair called for an expression of sentiment on the part of those present. After a short pause, Dr. O. B. Gause was named and spoke as follows:

I am sure the reluctance which is apparent here is only apparent. I have no doubt the majority of the persons in the room have that in their hearts and minds which they would like to say on this sad occasion.

I myself had not as intimate an acquaintance with Dr. Hering as many who are here, but I was frequently with him during several years, in connection with my college duties, and was frequently at his house enjoying his courtesies, and I am here to testify that I always found him an exceedingly generous man, an earnest man, and a wise man in the matter of medical education; and if I were to talk a long time I could not say more than to testify this much to the ability, and earnestness, and wisdom of the great man I was glad to call my friend.

Dr. John C. Morgan then being called upon addressed the chair, as follows:

It is honorable to mankind that we love to praise the dead. But it is no ordinary eulogy that we pass upon him of whom we speak to-day. A personal friend has been torn from us; our most venerable leader has departed. Nestor no longer lives. How shall we fitly recount his worth? And where begin? The magnanimous generosity of Dr. Hering to his colleagues and pupils in this city ought not to be unrecorded. In one respect he was lavish—exceeding anything I ever saw. One has well said: "A man of such abundant literary productiveness, and of such great usefulness to the profession, and to the interests of Homœopathy, could not have found much time for making money by practice." A large and select practice he always had; and he acquired a modest competency; only that. But I confidently venture the assertion, that no homœopathic physician ever enjoyed intimacy with him, but he has been not only deeply instructed, but also more than once or twice surprised by his transfer to him of valuable cases, and of excellent families, who had applied to him. The practitioners of surgery and midwifery, especially, have reason to remember the unexampled friendship of Dr. Hering. Unflinching in devotion to law and principle; merciless, possibly, in denouncing license under the law of our art; upright and downright in his consistency; successful in his practice; classic in his teaching; to these traits he added the humanities which to-day bind to his memory that innumerable host, who, in all ways, are the better and the happier for his living; and above all, that phalanx of true workers who ofttimes filled their exhausted pitchers from his never-failing fountain of knowledge and encouragement.

I thought this morning of that unfinished work, "The Guiding Symptoms;" who will take it up? Who will take up any of the work he has been doing? Upon whom shall his mantle fall? May we not pray that his mantle may fall upon all of us, and shall we not all take up the work upon which he has so nobly spent his life?

I must refer for a moment to another aspect of the subject—must allude to the life-long hostility of some who are to-day reaping where he has sowed. For many years I myself was kept aloof from him, whilst practicing Homœopathy, by the assertion of some who professed to know him, that he was dogmatic, like his master Hahnemann; that he was visionary, like his master Hahnemann; that he was unreliable and ultra, like his master Hahnemann. Great, then, was my surprise when I came to know him for myself.

I thank Providence that I have lived long enough to learn better of him and of his master Hahnemann. I have ever found Dr. Hering most pliable to the force of sound reason, and thus ever open to conviction. I have never met a man so willing to take suggestions from juniors as was Dr. Hering. I never met a man so humbly a learner from all sources; never met a man in the homœopathic ranks who was so completely *en rapport* with all the departments of modern science.

Were there new discoveries made, who was so eager to grasp them as Dr. Hering? When the spectroscope was introduced, who knew it so soon and so well as Dr. Hering? When Hausmann, the homœopathic professor in the University of Pesth, Hungary, published his great work, showing, from the homœopathic standpoint, the parallel lines of evolution of both organic beings and their inorganic pabulum—when, I say, that great book, hardly understood to this day in Europe or America, appeared, who introduced it? Who, of all the homœopathic profession, took up that book and interpreted it to the profession?

Who, but Dr. Hering? In all these things Dr. Hering has been found in the very front rank of medical and collateral science; and I wish to give this testimony as one somewhat intimate with him. He was as far from being the dogmatic extremist—the visionary symptomist—he has been represented, as was possible; nay, who does not admit, now, that he was in the very front rank of the medical men of our day?

Dr. Hering's influence as a teacher in Homœopathy is to-day felt everywhere. An incident will illustrate it. A very successful physician in Illinois, a graduate of the Philadelphia college, said to me that while a student he attended Dr. Hering's private lectures also—and added, "I studied general medicine from a homœopathic standpoint in the college; but I really learned *Homœopathy* from Dr. Hering, in that back office of his."

Dr. Hering was not only, however, a teacher of men. He humbled himself in an unusual way. His love, I may say *reverence for children*, was characteristic and unique. The simplicity of his own heart found its counterpart in them. When the Homœopathic Hospital Fair was organized in 1869, he insisted that a prominent place must be assigned to a "Children's Table," asserting that no good would come of the enterprise were the children left out. He poetically said that they, having lately arrived from heaven, have the angels still with them; and that they are ever nearer heaven than their elders.

He had convictions—strong convictions, why not? And he felt that he had a mission in life!

It has been said, "whosoever wishes to live in this world in comfort and in quiet let him beware of a man with a mission." That is a true saying. Let a man who wishes to be at his ease keep at a respectful distance from a man with a mission. Dr. Hering was such a man. He was alive to the questions mooted, and particularly to the recent departures from first principles by some in the homœopathic rank. He had the convictions that he should resist them to the utmost. He believed in his own mission. Only a few weeks ago he said to me, referring to recent departures from fundamental Homœopathy, and his purpose to defend it, "The Lord has kept me alive for that." A man with such a conviction of his mission and of the divine origin of it, and with such a knowledge of his subject, might be expected to appear dogmatic. Coming in contact with generation after generation of dogmatic tyros, let us rather say, such a man could not be expected to pause in his great life-work, to come down on demand, and wipe away all the cobwebs woven by their inexperience with a gentle hand. Dr. Hering has been among us as a *teacher!* Let us then revere, for their great worth, his teachings, as we all do revere his memory!

Dr. Augustus Korndœrfer then rose, and spoke as follows:

I scarcely know how to express myself on this occasion. In fact, I had thought that I should say nothing, as being truly unfitted to express the depth of my feelings, at the death of our old friend, Dr. Hering.

I have been intimately connected with him during a decade. From the first of my acquaintance I felt that he was my friend. He had a firm and an abiding friendship, and even at times when it seemed as though he were not the friend that you thought him, it was that he might do you good.

I would like, in addition to what has been said, however, to speak more fully of his great friendship to the young practitioner. His knowledge, his labors, his wondrous store of information, we all of us know; but not all knew how uniformly kind he was to the beginner in medicine. Hours were all as minutes to him, if he might help the young men, and the labor was pleasure to him, if he could render assistance to them. I well remember during the early days of my acquaintance with him how utterly he abhorred the idea of keeping a secret from the profession ; how earnestly he insisted on every member of the profession making known, in season and out of season, every fact which might tend to the healing of the sick, or rendering assistance in the slightest degree to the suffering. It is this phase of his character which has attracted me more than any other, for he showed it so freely during so many years.

In regard to his work, it has been said by some, as intimated by Dr. Morgan, that his work was unreliable because dogmatic. I can only say, that the man who says that, utters what he knows to be worse than a falsehood. It is infamous! Dr. Hering never put his pen to paper except where he had the fullest authority for the truthfulness of what he wrote. Every word and line he wrote bore not only the evidence of having been taken from some authority, but of being from his own authority, because he accepted the dictum of no man. He received as an authority no one, save that that authority could be verified.

It has been said by some that he made notes and memoranda of the most ridiculous experiences of physicians; but, as the doctor remarked to me in reference to this thing, "Yes, I do take notes of everything; a very great deal of it I only find fit for the waste basket; but I take notes. There may be some truth in it, which the future only will reveal." This exactness, this exactitude, this slow work, was simply the result of the over-carefulness that characterized him—his perfect desire to give everything in its most perfect shape to the profession. This I learned from intimate acquaintance with him.

He lived in faith; in faith in Homœopathy and the mission, the divine mission, he was called to fulfill. And he left it almost fulfilled. He left it with the conviction that he could now leave it where it could be finished by other hands. He said to me only a short time ago that we had men left in the ranks who could go on and finish now what he, for want of time, could not complete.

There is not one here but feels his loss, and will continue to feel that a good, earnest, true man has been called from our midst.

Before resuming his seat, Dr. Korndœrfer made an apology for the absence of Dr. E. A. Farrington, who, owing to sickness in his own family, was detained at home; but who desired the speaker to express his regret at being absent, and his sympathy with the family of Dr. Hering.

The chair then called upon Dr. Bigler to relate the circumstances of Dr. Hering's decease. Dr. Bigler thereupon said:

I was not present at the time of the death, but was in the house a few moments after. I can only tell what I learned from my father-in-law, Dr. Koch, who was called in. When he arrived Dr. Hering was already dying; his hands and wrists were cold, though he was perfectly conscious. He was restless, and moved from side to side of his couch, suffering greatly from dyspnœa, and breathed his last very soon, before Dr. Raue, who was Dr. Hering's regular attendant, came in.

I was present at the post-mortem and took notes for Dr. Thomas, who could not be here to-day; but I will presently read the results of the examination. The doctor before his death seemed to be entirely well. The whole trouble did not seem to last more than half an hour from the time he was seized to the time he died. He had, according to his custom, taken tea with his family in the garden, and after an hour's spirited conversation went into his upper office—his study. At about half-past nine o'clock Mrs. Hering heard his bell ring, and proceeding to his room found him in the condition I have described.

The post-mortem was made by Dr. A. R. Thomas. The notes are as follows:

POST-MORTEM EXAMINATION BY A. R. THOMAS, M.D.

The post-mortem examination was made at 12 o'clock M., on Saturday, the 24th day of July, fourteen hours after death. There were present Drs. A. W. Koch, H. N. Guernsey, C. B. Knerr, W. H. Bigler, J. C. Guernsey, C. Mohr, and C. M. Thomas, of Philadelphia; Dr. J. C. Burgher, of Pittsburg; Dr. J. C. C. Hill, of Mexico; Mr. Herman Faber, the artist, Mr. A. Oliver, the embalmer, the undertaker, and assistant.

The body was found well developed and with abundance of adipose tissue. The chest was remarkably full and large.

Upon opening the cavities of the body the lungs were found to remain fully distended, no appreciable collapse taking place. Extensive adhesions of the right lung to the thoracic walls were present, which were at first supposed to have interfered with the collapse, but the removal of these was followed by no change in the volume of the lungs. Slight adhesions of the left lung at apex. As the lungs were lifted from the thoracic cavity they were found extremely light, with very slight hypostatic congestion at posterior portions, and in a condition of extreme vesicular emphysema.

The heart, moderate in size, presented a large deposit of fat beneath its serous covering, about the base and along the course of the coronary arteries. The cavities contained a small quantity of uncoagulated blood. The valves were normal, except a slight thickening of the aortic semilunars. The muscular walls were firm and of good color. The coronary arteries were distinctly calcified. The liver was about normal in size, yet considerably congested, and presented a line of firm adhesion extending from the anterior to the posterior border to the right of the falciform ligament. The kidneys were both slightly congested, the right gland being smaller than the left. The spleen, pancreas, stomach, and bowels were normal. Large quantities of fat were found within the omentum, mesentery and around the kidneys.

No examination was made of the brain, it having been the expressed wish of the family that the head should not be opened. It having been also the desire of the family that the body be embalmed, the post-mortem was conducted in such a manner as to divide as few large vessels as possible, in order that the preserving fluid might permeate all the tissues. From the manner of death and from post-mortem appearance, the cause of death was considered paralysis of the heart.

At the request of the chair, Dr. J. C. Guernsey then read the following communication from Dr. A. R. Thomas:

Sunday, July 25th, 1880.

DEAR DOCTOR:

Having an urgent professional call to the country, one which will make it impossible for me to be present at the meeting called for this P. M., I desire to take this method of expressing my full sympathy with any action which may be taken with the view of doing honor to the memory of the illustrious and lamented deceased.

While all will admit the wide influence of the labors of Dr. Hering in the past, and the fact that this influence must extend far into the coming future, what more fitting memorial of our appreciation of his labors, on the part of the profession, than a united and vigorous movement for securing what he has so long labored and prepared for, what this community and the country have reason to expect of Philadelphia—a permanently established and large general hospital.

During the life of Dr. Hering, the ultimate purpose of every act or thought was the promotion of the one great aim of his life —the development and dissemination of the principles of Homœopathy. No sacrifice of money, time, or rest, was too great when required for this object, and now, that the largest and ripest fruit of this labor may be gathered, there remains a work for us to perform, and one that should command the united and hearty co-operation of every member of the profession.

Regretting that I am unable to join personally in the action of the meeting, I am, Very truly yours,

A. R. THOMAS.

Dr. Pemberton Dudley then rose and said:

I feel no words of ours can at all express what we feel at the loss the profession and the world has sustained in the death of Dr. Hering. I think and know that the homœopathic profession should feel to-day very much as the passenger feels, away out from the coast, when the pilot takes leave of the ship; because whatever may have been the perfection with which the law under which we labor was developed by Hahnemann, it required something more than Hahnemann to establish the art and principles of medicine under that law throughout the world. Hahnemann was a man of research, as Hering was, but Hering was a man of different mould; he was the man to establish the new system in a new world.

The question is asked, who will take Dr. Hering's place? Nobody will take it! The world does not need another Hering. Homœopathy does not need to be established a second time in America. We no more need another Hering than we need another Newton, another Kepler, or another Washington! Homœopathy is established now, and will go on doing universal good throughout the civilized world.

There were very few men, perhaps none, who could do the work that he has done. But there are other men, weaker perhaps, who can take up the work where he has left it. I believe there is a Providence watching over Homœopathy; and I believe we should take the death of Dr. Hering as an evidence that God watches over our cause. It will occur to all that the death of Dr. Hering fell upon an anniversary—fifty-two years from the day when Homœopathy was first introduced into the State; and his funeral occurs upon another—fifty-two years from the day when he first secured his " Lachesis."

But we have other evidences that Homœopathy is going right on with renewed vigor. There is a tendency in men to lean on each other; and in order to strengthen a man he must be made to lean upon himself—to strengthen the spinal column put a weight on the shoulders. I question whether we have not been leaning on him too much, and now that he is gone, whether we will not feel that there is more resting on us; whether the rising generation will not feel that there is a burden resting on them that their predecessors did not feel; whether, when we feel that the death of Dr. Hering has severed a link between us and Hahnemann—cut us loose from the time when there was no Homœopathy—it will not give us a new impetus that will carry us on to victories still more glorious than those we have already achieved?

Dr. Lee, the chairman, then said:

It is hardly necessary for me to say anything, after the liberal expressions already made, of the high respect I have for the memory of Dr. Hering. I felt, when the announcement was made of his death, that truly a great man had fallen. But perhaps, as Dr. Dudley has said, it may produce a distribution of labors which may lead to good. A superintending Providence never leaves a work that needs its protection; and I would merely express the exhortation: let us try and imitate the illustrious example set by Dr. Hering, who was willing to sacrifice fortune, and reckless of all personal interests to further the cause of Homœopathy. If we all had his enthusiasm, victory would be far nearer than it seems.

Responding to a call, Dr. H. N. Guernsey said that he concurred heartily and fully in the preamble and resolutions offered by Dr. Lippe.

The question then being upon the adoption of the preamble and resolutions, they were carried unanimously.

Dr. Jos. C. Guernsey then read telegrams from a number of physicians, in various parts of the United States, expressing the great loss the medical profession had sustained in the death of Dr. Hering.

The chairman then extended to the meeting an invitation to be present at the funeral ceremonies, and said: " It is the desire of the family that this meeting shall designate the pall-bearers."

On motion it was resolved that these be appointed by the chair, who then named the following gentlemen, being friends of Dr. Hering, intimate with him in former as well as in late years:

PALL BEARERS.

CHAS. G. RAUE, M.D., Philadelphia.
JAMES KITCHEN, M.D., "
AD. LIPPE, M. D., "
H. N. GUERNSEY, M.D., "
C. NEIDHARD, M.D., "
A. W. KOCH, M.D., "
A. R. THOMAS, M.D., "
J. H. PULTE, M.D., Cincinnati.
W. WESSELHŒFT, M.D., Boston.
F. R. McMANUS, M.D., Baltimore.
H. DETWILLER, M.D., Easton.
JOHN ROMIG, M.D., Allentown.
P. P. WELLS, M.D., Brooklyn.
EDW. BAYARD, M.D., New York.
JOHN F. GRAY, M.D., "
SAMUEL LILIENTHAL, M.D., New York.

Dr. J. C. Guernsey then moved the appointment of a Memorial Committee, to prepare a pamphlet containing an account of the life and works of Dr. Hering. He suggested the following names:

   Dr. Ad. Lippe, *Chairman.*
   Dr. H. N. Guernsey, *Secretary.*
   Dr. J. K. Lee, Philadelphia.
   Dr. Edw. Bayard, New York.
   Dr. Wm. Wesselhœft, Boston.

Dr. Korndœrfer suggested the propriety of a memorial meeting, to be held in the near future, where all who wished might give an expression of their sentiments, and those who could not attend could write. He then moved that the committee named be appointed a committee to call such a meeting. This motion was carried, as also an additional motion to place the whole matter in charge of the Memorial Committee, as named above.

The meeting then adjourned.

MEETING OF NEW YORK PHYSICIANS.

In consequence of the announcement of the sudden demise of Dr. Constantine Hering, a number of his friends met informally at the house of Dr. Alfred K. Hills, on Sunday, July 25th, 1880, for the purpose of condolement, and such other action as might be thought proper and fitting to the occasion.

There were present Drs. Bayard, Burdick, Finch, Bauer, Hofmann, Wilder, Linsley, Cowl, St. Clair Smith, Berghaus, Arthur Hills, Scherzer, Lippe, Wright, Hartley, Brown, Ostrom, B. G. Carleton, and Alfred K. Hills. Letters of regret were received from Drs. Blumenthal, E. Carleton, Jr., F. J. Nott, Deschere, W. H. White, and Doughty.

Dr. Alfred K. Hills called the meeting to order, stated its objects, and there being no objection, requested Dr. Edward Bayard to preside. Upon motion, Dr. Hills was elected secretary, and formally stating his reasons for the action so hurriedly taken, moved that a committee of three be appointed on resolutions, to which the president should be added; Drs. Finch, Burdick and Bauer were thus appointed. The following resolutions were reported and adopted:

WHEREAS, The sad intelligence has reached us that our revered friend and colleague, Dr. Constantine Hering, has passed from our midst; therefore,

Resolved, That we deeply lament that he could not have been spared to finish the great work of his life, the "*Guiding Symptoms of our Materia Medica.*"

Resolved, That in Dr. Hering's death we lose one acknowledged as first in his profession, a man of science, a ripe scholar, a genial friend.

Resolved, That to the afflicted relatives we extend our deepest sympathy and regret.

Resolved, That a copy of the minutes of this meeting be transmitted to the family of the deceased.

Resolved, That delegates be appointed to attend the funeral.

The following delegates were elected: Drs. Edward Bayard, Alfred K. Hills, S. P. Burdick, Chas. A. Bacon, W. I. Bauer, C. Lippe, L. deV. Wilder, St. Clair Smith, E. F. Hofmann, Wm. Scherzer, H. A. Wright, C. E. Blumenthal, M. Deschere, W. H. White, H. I. Ostrom, W. Y. Cowl, Jas. E. Lilienthal, M. A. Brinkman, M. W. Noxon, E. Carleton, Jr., John F. Gray, R. McMurray, F. Franklin Smith, and B. G. Carleton.

Adjourned.

Attest— ALFRED K. HILLS, *Secretary.*

MEETING OF THE PHYSICIANS OF BOSTON AND VICINITY.

The following resolutions were unanimously adopted at a meeting of the homœopathic physicians of Boston and vicinity, on Monday, July 26th, 1880:

Resolved, That in the death of Dr. Constantine Hering, of Philadelphia, the medical profession has met with an irreparable loss; that we recognize in him a man of unusual scientific attainments, accompanied with great power of original investigation, one who devoted a long and busy life to the improvement of medical science, and who, by indomitable energy and industry in the advancement of Homœopathy, has accomplished a work in this country and the world, which shall ever redound to his honor.

Resolved, That we extend to his family and friends our heartfelt sympathy in the great loss they are called upon to bear.

I. T. TALBOT, } *Committee*
C. WESSELHŒFT, } *on*
J. B. BELL,   } *Resolutions.*

M. P. WHEELER, *Sec'y.*

THE FUNERAL SERVICES.

The funeral rites were observed on the morning of July 28th, 1880.

A large number of the relatives and friends, including many homœopathic physicians from other cities and the greater proportion of the profession of Philadelphia, assembled at the house, where the services were conducted by the Rev. S. S. Seward, pastor of the Swedenborgian church, of New York city.

The remains were placed in the rear parlor, and, according to the custom of the Swedenborgians, in, which faith Dr. Hering was a believer, they were encased in a white cloth-covered casket and strewn with flowers. A number of floral tributes placed around the room testified the affection of friends and relatives, and the release from life and its cares was looked upon more as an occasion for joy rather than sorrow, according to the articles of the Swedenborgian faith.

The services were opened by the singing of Dr. Hering's favorite hymn, "Befiehl du deine Wege," (" Let all thy works be guided by the law,") by a quartette choir. The Rev. Chauncey Giles being absent from the city, Rev. S. S. Seward from New York then delivered the following address:

On the first of January, 1800, on Sunday morning, as the organist of a church in a far-away German village was seated at his instrument, word was brought to him that a son and heir had been born to his house. Engaged as he was, he took the only means at hand to express his joy that a man-child had been born into the world, and burst out with the grand old German hymn, "Give thanks to God."

It is now nearly five days since that child, after a most busy and active life, quietly breathed his last on earth, in an upper room in this house; and if we may believe, as many of us do, the promise of the old prophet,

"After two days He will revive us;
In the third day He will raise us up;
And we shall live in His sight"—(Hosea vi, 2),

if we may accept the later promise of our Saviour, who Himself rose "on the third day," that whither He has gone we shall follow Him afterwards, then we may be sure that long before this a far grander hymn has been heard in the spiritual world, in honor of the birth of a man into spiritual and eternal life.

It is a matter of exceeding regret to me on this occasion, that I did not enjoy a personal acquaintance with our departed and beloved brother. But such has been his busy and active life, since I have known him by reputation, both as a physician and member of the church of his and my adoption, I have always felt that any advances in that direction would be improper on my part, and a return impossible on his. I regret it, because it is impossible for me to speak with the same intelligence and warmth that I could do if I had enjoyed more friendly relations with him, and more especially that most intimate and sacred relation which obtains between pastor and friend.

It must be only evident to every candid and thinking man, that if we could understand the relation between this world and the next—if we could clearly and rationally perceive, in other words—why we are born first in this world, to live here a few short years, and then to be transported by what we call death to the other world, there to live to eternity, it would go far both to console us for our own loss, and to remove our fears for our departed friends. Nor is the truth in this case far distant. Like every other truth—like the great medical truth, to the promulgation of which our dear brother devoted his life—it lies at our very door. The facts of the case suggest the solution of the problem. The facts are that we are born in this world, we die, and pass on to the spiritual world. The very fact, therefore, that this life precedes the other is *prima facie* evidence that it is intended, in some way, as a preparation for the other, and that the death which introduces to the latter is but a necessary step in the development of our life. But in order to understand the relations of this life to the other, it is necessary to know something of our relations to the Lord. The Lord is the only source of love, or, what is the same thing, of life. He alone has life in Himself. All other life, whether that of angels or men, is derived from Him, moment by moment. All the life we enjoy to-day is due to a direct and constant influx from Him; and if that influx should be cut off we should cease to exist, as a ray of light ceases to exist as soon as its connexion with the sun is interrupted. But the Lord not only gives us life; He gives it to us in such a manner that it may be our life; or, in other words, in such a manner that we may receive and use it as if it were absolutely our own. For this purpose He created us in this world, on the natural plane, so far removed from His immediate presence that we can receive and enjoy the influx of life from Him, without being directly conscious of the infinite source from which it comes. This could not be the case in the other world. Some of the angels, we are told, "behold His face." They are all near Him, so near that they can at times perceive the influx of His love in their hearts, as we sometimes feel the effect of the sun's warmth in our bodies. Hence it was a part of the Divine economy from the beginning, to create man in this world, where, in the enjoyment of perfect freedom and rationality, he could form a character of his own, capable of receiving the influx of the Divine life to all eternity; and when this was accomplished, to transform him to the other world by the gate of death. This would have been the case if sin had never entered into the world, and man had never fallen. The death that was brought into the world by sin, was the death, not of the body, but of the soul. If the first race of men had not sinned they would have died as to the natural body, just as we do now; except that their lives would have been peaceful and free from hereditary taint, and their deaths quiet and pleasant, like one who lies down to pleasant slumbers. Now that this is the truth with regard to this life, we know by experience. We know, as a matter of theory, that we receive all the life we enjoy from the Lord, moment by moment. But we know, also, as a matter of fact, that we use our life as if it were absolutely our own and self-derived; and it is in view of this grand but simple truth that we find the relation of this world to the other so often alluded to in the sacred scriptures. "He that confesses me before men, him will I also confess before the angels in heaven; and he that denieth Me before men, him will I also deny before My Father and the angels." "He that is faithful in that which is least,"—that is, the lesser things of this world, "is faithful also in much,"—that is, in the greater things of the other world; "and he that is unjust in the least, is unjust also in much." And because the Lord removes men far away, in the beginning of their immortal career, by creating them in the natural world, it is said, in the parable of the talents, that after he had given to one ten, to another five, and to another two, he "went into a far country;" and that afterwards, when he came to reckon with them, he said to those who had faithfully used the talents he had bestowed upon them, "Well done, thou good and faithful servant, thou hast been faithful over a few things, I will make thee ruler over many things; enter thou into the joy of thy Lord."

But we have not time to amplify the subject, though it might be done to an almost unlimited extent; nor is it necessary. Sufficient has been said to answer the purpose of this occasion. For if this doctrine is true, it teaches us that death—I mean the death of the body—is a blessing, instead of a curse; that it was not brought into the world by sin, but would have taken place just the same if man had never fallen; that it is not an interruption, or partial defeat of the purposes of Divine providence, but an orderly step in the development of human life; that it is not in any sense a judgment upon man for his sins, but in the case of every well-disposed person, the crown of his life, the door by which he is admitted to his everlasting reward.

It seems to me, dear friends, that this simple thought affords us especial consolation on this occasion. It teaches us, in the first place, that the great change which has come to our dear friend, is not an end, nor even an interruption, but rather an enlargement of his immortal career; and such being the case, it leaves us nothing to mourn in his behalf. When one of our children, after long years of painful study and preparation, graduates from the university where he has matriculated, into the broader arena of the world around him, we call the event the " commencement," and not the end of his course, and instead of mourning over it, celebrate the occasion with joyful ceremonies. So it seems to us, that now our dear departed brother has graduated from the world, which is the seminary of heaven, into heaven itself, after a longer and far more useful life, a fuller preparation than often falls to the lot of man, it is an occasion of deep gratitude and thankfulness on his account, rather than of sorrow or regret on ours.

But this will appear the more patent to us if we will review for a moment, in the light of this truth, the busy life that has now been ended. To do this it will be necessary to glance for a moment at the work in which he has been engaged. If I may speak as a layman of the system of medical practice of which he was the foremost exponent, I do not hesitate to say that it seems to me one of the greatest blessings vouchsafed to the human race, even in this age of marvels. Indeed, I believe it stands second to but one other—to the revelation of the doctrines of that church of which our beloved brother was a member, and which, though little known to the world as such, are nevertheless spreading themselves throughout the earth, and modifying and uplifting every other system of religious truth of which we have any knowledge. Nay, I may run a little extravagant, but I believe that these two discoveries are intended in the divine providence of the Lord to go hand in hand; the one to do on the natural plane, a work corresponding to that which the other is to do on the spiritual. For, as I believe that the doctrines of the New Jerusalem Church contain within themselves those traits which are capable of removing, by slow degrees, the hereditary evils which have been accumulating for ages in the human soul, so it seems to me that the great law which lies at the foundation of homœopathic practice, if faithfully applied, will gradually remove the hereditary tendency to disease in the human body; and thus that the operation of both taken together, will bring back to man, by a process necessarily slow and painful, but nevertheless sure and certain, the pristine state of innocence and purity he enjoyed in the beginning, and restore the Paradise which man has lost by his evils.

Now, in the work of establishing this system of medicine, Dr. Constantine Hering took an early and prominent part. He went into it when it was little known, and its practitioners few in number, subjected to misunderstanding and contumely, and almost social ostracism. Next to Hahnemann himself he was its most devoted exponent, especially in this country. He consecrated all his energies, not only to the practice but to the teaching, and not only to the teaching, but to the development of this system; and left a name which, if not as widely known outside of professional circles as it deserved to be, will be more known as the years go by. The result is the most wonderful revolution in medical science that the world has ever witnessed, the beneficent fruits of which it is impossible, as yet, to estimate.

But I should do great injustice to the character of him, in honor of whose memory we are gathered here to-day, if I should rest his laurels upon the work he accomplished. It was not so much what he did, as the spirit in which he did it, that glorified his career. A man may accomplish more prodigious results than he did, and yet not be a great man in the true sense of the term. But this cannot be said of Dr. Hering. The work he did, remarkable as it was, was of little importance in comparison with the high principles he brought to bear in doing it. It was the simple integrity—wholeness—of his character that led him to give up the old practice in the beginning. The same fidelity to truth led him afterwards to turn his back upon kingly favors rather than give up, even temporarily, his convictions. And all through his long and varied life, it was this lofty devotion to principle that made him true, not only to the system, but to the highest and best interpretations of the system, and enabled him to imbue, with something of his own faith, all those with whom he was associated. He lived and labored for the cause; not for success, nor popularity, nor even renown. Never was priest or missionary more unselfishly devoted to a noble calling, than he to maintenance of the great idea of Homœopathy. Nor was this due merely to the honesty and earnestness of his character. It was due more, perhaps, than he was conscious of himself, to a deep and strong religious faith; a faith, not merely in a Divine Being or Power who created and preserved the universe, but in a personal and loving God, who yearns over him and all men, and who loves nothing so much as to inspire them with lofty purposes for the good of their fellow-men.

But Dr. Hering was not by any means a one-sided man. On the contrary, his affections went out in sympathy toward every good cause. He fulfilled all the duties of life with something of the same devotion he applied in his professional labors. He was a faithful and tender husband; a kind and affectionate father; a true and steadfast friend; a lover of his country; an earnest admirer of everything that was true in science and beautiful in art; one of the most perfect and completely rounded characters which it is our good fortune to meet in this world.

And now, in conclusion, let us put this and that together— what we have learned with regard to the relation of this life to the other, with what we know of his character and aims. If it is true, as we have said, that this life is a preparation for the other, then his preparation has been more complete than that of most men. His life has been a long and exceedingly active one. He has assumed and discharged all the responsibilities which usually fall to men in this world. In all this he has been actuated by lofty and noble principles, and inspired by a firm and consistent faith in the one God, the Lord and Saviour Jesus Christ. And now that death has come, it comes to him, not as a dread destroyer, but as a loving friend, to introduce him to his final reward. In view of all these things, who is there of us here—who among his professional associates, who among the thousands who have received healing at his hands, who even in his immediate family—who that would call him back again if he could; who that can find it in his heart to do anything but rejoice that his long and active life has been crowned by such a quiet and peaceful death, and that he has at last entered upon the reward of his earthly labors. For him the life that now is has subserved its purpose. By the exercise, in noble undertakings and for praiseworthy purposes, of his great powers here, he has gained a spiritual stature as robust and symmetrical as his physical stature was beautiful and imposing; and now death has come, not to claim him as his own, but to introduce him into the free, and joyous, and never-ending exercise of those powers, in the more immediate presence of the Master, in the spiritual world.

But this is not all. Not only does this line of thought, if true, go far to remove our doubts and fears for our departed friends; it affords ample consolation and encouragement to those who are left behind. Far be it from me to choke one single tear that may be shed upon this grave. The natural affections—of a wife for a husband, and a husband for his wife, of a parent for his child and a child for his parent, and of a friend for a friend—are right and proper. They were implanted in our hearts by the Lord Himself for a good purpose. Without them this world would be a wilderness, full of enmity and discord. By means of them we are drawn together by indissoluble bonds, and the most sacred and tender relations made possible. It cannot be expected that such affections can be overcome in a moment. The

Lord Himself does not require it at our hands. "He knoweth our frame; He remembereth that we are dust." Nevertheless it should be our effort, even in the midst of our deepest sorrows, to look up; not to seek consolation in forgetfulness, but to follow our departed friends, in affection and thought, to the higher and better world to which they have gone. And it will help us to do this to remember that this life is but a preparation for the other, and that every circumstance by which we are surrounded here is intended, if we will take the right advantage of it, to conduce to our happiness there. Nor in the meantime, before we can join our loved ones on the other side, need we give up to despair. That love for them, which made up so great a proportion of our life, and which now seems as if it must die out of our hearts for want of an object, need not cease its outward flow for a moment. On the contrary we can love them more and more unselfishly now than we ever could before. While they were yet with us there was more or less of the taint of selfishness in all that we did for them, because it could not fail to meet with at least the reward of their approval. But now we can do what we know they would have us do, and be what we know they would desire us to be, without the possibility of any other reward except such as is to be found in doing good for its own sake; and thus we can love them with a purer and more spiritual affection than while they were yet present with us on earth. Let us, therefore, try to find consolation for our great bereavement in these thoughts. Let us no longer selfishly mourn for our departed brother, knowing that the change which has come to him is but an orderly step in the development of his life, and that his preparation for it has been all that our fondest desires could ask. Let us not give up to doubt and despair, but let us follow him in thought into that brighter world whither he has gone. Let the lesson of his life reflect a clearer and stronger light back upon our own, teaching us the meaning of that which now is and the important bearing of the things which surround us here upon our state hereafter. In the meantime, let not our love for him be choked in the slightest degree; but let it find a fuller expression and exercise, if we are his professional friends, in greater devotion to the cause he had at heart; and if we belong to his immediate family, in realizing, as far as possible, his tender wishes in our behalf.

At the conclusion of Mr. Seward's address the choir sang a hymn composed by K. E. Hering, a brother of the deceased, entitled, "At the Grave," and at its close the casket was carried by the selected pall-bearers to the hearse in waiting, and then conveyed to North Laurel Hill Cemetery. Here the cortege was received by the members of Concordia and Sængerbund singing societies, who united in singing hymns during the interment, which was very impressive, scarcely a dry eye being seen among the numerous persons surrounding the place of burial.

As the dull thud of mother earth was heard, shutting away from mortal sight the remains of the departed, the relatives and friends slowly and sadly wended their way homeward, feeling bereft of as sincere a friend as ever lived. Drs. W. B. Trites, J. C. Guernsey, and C. Mohr remained until the grave had been filled, and after paying a last tribute of respect and affection, by placing on the new-made grave the floral devices stricken hearts had lovingly tendered, they too proceeded homeward, leaving all that was mortal of Constantine Hering to the watchful eye of his Creator.

MEMORIAL MEETINGS.

The committee appointed at the meeting of the homœopathic physicians held in Philadelphia on Sunday afternoon, July 25th, 1880, met at the call of its chairman, Dr. Ad. Lippe, and resolved to request the holding of memorial meetings on Sunday evening, October 10th, 1880, in all cities of the world where homœopathic practitioners are to be found. Pursuant to this request, meetings were held, but not all on the same day, that being found impracticable. The proceedings of these several meetings are here published in the chronological order of their occurrence.

ONONDAGA COUNTY HOMŒOPATHIC MEDICAL SOCIETY.

A meeting of above named Society was held in Syracuse, N. Y., August 3d, 1880, at which were present Dr. J. R. Long, President, Dr. C. D. Hale, Secretary, and seventeen of its thirty members.

The president, in a few appropriate remarks, announced the decease of Dr. C. Hering, of Philadelphia. On motion, the president appointed a committee of three, consisting of Drs. Harris, Jennings and Seward, to prepare suitable resolutions in reference thereto.

The committee, in due course, reported the following:

Constantine Hering departed this life the 23d of last month, at his home in Philadelphia. He has fallen full of years and full of honors. For more than fifty years his services to Homœopathy have been so unremitting, so unselfish, and so eminent that it is a duty to place a memorial to him upon our minutes. Oschatz, in Saxony, has the honor of being the place of his birth, which occurred January 1st, 1800. The University of Leipsic was his Alma Mater. Such was his standing while yet an undergraduate that he was selected to write a work against the system of Hahnemann. He entered upon his task with undoubting zeal, but his investigations led him to adopt the new faith. March 27th, 1827, he received the degree of M. D. from the University of Wurzburg. His thesis was entitled " De Medicina Futura." In it he vindicated Homœopathy " *con amore.*" He came to Philadelphia in 1833. He assisted in establishing the school at Allentown, Pa., and became one of its teachers. It was the first school opened anywhere in the interests of Homœopathy. In 1846 he took the chair of Materia Medica in the first Homœopathic College in Philadelphia. He was one of the originators of the American Institute of Homœopathy, itself the oldest national medical society in the United States, and was chosen its first President. He was a voluminous author. Many of his works have been translated into foreign languages, and their worth will ensure their survival. The industry of the man is represented in his study, three sides of which from floor to ceiling are lined with manuscripts from his prolific pen. Gifted with intellectual strength and with rare powers of discernment, he knew how to gather and classify facts and formulate their general laws. His varied and accurate learning, his tireless industry, his genius for observation, and his single-hearted devotion to medical science fitted him to be a master workman in our school. He was its Coryphæus. His death creates a large void which it will not be easy to fill.

We join in the general grief over the heavy loss, and we tender to the bereaved family our condolence and sympathy.

The report was adopted, and on motion it was resolved to send to the family of deceased a notice of the action of the Society, duly authenticated.

HOMŒOPATHIC MEDICAL SOCIETY OF NORTHERN NEW YORK.

The Homœopathic Medical Society of Northern New York met in annual session at Saratoga Springs, August 10th, 1880. During the session, Dr. H. M. Paine, of Albany, offered resolutions of respect to the memory of Dr. Constantine Hering.

Dr. Gray, of New York, in seconding the resolutions, spoke feelingly of the high estimation in which the deceased was held, and of his great services in the department of the Homœopathic Materia Medica.

The resolutions were adopted as follows:

WHEREAS, This Society has learned with deep sorrow of the decease of the venerable Nestor of medicine, Dr. Constantine Hering, of Philadelphia ; therefore,

Resolved, That in the death of this veteran physician, one of the pioneers of Homœopathy in this country, we have sustained an irreparable loss; our school a wise and influential leader, an original thinker, a sagacious counsellor; and the public a prudent and eminently successful practitioner.

Resolved, That his untiring labors in the unexplored fields of homœopathic provings, and in his admirable tact and genius in elucidating therefrom an accurate and eminently practical system of therapeutics, comprise voluminous contributions to standard medical literature of great practical utility to the medical profession.

Resolved, That his genius, his intuitive perception, his indefatigable industry, his powers of analysis, inductive reasoning, sound and logical discrimination, placed him in the foremost rank of homœopathic physicians.

Resolved, That his noble qualities of mind, his genial and courteous manner, his ingenuous, child-like simplicity of character, his readiness to draw from his vast stores of medical research which he had long and patiently accumulated, endeared him to the medical profession, and prompt us to hold his name and memory in the most affectionate remembrance.

Resolved, That while we deeply mourn his loss, we gratefully revere his memory, and emulate his unselfish and life-long devotion to the promotion of the best interests of humanity.

MICHIGAN COLLEGE OF PHYSICIANS AND SURGEONS.

A special meeting of the College of Physicians and Surgeons of Michigan, called to take appropriate action upon the occasion of the death of Dr. Constantine Hering, of Philadelphia, convened in Detroit, on the evening of August 16th, 1880, a full quorum of members being present, with Drs. E. R. Ellis and P. B. Morgan as visitors.

In the absence of the president, Dr. Wm. M. Bailey, vice-president, occupied the chair.

The recorder, Dr. J. G. Gilchrist, stated the object of the meeting and spoke in eulogy of the life and labors of the great man whose recent death had startled the profession, after which a motion was passed that a committee be appointed to prepare suitable resolutions. Drs. J. G. Gilchrist and P. B. Morgan were appointed.

After further remarks, many of the speakers recalling instances of personal communion with Dr. Hering, the following preamble and resolutions were unanimously adopted.

WHEREAS: This College has received the painful intelligence that Dr. Constantine Hering has been called away from the scene of his labors, in the hope of entering upon another and higher life; and,

WHEREAS: The officers and fellows of this College realize that in his death the profession of medicine has lost one of its brightest ornaments, and most earnest workers; therefore,

RESOLVED: That we publicly express our keen appreciation of the loss we have sustained, in common with the whole profession.

RESOLVED: That while we regret that his labors have been terminated, we recognize the inestimable value, and enduring character of the work he has been permitted to accomplish, and left as a heritage to us, his successors in the cause he loved so well.

RESOLVED: That these resolutions and the accompanying preamble, be spread upon the minutes of the College, and a copy transmitted to the Memorial Committee in Philadelphia.

BRITISH HOMŒOPATHIC CONGRESS.

At the British Homœopathic Congress, held at Leeds in September, 1880, the following resolution was duly presented and unanimously passed:

That this meeting of British homœopathic practitioners has

heard with the deepest regret of the recent death of the venerable Constantine Hering, of Philadelphia; that they desire to place upon record the strong sense they entertain of the value of the services that Dr. Hering has rendered to the science of medicine during the whole of his professional career, and of the great zeal and energy he has ever shown in the advancement, development, and propagation of Homœopathy; that they at the same time desire to express their sympathy with the members of his family, his colleagues in the Hahnemann Medical College, and his professional brethren in Philadelphia, at the loss they have sustained by his death.

NEW YORK STATE SOCIETY.

At the semi-annual meeting of the New York State Homœopathic Medical Society, held at Brooklyn, at the afternoon session, Tuesday, September 7th, 1880, Dr. Samuel Lilienthal spoke as follows:

I am sure the Society will pardon me for interrupting its proceedings at this time, for I have a matter to bring before it which it seems to me should receive attention to-day. We all know that we have lately lost one whom we called Father, Constantine Hering, of Philadelphia. I think it is one of the greatest losses Homœopathy has sustained in this country, and I would move that the president appoint a committee to draft suitable resolutions in relation to the death of Dr. Hering, the Father of Homœopathy in this country.

The motion was carried, and the president appointed as committee, Drs. P. P. Wells, of Brooklyn, and Samuel Lilienthal, of New York, with instructions to report at the session on Wednesday.

At the session on Wednesday morning, Dr. P. P. Wells spoke as follows:

Mr. President:—Before proceeding to read what I have written, it will be, perhaps, but just to myself to say that I was taken altogether by surprise last evening on receiving notice that I had been appointed to prepare resolutions commemorative of the death of our colleague, Dr. Hering. The time given in which to arrange my thoughts appropriately to so vast a subject and put them on paper, was so brief that it was exceedingly embarrassing. The interest I have in the memory of that great man, and the many years of intimacy I have had with him, forbade my declining to attempt, as best I could, to present to you this morning the brief preamble and resolutions which I now read:

In Oschatz, in Saxony, on January 1st, 1800, it pleased Almighty God to give a great blessing to the world of science and to the world of suffering in the birth of an infant, who afterwards became known to us as the man, Constantine Hering. It pleased the same Almighty goodness to remove him from us by death on the twenty-third day of July, 1880. In view of the life and its labors which filled the space between these points of time, we resolve,

1st. Gratitude to Him who gave so long life and so great powers for good to our friend and brother, and that for so many years He gave it to us to receive inspiration from his great knowledge and generous spirit, becoming to us our leader and teacher, our father and friend, our light in the art of healing, and our example in his never-failing devotion to the cause and interests of truth in all the time and circumstances through which he passed.

2d. Gratitude to the memory of him by whose labors we have been so greatly enriched.

3d. That in Hering, the philosopher, we remember his vast extent of knowledge, his vigorous pursuit and grasp of facts, his ready appropriation of these and his facile tracing of the relationship of new facts to old, and their sure reference to their proper place in the circle of facts known.

4th. That in him, as a teacher, we remember his clear perception of facts, and of just those his pupil needed first to know, and his skill in imparting them in the manner and sequence best adapted to meet these needs, and his heart-felt gladness in giving from his fulness to the wants of all who would learn. That he never was weary of adding to the knowledge of others from the vast treasures he had gathered in his long life of unexampled activity.

5th. As a physician, we remember his loyalty to his convictions of truth, and to the law of healing he had accepted from the great master; his clear perception of the facts of disease and of the specification of the agencies he employed for its cure, and his never-failing or faltering endeavors to add to the number of these, and that from these endeavors have come to us a knowledge of many of our most precious remedies.

6th. As an author, we remember the great number and excellence of the productions of his pen, each bearing in clear characters the impress of the individuality and genius of the writer, the whole making a series of unexampled extent, interest and value. We remember these as abounding in compact thought, with facts contributed to our knowledge, with suggestions of relationships of these to other facts and to each other; all so luminous with the effulgence of genius, and so astonishing by reason of the great labors they disclose. We remember that it is to these labors the literature of Homœopathy is indebted for more than half its wealth.

7th. As a man, we remember him as largely endowed by nature with the noblest qualities; frank, generous, affectionate, true, noble in his aspirations, loving the good and hating all that was mean, he has left to us a memory to which we can always recur with pleasure and profit. As an embodiment of great knowledge and learning, by his death he impresses us with a sense of our great loss, and we are constrained to feel and say we shall never look on his like again.

Dr. Samuel Lilienthal spoke as follows:

Will you allow me, in seconding these resolutions, to say a few words about our departed friend. One thing which endeared him to all those who were acquainted with him was the great encouragement he always held out to the young. There was no difference manifested in him, no matter who it was that came. Any one who came to him poor went away rich. Another thing which I always admired so much in Constantine Hering was, that you never heard him say, "Homœopathy will go down." He knew, as one of the founders of Homœopathy, that the legacy was left in good hands, and I am pretty sure our young men will take pride in following such a good example as that which Constantine Hering left them. I remember on one occasion he said, "I have no fears for Homœopathy; we shall mix with other schools, and I am pretty sure that the other schools will come to us." Dr. Hering died in harness. At six o'clock on the evening of his death he made his last prescription. It was for a poor German in broken health, who had been treated by the old school without any benefit; he examined him and expressed a doubt whether he could be made a whole man again; but he said he must relieve him, so he gave him a prescription. This was another beautiful trait in his character, that he knew the great resources of the Materia Medica, and when others despaired he was hopeful. His memory should be sacred to us. I hope the resolutions, as prepared by Dr. Wells, will be accepted unanimously.

The resolutions were adopted by a rising vote, every member of the Society rising.

PENNSYLVANIA STATE SOCIETY.

At the annual meeting of the Homœopathic Medical Society of the State of Pennsylvania, held at Easton, September 8th and 9th, 1880, the president, Dr. John K. Lee, concluded his address with the following words:

As an appendix to these desultory thoughts, I would ask your permission to pay a brief tribute to our late colleague and co-laborer, the illustrious Dr. Hering. With natural ambition of a high order, strengthened and developed by careful culture, he in early life, for the purpose of refutation, applied himself to the study of Homœopathy, and as his logical mind advanced in this investigation and he turned the clear light of reason upon its alleged principles, and placed their proofs in the crucible of experience, the vigor of his prejudice relaxed and gave way to convictions, and these convictions gradually hardened into firm belief until, like Paul who went out with threatenings to persecute the saints, he renounced his hostility and became the champion of a new medical faith. Placing himself in communication with Hahnemann, he received a full revelation of this great truth and its corollaries, and imbued with the sentiments of his master and an ardent desire for their triumph, he sought an asylum in the New World, where, under the protecting ægis of our free institutions, he could accomplish his mission without embarrassment or interference.

Here, for nearly half a century, with untiring industry and zeal, he prosecuted his researches, and from the perennial fountain of his pen flowed a continuous stream to fertilize the seed he had planted; and ere his great heart had ceased its pulsations, his eyes were ravished with a view of the waving harvest as a reward of his benevolent and useful labors.

Truly a great man has fallen—great intellectually, and great in the simplicity and grandeur of his character, but greater still in the possession of those moral attributes which elevate man to that exalted plane where he can abnegate himself and make all personal considerations subordinate to the higher and holier interest of a common brotherhood. His last moments were a fitting climax to his distinguished labors, since amid the undisturbed repose and endeared associations of his study, surrounded by his unpublished manuscripts and other evidences of his unremitting toil, he at once ceased to write and to live.

He requires no marble shaft to preserve the reward of his life or tell the story of his achievements, for his history is the warp and woof of nearly every page of our literature; his memory will be cherished by thousands yet unborn, and his fame will only brighten by the lapse of time. Whilst we may not be able to receive the mantle that has fallen from his shoulders, we can imitate the brilliant example of his devotion to the cause he so ably espoused; and ere his lifeless form has faded into dust and the wintry winds wail their plaintive requiem over his grave, let us renew our vows of fidelity to Homœopathy, and endeavor to realize, as he eminently did,

"He most lives who thinks most—feels the noblest—acts the best."

At the conclusion of the address, a committee consisting of Drs. J. H. McClelland, Aug. Korndœrfer and H. Detwiller was appointed to draft suitable resolutions of respect, and in due time the chairman of the committee presented the following:

The Homœopathic Medical Society of Pennsylvania, in annual session assembled, with unanimous voice adopts the following minute:

The death of Dr. Constantine Hering, of Philadelphia, on the 23d day of July, 1880, is recognized as an event of signal import in the history of medicine. It marks the close of a life, remarkable for unflagging and long-sustained industry in the cause of medical science and in promoting the good of his kind. With full recognition of his prodigious labors in the field of Materia Medica and Homœopathic Therapeutics, the attainments of Dr. Hering in general science and letters entitle him to a high place among men of learning in this enlightened age.

This Society, therefore, records with willing hands its high appreciation of the distinguished dead, and with sentiments of high regard, offers heartfelt sympathy to the bereaved family.

By a rising vote the report was unanimously adopted.

NEW YORK COUNTY HOMŒOPATHIC MEDICAL SOCIETY.

Pursuant to call a special meeting of the Homœopathic Medical Society of the County of New York, convened on the evening of October 7th, 1880, the president, Dr. W. Hanford White, occupying the chair, and Dr. Alfred K. Hills acting as secretary.

There were present, Drs. W. Hanford and J. R. White, E. Bayard, S. Lilienthal, L. Hallock, H. D. Paine, T. F. Allen, E. M. Kellogg, H. M. Smith, Jos. Finch, C. Th. Liebold, S. P. and A. H. Burdick, H. A. Wright, E. Carleton, Jr., H. Von Musits, G. S. Norton, M. Deschere, E. A. Jennings, M. Leal, J. H. Demarest, M. C. Man, John Butler, J. W. Dowling, C. Williams, W. Y. Cowl, F. Oertel, J. A. Carmichael, J. and F. Donavan, and Alfred K. Hills.

The president, after announcing briefly the object of the meeting, called upon Dr. E. Bayard, who responded as follows:

If a great man is one to whom God has given large gifts, and who has cultivated them to the extent of his powers for the best interests of his fellow-beings, then Constantine Hering was a great man. He was not a money-getter. His powers did not work in the direction of accumulating property. He did not care to amass this world's goods; but he wanted to be rich in learning, especially in all that pertained to his profession.

He was logical, discriminating, a great lover of nature, and a close observer of her. He was a hard student, of unwearied industry. He "sought Truth earnestly, and he found it." He made note of all his observations; hence he left behind him a large amount of valuable writing.

He was engaged at the time of his death in a great work, his "Guiding Symptoms," and would to God he had been permitted to finish that work; but it was otherwise ordered. I am told by those who knew his habits, that every sentence in that work was studied over sometimes for hours, that his true meaning might be expressed. That he might lose no time, his writing-desk and materials were brought close to the side of his couch, so that he could arise in the night, light the lamp and continue his work. As for recreation and amusement, he knew little of either outside of his profession.

While a subject of the Saxon Government, he was commissioned to make collections as a naturalist in Surinam, South America. In the course of this study he found facts illustrating the truth of Homœopathy, and gave account of them to a homœopathic journal in Germany. His Government objected to this work as heterodox. Dr. Hering thought he ought not to be controlled in any respect in the service of scientific truth. Upon the instant he resigned his commission and sought a free land, where his thoughts or the expression of them for the advancement of his race would not be controlled. He found such freedom in this country.

This showed his noble independence of character, and his earnest search and love of Truth, which would not permit him to weigh against her a social position and a money consideration. He sought this New World to work and plow the field the providence of God assigned to him, with gifts to carry out fully and nobly his work, ere he was called away to be set in the heavens by the side of Hahnemann, Bœnninghausen, Stapf and Jahr—a galaxy whose light will continue when the things of this earth and its monuments of brass and stone have crumbled.

Is it not wise and right that we should look into the sheaves of the rich harvest garnered by our late beloved colleague for our own instruction, and that we should examine into the principles that governed him in the profession and practice to which he devoted his life, and in which he stood out so eminently the acknowledged leader?

Dr. Hering made this the essential point of doctrine and practice: to cure the sick easily and permanently, by medicines capable of themselves of producing in a healthy person morbid symptoms similar to those of the sick. He sought no other cure, nor recognized it as one, unless it was under the law proclaimed by Hahnemann. He sought no palliation, except under this law, believing that it hindered and endangered a perfect cure. He believed that the morbid condition of tissues and organs are the result of the dynamic disturbance, and not the cause of the disease. He was therefore a Vitalist—believing disease to be the disturbance of the vital force, and its equalization the state of health. He believed that the totality of symptoms, subjective and objective, are the only indications for the choice of a remedy. He did not believe that prescribing on the pathological states, nor diagnosis where the vital powers were tending to those states, were sufficient to effect a cure. The symptoms in their totality alone were the only guide for a cure to him.

He believed that the only proper way to ascertain the disturbing properties of medicine on the vital force is to prove them on the healthy; that thereby only the true expression of that disturbance can be observed. And he believed that in order to obtain and secure the highest curative results, medicines must be administered singly and in a dose just sufficient to cure, because he knew that all action is followed by reaction (there is no exception to this law); that all action on the vital powers is, by an inherent law, followed sooner or later by reaction, which terminates in cure and health. Hence an overdose must, by its intensity of action, delay or prevent reaction and cure.

I remember on a certain occasion, early in my practice, I told Dr. Hering of my suffering. He asked me the remedy I had taken, and seemed to think it well chosen. He then asked the dilution. I told him the third. "Ah," said he, "you have stopped it, but perhaps not made a cure." He shook his head and seemed disappointed. He said no more; but he caused me to reflect that it might well be so—that I had thrown an obstacle before the diverted vital force—that I had stayed its forward movement by a shock that injured its reactive power—as a boulder thrown before a carriage wheel in motion stops it, but cripples the wheel.

Dr. Hering believed that when he produced the impression at the right point, and in the right direction, the force must be permitted to be exhausted; therefore he waited. Shorter or longer the time, he waited, his eyes wide open, and his observation on a stretch, looking for that action which is to end in equalization.

Dr. Constantine Hering was a true Homœopathist. He believed in Homœopathy and lived up to it. He believed that the highest results in his art were obtained by close individualization alone, not by generalization. I loved him for his simplicity and directness of character; for his large, brilliant inquiry after truth, and for his resting on principles derived from a patient examination of facts.

He enriched our Materia Medica by his severe labors. I will not name the many remedies he has proven, arranged and published. You know them all. The diligent student of our Materia Medica must have observed how full, exact and characteristic were the medicines proved and arranged by Hahnemann. Just so were the provings and arrangements by Dr. Hering equally clear, full, exact and characteristic. He took his great master, Hahnemann, as his model, and we only hope that those who may have the direction of arranging and publishing his writings will give them to us just as he set them down. Then we shall feel that the seal of reliability is placed upon them.

When some patient astronomer, who night after night has been watching the stars, brings to light some unknown planet, to do him honor the new-born world is called after his name, and the discoverer is never to be forgotten. If the astronomer is worthy of distinction, what shall we say of the man who brings to light a new remedial agent to relieve suffering humanity, ward off death, and bring back health? He, methinks, has done a greater work. And so the great discoverer of Lachesis will be gratefully remembered by those who know how to apply this remedy in all its varied forms, for which in the provings he suffered; and his only suffering was from the seal set by Lachesis, from which he never wholly recovered. That suffering was a crown of glory to him.

Constantine Hering showed in his death his medical principles, and showed that if the homœopathic law, the law proclaimed by Hahnemann, was followed, a man would live longer and die easier than under any other practice; for he that is filled with disturbing drugs must die as the hunted fox, torn and rent by the bloody mouths of a pack of hounds. But he that follows the practice of our beloved colleague, will have sleep rather than death. The forces equalized, he has rest. He ceases to exist by the withdrawal of his life by the Giver of life; as some locomotive running smoothly upon the track, after exhausting her fuel, slows down and stops—not thrown from the rails by broken machinery, and rushing to ruin with terrible violence.

At six o'clock in the evening he made his last prescription to a patient, observing to his wife with great animation and interest, that this patient had been prescribed for by many physicians, and he believed he should help him. Then he went, as he was accustomed, to take his evening meal with his family, which he greatly enjoyed in that social circle under an arbor in his garden. At eight o'clock, the meal being over, Dr. Hering said he would retire to his study and his couch. His devoted wife went with him to aid him in preparing for bed. He said to her: "I believe I shall sleep." She left him to his repose. At ten he touched his bell, which summoned her at once to his side. He remarked that his breathing was embarrassed, accompanied by constant yawning. He asked her to get a book in his office that he might examine this symptom. She did as directed; but being alarmed sent for a physician. I believe he selected the remedy and laid down to sleep. In a short time, without pain, without a struggle, he passed into that sleep which knows no waking—and the great physician demonstrated the benign, gentle, but controlling influence of the action of the great law to which he devoted his life. Thus died Constantine Hering, dear to Homœopathy, and to be forever honored by its true practitioners.

Dr. S. Lilienthal said:

For the little that I am, the little I ever accomplished, the little reputation I have gained, I have to thank two men, who have gone home to do more precious work in higher spheres—I mean Carroll Dunham and Constantine Hering.

The day I made the personal acquaintance of Father Hering will never be forgotten, as long as I live. In the beginning of the year 1870 I had received an invitation from the faculty of the Hahnemann College, in Philadelphia, to deliver a lecture during the preliminary course. Our mutual friend, Dr. Raue, introduced me to the Father of Homœpathy in America. With that even, cheerful smile on his face, he looked at me attentively, and then, with a sonorous laugh, he addressed Raue, "I thought I would see a young man before me, and now that hard-working Lilienthal is as grey as I am." I soon found myself at home, in the full sense of the word, in his company, and when after that lecture we met at Raue's house, to spend a few hours in convivial conversation, Constantine Hering was the life of the whole company. It is just ten years ago or, perhaps, eleven, when the firm of Boericke & Tafel bought out Mr. Radde, in New York, and they seriously intended to give up the *North American Journal of Homœopathy*. Hering would not listen to it. "There is your editor," he said, pointing to me, "and we must support him." Relying on this great support, not in words, but in deeds, I accepted the trust, and Hering has never disappointed the readers of the Quarterly. In fact, this was one of the great traits of this great and good man, that his word was as good as his bond, and as number after number appeared for the last ten years, he kept on cheering to the last; and now that he has departed, I consider it my duty to collect from the old German literature the writings of our Father, and give them to you in that old Quarterly of mine.

During the Centennial World's Convention at Philadelphia, friend Raue was again my host, and one day, visiting Papa Hering, he requested me to invite some congenial spirits and meet that night quietly at Raue's. Though it was the night of the big ball and it rained torrents, the old man came to 121 North Tenth street, according to promise, and I never can forget the happy hours passed there. Hering and Dunham were sitting on the sofa together, Dunham asking and Hering answering, and we, a dozen or so, listening to that interesting conversation. The rain had stopped; it was a clear night, and when we broke up Hering felt so happy he would not ride home, and invited us as his bodyguard to accompany him the short distance. The next morning Dunham and myself compared notes at the Continental hotel and as Carroll Dunham said: "We felt better to have spent such an evening with such a master, and we envied the physicians who could enjoy (night after night) such a privilege."

It was my habit to make, year after year, my pilgrimage to this holy shrine, and I always left it highly satisfied with my gain. If I learned my lessons in liberality and charity from Dunham, I learned from Hering to value the opinions of others, and to despise those who preach one thing and practice another. Any falsity was an abomination to his straightforward manner, and the language which he then could use, was more forcible than elegant. He always felt happy in the midst of the young and rising generation, and none ever left him without an encouraging word. Envy was unknown to him, for he knew that he had done his duty to humanity, and no one was more pleased than Father Hering with the increase of our homœopathic literature. The one great fault which this master had, was, he tried too much, he began too much, as if life would last forever. His restless mind knew only work, work, work, and if tired of one thing there were so many wakeful ganglia in that large brain that other work could be accomplished, and thus we find in that glorious room up stairs, and in those safes down stairs, treasures garnered, which he intended to give us, piece by piece, but threescore years and ten and perchance four more is the allotted time, and though a gracious Providence spared him so long to us, the clock has run down. Let us honor the memory of Constantine Hering by continuing those masterly works which he laid out for us during his lifetime. Thus, though departed, he still lives in us and with us.

Remarks of Dr. T. F. Allen :

Mr. President and members of the Homœopathic Medical Society of the County of New York.

Some of our colleagues can speak of the departed hero, whom we commemorate this evening, as a fellow-laborer, as one with whom they toiled in their earlier as well as during their more mature years; to me, he seems like a pioneer, one whose labors were to be built upon, one who prepared the way, who hewed straight paths through the thickets and let light into dark places. This feeling toward him had birth when one winter's evening, twenty years ago, my revered preceptor, Dr P. P. Wells, took me to a meeting at the house of Dr. Joslin, the elder, on the corner of University Place and Thirteenth Street. How vividly I remember that evening, the calm, philosophical Joslin, the earnest Bayard, the positive Wells, the dogmatic Reisig, the keen-eyed Fincke, and the enthusiastic life and centre of all— Hering. I was the only young man present, fresh from the University, full of the teachings of the scholastics, full of the old time prejudices of my father. That group of men, that enthusiasm of Hering, the whole tone of thought was so different from that of the schools, that I was forced to believe in a vitalizing truth in Homœopathy. I ventured one little remark to Dr. Wells during the evening. Dr. Reisig was explaining some preparation of *Castile soap,* which he considered a specific for burns. He was in the habit of applying it locally and of giving a potency internally, and Dr. Hering was combatting the local application. I asked Dr. Wells, almost in a whisper, "but does it cure?" "*Cure,*" thundered Reisig, " of course it does." Hering looked at me, smiled, and said, "That was a good question." My heart warmed toward him, and from that time we were friends, though he did not always approve of my way of doing things. Hering was always searching for truth; he despised no contribution to his large knowledge, however humble its source; *he proved all things and held fast to that which was good.* One can but be impressed by the avidity with which he sought for the truth, while reading his earlier contributions to homœopathic literature. His first article is in the *Archiv f. Homœopatische Heilkunst,* for 1828, a letter to the editor, Dr. Stapf, from Surinam, dated Sept. 28th, 1827. Prefacing the letter the editor remarks: " These communications from Dr. Hering, of Dresden, who is well known to several readers of this *Archiv* and highly esteemed as a zealous naturalist and warm friend of Homœopathy, now for more than a year journeying in South America studying the natural sciences and medicine, deserve a place in this journal, on account of interesting notes concerning the diseases of those countries and their homœopathic treatment; they will also be peculiarly welcome to those more nearly related to him giving, as they do, information concerning his life and doings." First he gives us a careful analysis of sea-sickness and his experience with Cocculus 12th, followed by Staphisagria 30th. In succeeding communications he relates his experience with Leprosy, the symptoms of which he studied most carefully. The enthusiasm with which he took up the study of Psorinum, the provings of which Hahnemann reluctantly, and after patient investigations, allowed to be published, was characteristic of the man; now was his restless mind content; he seemed to see boundless possibilities in the "nosodes" and took up the fascinating, but fatal, doctrine of Isopathy, and enlarged, embellished and generalized from it, till he found the bottom of soft, slimy ooze, which he then struggled out of and hastened to wash clean off his skirts. In his latter years he saw clearly that it was fatal to Homœopathy, and, like a true savant, he retracted all he had said in its favor.

I can testify, with thousands, to his large heartedness, to his never-failing generosity. In the special work on Materia Medica which I have undertaken he has always been ready, even anxious, to help me; from the time when I translated his provings of Aloes, Apis, etc., for the *American Hom. Review*, to my latest task, I am proud to acknowledge with gratitude the encouragement and assistance received from Dr. Hering. We differed in some things and he has berated me soundly for differing, but his help continued.

His faith in the homœopathic law of cure was boundless, his faith in his friends almost equally boundless; by nature, trusting as trustworthy, he gathered from everybody, and his shelves, groaning beneath the weight of the harvest, testify to his unwearied industry.

We shall do highest honor to Constantine Hering by imitating his example. Could he have desired more than that? There has never been a time in the history of Homœopathy when it was more necessary to hold fast to the first principles of our faith; never a time when more were inquiring the way to save the sick than now, and shall we relax our firm grasp upon what we know to be right, for the sake of gaining popularity? Hering knew, as we know, that the right would prevail; he knew, as we know, that the chief principles of Hahnemann are laws of nature. Let us then imitate him. Let us be *enthusiastic*. Let us be *scientific.* Let us be *industrious.* Let us seek the good that is in everyone and help one another. So shall we honor Hering.

Dr. Joseph Finch said:

Mr. President: I wish this evening to add my humble testimony to the worth of the great and good man who has gone from us.

In regard to the death of our friend, Dr. Constantine Hering, there can be but one sentiment, one feeling, viz., that of loss, irreparable loss, the extent of which we do not realize to-night, but shall more and more in the days that are to come.

The immediate circle in which he lived and moved has parted with its brightest light and its sincerest friend; and those who have only known him through the medium of his zealous labors with the pen, missing the profoundness of his research and the unusual clearness of his statements, will gather up and cherish what he has given with a double care. Homœopathy has lost her eldest son, her clearest-sighted pioneer, her bravest defender.

He was her Nestor in America, and when she writes his epitaph many words will be required, each a picture in itself, to describe the hero she has lost, the friend she has buried.

His unparalleled devotion to Homœopathy was not the outgrowth of fidelity to a school, nor could it be justly attributed to the impulses of an ambitious nature. It was founded in the deepest conviction of an earnest heart, and stimulated by a manly love of truth.

He was not partisan in feeling. He was not a hobbyist, but a scientist that commanded the admiration of his friends and the respect of his foes. But he has gone, and our grieving shall be tempered by submission to the will and wisdom of that Divine Providence which gave him to us at the first, which sustained him so long and well in his professional career, and hath in the full harvest time gathered him so peacefully to the garner of refined and ripened life—his home in the skies.

Dr. C. Th. Liebold said:

Mr. President: I am not a convert to Homœopathy, I have been brought up in the faith. In fact, among my earliest recollections is the magic relief of a very severe pain by two or three diminutive sugar pellets, administered after careful selection in "Hering's Homœopathischer Hausarzt," by my parents. I have never wavered in my faith, neither the ridicule nor the scientific contempt of greater or lesser medical and non-medical lights has ever for a moment been able to extinguish the memory of the fact that it did help. Not that I have ever remained faithful to the smallest possible pellets or to any other "dictum" about the "dose," but nothing has struck me more forcibly or made me a more confirmed homœopath than the attendance on lectures on Allopathic Materia Medica. On one side the advice never to give more medicine than just enough to cure; on the other from Arsenic down to Zingiber, how much a patient could possibly bear without doing him serious harm, and so and so much will kill a large dog, while so and so much will finish a puppy.

Reminded to present also my mite at this memorial meeting, I rummaged among my old papers and found a copy of a letter addressed to Dr. Hering, nearly fifteen years ago, soon after I had settled in this city. The occasion was a letter written to a mutual acquaintance but indirectly to me, inquiring about information on some questions concerning the eyes. The first was the dilatation of the pupil by atropia to facilitate ophthalmoscopic examinations, and whether it would not cause permanent mydriasis in some cases? The second: what was really the cause of the sparkling of the eyes (augenglänzen)? The third: what are the crossed (rhombic) lines in the field of vision? It does not matter about the answers, I only mention the fact because the inquirer was then three-score and six, but still young enough to learn a lesson and an example, which I only hope to be able to follow.

Some years later I remember he asked my opinion about that

mischievous but plausible humbug of dry cupping of the eyeball.

The last years have brought some antagonistic views to light, about the enucleation of a diseased eyeball in certain cases, to prevent the loss by sympathetic ophthalmia of the other sound eye; in regard to which I will only say that every oculist will be glad to learn that medicine will be able to prevent permanently such a disastrous result. All such controversies not only do no harm in the end, but they are absolutely necessary to elicit the truth, and if they are conducted in the sole interest of the truth, they will benefit both sides. I do not believe that his hottest, but honest opponent will ever say that Constantine Hering ever had any other aim in view in his whole life. Blessed always be his memory among us.

Dr. J. W. Dowling said:

If anything could be added to the perfect happiness that exists in Heaven, I should say that our dear old patriarch brother and friend, as he looks down upon us from his celestial and eternal home, is rendered supremely happy at listening to the kind words which, with stirring eloquence, have been spoken, and which have come from the hearts of warm friends and admirers to whom his memory is still fresh and dear.

It seems as if nothing was left for me to say. Those who are my seniors—who have known him perhaps longer than I—have justly sounded his praise, have pictured his virtues, his honesty, his earnestness and zeal in advocating a cause dear to him, not for advantages he himself derived, but because of the benefits it conferred upon suffering humanity.

This is not an occasion for mourning, but rather of rejoicing.

It is true he has left us; his earthly remains have been laid in the ground, but why should we be sad? Was he not with us half a score of years beyond the allotted time of man? Should we not rejoice that this long, this spotless life had been one of usefulness and of unremitting labor in the cause he loved so well—to the very last? Should we not rejoice that the results of those labors of his later years are living, and will live to aid us and our children in the work to which our lives are being devoted? Should not we who respect and love him rejoice that through all his long and active life, not a truthful word had ever been uttered that could reflect upon his character as a man—as a christian—and that at the last his death was peaceful, calm and free from protracted suffering? Should we not rejoice that his sorrows—for he had sorrows—sorrows hard to bear, too, are at an end, and that there is before him an eternity of happiness? For I believe of such as he is the kingdom of heaven.

The following note was sent by Dr. B. F. Joslin:

I am prevented by a cold from being present at the meeting this evening, but I desire to contribute one word of praise to the memory of the illustrious Hering.

I wish to say that if in his long and useful life he had but given us the proving of Lachesis, he would have been entitled to the everlasting gratitude of mankind.

Dr. E. Guernsey said:

It is my misfortune never to have had a personal acquaintance with Dr. Hering, but the magnetism of his mind was so diffused through all his works, that a personal acquaintance was hardly necessary to know the man. Were I asked to write his epitaph I should say, as was said of Sir Christopher Wren, beneath the stately dome of St. Paul, reared by his genius—Look around you! Dr. Hering can have no nobler epitaph than his pure, almost blameless life and the broad, catholic spirit and the earnest scientific research found in all his public works, which have placed him in the first rank of profound, practical thinkers in the medical world. Aside from the scientific value of his life's work, we are forcibly struck with that spirit of christian kindness and charity, which we shall all do well to imitate. He was, in every sense of the word, a christian gentleman, and illustrated in his life and writings how a man can be truly great and noble when divested of bitterness and selfishness. By none will he be more deeply mourned, and his memory held in greater reverence, than by the younger workers in the field, who looked to him as father and friend.

Dr. George S. Norton said:

Having known Dr. Hering for several years, both in a professional and social way, it gives me pleasure to record my high appreciation of him as a physician and as a man. In his home life there was much to admire. Wife and children were devoted to him, and he to them. His hospitality was well known, and it always gave him great satisfaction to see his friends gathered at his table; all were made welcome, and all could not help but enjoy those delightful, instructive talks with the gifted Father Hering.

One of his chief pleasures and relaxations from work was on Sunday afternoon, when a circle of old friends assembled in his reception-room, and over their cigars and coffee compared experiences and discussed various subjects. Neither hot, cold, nor stormy weather interfered with those social gatherings.

Of his investigations and teachings of our Homœopathic Materia Medica, I need not speak, as his extensive knowledge, diligent researches, and practical additions in this important department of medicine are known to you all—yes, not only to us, but to all, every land and every clime, who have studied the law of similia. It therefore seems to me as if the most comprehensive and fitting eulogy to his worth is expressed in the words, Constantine Hering, a Father to Homœopathy.

Dr. Alfred K. Hills said:

Mr. President, Ladies and Gentlemen:

It is with no small degree of effort and embarrassment that I attempt to find words in which to express my respect for one so great as he in whose memory we meet to-night.

As we younger members of the profession glance reflectively over such a life as that of our late colleague, it inspires us to greater energy in the living of our own. His was filled not only with the most industrious effort, but he gave freely of what he had and without the asking, to all those who chose to avail themselves of the results of his researches.

With him nothing professional was secret, could not possibly be kept as such, and he had the greatest abhorrence for any who attempted this practice. His precept always was, make everything known that may by a possibility be of service to another. We could scarcely find his equal in the world of science as a student, and few have originated more than he.

What greater epitaph could be placed over his resting-place than the words "Lachesis," "Glonoine," and the "Guiding Symptoms of our Materia Medica." Certainly no one individual could hope for more than this would express.

Our appreciation of his devotion to that cause which we all hold so dear, justly emphasized by many, cannot be repeated too often for those who love and cherish his memory.

Let us, therefore, emulate his example in our faithfulness, and then we may hope for that reward which is vouchsafed only to such.

Remarks of Dr. L. Hallock:

Dr. Constantine Hering may, I think, be regarded as next to Hahnemann in the value and amount of his labors for the interests of Homœopathy.

Every reader of the periodic literature of our school must have been surprised at the number and variety of his contributions. Nothing but talents of the highest order, united with earnest zeal and untiring industry, could have furnished so many and so valuable practical essays as he has given to the profession. Besides his large and systematic works, the numerous additions to our Materia Medica furnished by his incessant labors, have placed our school under lasting obligation to respect and honor his memory. Among these additions Lachesis has long been prominent as one of the most valuable remedies at our command. More recently his elaborate and minute articles on the history, effects and therapeutic value of Lyssin evince an amount of patient research and self-denying devotion truly surprising in one so occupied in active professional duties. The thoroughness of his work is well illustrated in the extended pathogenesis of this potent remedy by experiments upon himself as well as others, until, as he expressed it, "terrible forebodings" warned him of the danger of further trials. Such bold and self-sacrificing labors for science and humanity certainly deserve our admiration and gratitude. The writings of Dr. Hering seem designed to be clear, forcible and practical, and when from their frequent novelty and boldness they were sometimes received with adverse or doubting criticism, were defended with the energy and ability of conscious integrity.

Remarks of Dr. E. Carleton, Jr.:

Mr. President:—In response to your request to speak, I will offer my humble tribute to the character of our departed friend, by saying that I felt love and reverence for him.

I remember, as if it were but yesterday, the first time we met. It was in his office as physician and patient. He stood and looked at me calmly, while I related my symptoms. Then, silently turning to his desk, he prepared three powders and handed them to me, with directions. I left him in wonder, for my case had troubled the physician who had sent me, and I had expected a long search. The remedy produced a violent aggravation, and I recollect that wonder temporarily gave place to a state of mind akin to resentment. Recovery followed, and so did my promised report to the doctor. The recital of the success of his prescription caused his face to smile all over, which ended with a hearty, genial laugh, and he said, "that was al-o-es; it was low; it was the five hundredth." Then seating himself and motioning me to a chair, he went on to relate how he had suffered similarly when proving the drug, and made me promise to write out and give to him a history of the case, which I afterwards did, and informed me that the medicine had been potentized for him by Doctor Fincke, from a choice bit of crude material furnished by himself. He then enlisted me in the search for a pure drug that he had not been able to procure, for a proving. When we parted, I had learned to place a high estimate upon him. He was a noble man.

Soon after that, we met again in the college lecture-room, as professor and student of medicine. His subject was Natrum muriaticum; and as the golden words fell from his lips, I made every endeavor to preserve and profit by them. It was my good fortune to hear his lectures upon various drugs, which in the hands of many prescribers have verified the provings, and demonstrated his sagacity in arranging them. I have often thought of him when difficulties would beset me in the sick-room; and I know that his contributions to our literature have enabled me to save lives. For this his memory is sacred to me.

But, sir, I must not detain you with extended remarks. You do not care to hear more of my personal experiences. It is enough to say that I loved and revered Constantine Hering; and when he died, I felt that I had lost one of my best friends.

Dr. Edward Bayard was appointed delegate to the memorial meeting to be held in Philadelphia on the evening of October 10th, and then the meeting adjourned.

PHILADELPHIA MEMORIAL MEETING.

A large meeting was held on Sunday evening, October 10th, 1880, at the Hahnemann Medical College, Dr. John K. Lee presiding.

On motion, Dr. Charles Mohr was appointed Secretary.

After numerous letters and telegrams were read from physicians in many neighboring cities, expressing regret at their inability to be present at the Philadelphia memorial meeting, the following report was submitted on behalf of the County Society:

The Homœopathic Medical Society of the County of Philadelphia, uniting with the friends of Homœopathy and medical progress everywhere, in mourning the departure of our late honorary member, Constantine Hering, M.D., offers this tribute of respect to his memory.

We recognize in the decease of Dr. Hering the loss of one pre-eminently adapted by nature and education to be a leader in the early struggles and sacrifices of a new medical dispensation. Cultured in literature and in general science, learned in all the medical wisdom of the allopathic fathers, careful in the formation of his opinions, zealous for the advancement of his chosen profession and ambitious to excel in the practice of his art, we yet find him fearlessly investigating the principles of a new system, accepting without reserve and without hesitation the overwhelming testimony to the truth of Homœopathy, flinging aside the temptations of professional honor and political preferment, fearlessly asserting his "liberty of medical opinion and action" in the presence of an arrogant and intolerable profession and in the face of his king, and deliberately casting his lot with the derided and persecuted pioneers of a new and hated system, devoting all his talents and energies to the perfection and dissemination of the newly-discovered art of healing, laboring with heart and hand and brain for its establishment over a whole continent; unswerving in his adherence to its teachings, unflinching in its defence and untiring in all labors for its advancement; he seemed ever to realize that he had been raised up for this, his heaven-appointed work. We rejoice that he was permitted to witness the vast results, towards which his own herculean labors had so largely contributed,—the shaken foundations of the old medical superstructure, the triumphant vindication of the once despised system of Hahnemann, the establishment of its hospitals, its colleges and its journals, the organization of its societies over the whole civilized world, and the spread of its beneficent influence by thousands of educated physicians into millions of homes.

We, his fellow members of this Society, among whom he walked and taught and labored for so many years, who enjoyed his intimate personal acquaintance and counsel, are proud to express our appreciation of his personal character, and his abounding services in the cause of progressive medicine—the cause of suffering humanity. We shall ever hold his name, his work and his worth in warmest remembrance, and our posterity will rise up to do him honor.

As expressive of the feelings of the Faculty of the Hahnemann Medical College, the following was communicated by Dr. O. B. Gause, Registrar:

We have contemplated the death of our venerable friend and co-laborer, Constantine Hering, M.D., Emeritus Professor of Homœopathic Institutes and Materia Medica, with unfeigned sorrow, believing that the Hahnemann Medical College has lost its brightest light, and the homœopathic school its most profound and learned exponent.

Dr. Edward Bayard, of New York, upon being introduced, made a few remarks, expressing his deep veneration for the man in whose honor this memorial meeting was held, and, referring to his address before the New York Society and the character of its meeting, begged to be excused from further remarks.

Dr. C. Pearson, of Washington, D. C., was next introduced, who responded as follows:

It was not my good fortune to be as intimately acquainted with the deceased as many who may be present this evening, but my acquaintance was sufficient to induce me to travel over a hundred miles to meet with you, his more immediate neighbors, on this memorial occasion, and to deplore with you the worth we have lost. That Dr. Hering should not live longer in the body was not at all strange, for eighty years he had seen the seasons come and go, over half a century he had devoted to the relief of suffering humanity, he had heard the call for help come up from a thousand tongues, and in response to this, he had endured the summer's heat and the storms of winter. With the key of energy, and application, and the lamp of knowledge, he penetrated the arcana of nature, and searched through her storehouse for the hidden remedy, which, when discovered, became the property of the entire world; his humanity was co-extensive with the race, which he left wiser and better for his having lived, and thought—

> A life thus long for others' comfort spent,
> Is human nature's grandest monument.

The end is not yet, Hering still lives, like the dynamic property of his Lachesis; and a hundred years hence the child will be born that will bless his name for the relief this medicine affords.

But he has gone to that great institution of learning, where we, his pupils, will, ere long, like irregular school boys, be dropping in one by one.

And who then shall say so much of us? No one; and yet I hope it may be justly said of each and all, that we contributed our mite of influence to that reform in medicine which portends to the afflicted a brighter and happier day.

But while we aspire to this, let us not forget that change is not always improvement, that belief is only temporal, while truths are eternal, that these are the golden particles that glitter in the sands of time, and the friction of years but adds to their lustre. If we cannot furnish another to that cluster of diamonds Hahnemann discovered, and Hering cut and set in his starry crown, let us not wilfully or ignorantly tarnish their brightness. If we attempt to travel the road they trod, let us be careful which end we take, for they certainly lead to opposite results, and it is better to be right with a minority, than with the majority wrong.

Four score years is a ripe age to attain, and yet it is far too short to reform a world; truth is of slow growth, and requires care and painstaking, and if it rise again when "crushed to earth," more than one generation may be required for it to do so.

Those truths then left us by Hahnemann, and so ably promulgated by Hering, Bœnninghausen and other pioneers gone before, should be guarded by us with zealous care, and as we too will soon pass to "that bourne from whence no traveler returns," may the young men who succeed us realize that "truth is ever the same, that time alters it not, nor is it the better or worse for being of either ancient or modern tradition."

It may be possible that no improvement could be suggested on the order of nature, but in some respects it seems unfortunate that the knowledge and experience accumulated during a long life of patient industry, could not be bequeathed to others to be used, and added to during their natural lives, and then to pass like a landed estate to the next of kin; but this seems not to be a part of the programme, or panorama of human life, but whoever would excel in knowledge and usefulness must do so by his own individual efforts. And however economical of time, his life, however protracted, will be too short to attain perfection.

We are only prospectors in the field of science. One finds a treasure here, another there, these become the support of the indolent, the wealth of the wise, and the sport of the ignorant; the patient toiler in the mine of knowledge is rarely appreciated, few take him by the hand and bid him God speed—he is called visionary, foolishly demented. Sir Joshua Reynolds says: "present and future time may be regarded as rivals, and he who solicits the one, must expect to be discountenanced by the other," and as men are the creatures of the age in which they live, not its creators, it is not difficult to see why they should desire, and court the flattery and commendation of their own times more than that of succeeding ages; for with such tenacity does mind cling to the dead traditions of the past, that the iconoclast is rarely popular during his lifetime; but it is the bold adventurer on unknown seas that tells us of other continents, and future ages build his monument.

"So runs the world away."

"We are such stuff
As dreams are made of, and our little life
Is rounded with a sleep."

It is unfortunate that amongst the unnumbered millions

"That strut and fret their hour on the stage
And then are heard no more,"

so many should be "poor players," hence when "after life's fitful fever" a good man "sleeps well," it becomes so difficult to supply his place.

But though a standard-bearer in our cause has fallen, our flag must not be lowered, and when we too shall have followed him, others, I doubt not, will close up the ranks, and still keep it floating in the sunlight of eternal truth.

Hering's earth life is ended, his conveyance was ready before ours, and he is still in our advance—we shall miss him, but

"He hates him
Who upon the rock of this rough world
Would stretch him out longer."

The night dew that falls though in silence it weeps,
Will brighten with verdure the grave where he sleeps;
And the tear that we shed though in silence it rolls,
Will long keep his memory green in our souls.

Dr. Ad. Lippe then rose and spoke as follows:

Like children who have lost their father, we meet here this evening to express our grief over the loss we suffered by the death of Dr. Constantine Hering.

As mourning children we vividly remember what the departed was to all of us, we remember how he instructed us, how he taught us by precept and example the way to obtain a perfect knowledge of the healing art, how he advised us to study the writings of Samuel Hahnemann, and we remember with gratitude his ceaseless labors in the field of Materia Medica.

Dr. Hering was chosen among many able medical students at Leipzig to write a pamphlet, and in it to expose the follies and absurdities of a new system of therapeutics by Samuel Hahnemann, and with that honesty of purpose which always guided him through life he undertook that task; his first step was to study Hahnemann's *Organon of the Healing Art*, and then he tried the correctness or the falsity of his teachings by the experiment.

The only true test, the experiment, convinced him that the follies and absurdities of the prevailing allopathic school of medicine were exposed by Hahnemann, that a rational system of the healing art was revealed to the world by him. Homœopathy but slowly gained ground in those days. The medical student who in 1824, dared to declare his conviction of the truth of the superiority of Homœopathy over all known systems of medicine had to be a brave and fearless man. Persecution followed

Dr. Hering at once, his friend and preceptor who had expected him to ridicule and demolish Homœopathy, summarily dismissed him, distressing privations followed, but his faith was firm, it was not to be shaken by early personal adversities, no more than the progressive development of Homœopathy could be retarded by innumerable adversities and persecutions which all the early adherents of it had to suffer. Finally, Dr. Hering bravely overcame all these obstacles and he found a true friend in the late Professor Schoenlein, the father of a well classified pathology, and protected by him the young student graduated at Würzburg. After teaching natural sciences and mathematics at Blochmann's Institute at Dresden he obtained an appointment from the Saxon government as naturalist. We find him at Surinam making collections for the museum of the Academy of Natural Sciences at Dresden. As an eminent naturalist the Saxon government provided for him, but he was, almost against his will, compelled to practice the healing art in Surinam. The Saxon government claimed all his time to be devoted to his appointment as their naturalist and were displeased with his practice and the papers published by him in the homœopathic journals; he had himself dismissed from the government service and was again thrown on his own resources. It was there and then that Dr. Hering obtained the few drops of the poison of the Trigonocephalus Lachesis, there and then he published the first provings of this poison on the healthy and earned the everlasting gratitude of the profession who thereby were enabled to cure sicknesses formerly considered incurable.

Again we find him devoted to the teaching of the healing art at the Allentown Academy, the first public institution of the kind chartered by a liberal government. The unselfish, self-sacrificing apostle, regardless of his own individual interests, but resolved to fulfil his self-chosen mission to its full extent, accepted a much smaller compensation for his laborious work to which he devoted all his time and energies, than was accorded forty years later to the Secretary of the American Institute of Homœopathy.

The teaching of students of medicine, the publishing of Hahnemann's *Organon* and a Materia Medica with a Repertory in the English language, the proving of drugs and the publication of the medicinal virtues of Trigonocephalus Lachesis occupied his time. He had finally the gratification to see the diplomas conferred by the Allentown Academy on its graduates, the first homœopathic diplomas ever conferred, accepted at home and abroad. Dr. Wahle presented this diploma to the Papal government when he came to seek permission to practice in Rome, and the Pope himself accepted this diploma and gave him the requested permission to practice Homœopathy in the Papal States. Later, Dr. Hering returned to Philadelphia after Dr. William Wesselhoeft had been appointed President of the Allentown Academy. With a large clientage he found in Philadelphia, this indefatigable man added much to the further development of our healing art by the proving of new remedies and by perfecting and re-arranging many proven ones. Not less active was he in guarding our school against innovations and perversions. Many posological papers were published by him in the homœopathic journals, his witty sarcasm silencing those who tried to modernize Hahnemann's plain teachings. He never rejected, *a priori*, apparently advanced ideas till he had patiently investigated the proferred claims of their superiority over the established principles and rules accepted by the early followers of Hahnemann, but when no convincing proof of the correctness of such innovations could be established, either by argument or by the test of the experiment, his powerful pen was brought into requisition and he very soon silenced these bold writers. One of his last acts was the signing of a paper declaring his unswerving faith in the essential principles of Homœopathy, and finally saying: "If our school ever gives up the strict inductive method of Hahnemann we are lost, and deserve to be mentioned only as a caricature in the history of medicine."[*]

---

[*] *North American Journal of Homœopathy*, August, 1880.

As children who have here assembled to mourn the loss of a father, we can do no greater honor to his memory than to always remember this parting instruction and warning; and, on this solemn occasion, let us resolve never to depart from the strict inductive method of Hahnemann, a method our departed friend followed most faithfully for more than half a century.

Dr. Henry N. Guernsey then addressed the meeting as follows:

Mr. President and Fellow-Members of the Profession:

In rising to offer this tribute of respect to the memory of our departed colleague, allow me to dwell for a little while upon the early reminiscences of my acquaintance with him, which dates back to the days of my medical pupilage.

In the autumn of 1842, I matriculated in the Pennsylvania Medical College, which then occupied the very building wherein we are now assembled, and I soon made the acquaintance of Mr. Hussman, a fellow student. He was then a private pupil of Dr. Hering, and later became his brother-in-law. My friend soon introduced me to the distinguished subject of this memorial, whose office at that time, nearly forty years ago, was located on the northwest corner of Eleventh and Spruce streets. During the session, Dr. Hering frequently came to our dissecting-room to examine the abdominal viscera of the cadavera, that he might the better establish the truth of some of his theories.

In my mind's eye I now see as I saw him then—his erect and commanding figure, his eager and piercing eye, his massive brow, his well-shaped head crowned with long, black hair, and his whole appearance so clothed with dignity as to render him apparently unapproachable.

At our first interview, however, I discovered my mistake; for he proved so genial, so friendly, and so communicative, that we fraternized at once. Thus, I am proud to say, our fraternal relations continued to our last conference, which was only a few hours before his demise. During all these years it has been my good fortune to have free access to him, even to his private study, at almost any hour.

His active and inquiring mind led him to continually search for, and gather up, all facts, particularly if new and of recent occurrence. As an illustration, I will mention the following circumstance. A short time after I had located in Frankford, I was quite astonished to find Dr. Hering at my door, early one morning, inquiring for the residence of a person who had been stung by a bee, whose sufferings had been published in the daily papers. I at once took him in my carriage to the house of the sufferer, where he carefully noted down every fact and symptom developed by the bee-sting. This case proved of great value in making up the pathogenesis of *Apis mellifica*, but it cost Dr. Hering the fatigue of a sixteen-mile drive, beside the loss of time to his professional duties of nearly the whole day. We all know the value of time to a physician in full practice. But for him, when in quest of knowledge, everything else had to give way; time, money, strength, sleep, and all else were sacrificed for the sake of science and Homœopathy. "Anything and everything for our cause," as he was often heard to say.

Dr. Hering, as consulting physician, has many times driven to Frankford to advise me on a bad case of sickness.

How mightily he would apply himself to find the proper remedy?

He never resorted to any make-shift; but, firmly relying upon the unfailing law of the Similars, he would persevere until the true Similimum was found, and the cure effected. As an invariable rule, the more dangerous the case, the more mightily would he apply himself to the letter and spirit of the law bequeathed to us by Samuel Hahnemann.

After my removal into the city proper, in 1856, the frequency of my visits to him increased, while my confidence in and reliance upon my dear old friend's judgment, were vastly heightened. His abiding faith in the true law of cure was exemplified in the treatment of his own person and of his family, when ill, as well as in the treatment of all his patients. Everybody was treated according to the same principles, and everybody shared equally with him one of the greatest blessings a merciful Heaven has ever vouchsafed to mankind.

I will briefly refer to one or two of the many instances, which might be cited, to illustrate this point. Some years ago he suffered from a very painful attack of hemorrhoids, which confined him to his bed. Dr. Lippe prescribed *Causticum*^{cm}, one dose, and admonished him to await the action of the drug for three days. The improvement appearing but slight, as the prescribed time drew near its close, he began to doubt that the true similimum had been found; so, he took up his books and brought his own great mind to bear upon the search for a remedy. Finding no better one, he concluded to await the full expiration of the time as agreed upon. Soon afterwards he fell into a sweet sleep, lasting several hours, from which he awoke, well. He enjoyed telling of this triumph of the single dose and the high potency, as an encouragement for all true healers to go and do likewise. Again, when one of his daughters was very ill with diphtheria, by my advice he had given a single dose of *Lachesis*, which was followed by so little improvement in twenty-four hours, that he was sorely tempted to either repeat the dose or change the remedy. But, as the little patient was no worse, he concluded to wait twelve hours longer, at the expiration of which time he had the satisfaction of seeing her greatly improved. He was ever faithful to the true cause he loved so well, because, *he believed it to be true!* As with all true men, believing with him was synonymous with doing.

About seventeen years ago Dr. Ad. Lippe was greatly prostrated by an attack of typhoid fever. So fearfully did the disease rage that I feared he would not recover. As was my custom in all such bad cases, I repaired to Dr. Hering, who had not yet seen the case, and told him my fears. Dr. Hering suddenly dropped his pen, and, giving me one of his searching looks, apparently to see if I was in earnest, said with great emphasis, "Dr. Lippe must not die yet! I will go with you." For over an hour, with book in hand, he applied his great mind to the case and finally declared "*Silicea* is the remedy." Drs. P. P. Wells and the late Carroll Dunham, who had been summoned, came in later and confirmed the wisdom of their teacher's choice—for they, too, had taken their first lessons in Homœopathy from Dr. Constantine Hering. Silicea stayed the ravages of the fever; its subject made a rapid recovery, and Dr. Lippe stands among us to-night, a living monument of one of Dr. Hering's good works.

And so it ever was with our lamented father of Homœopathy in this country. I never knew him to deviate from the true line of action in his efforts to heal the sick or to relieve the dying. For he knew this to be the best, and indeed the *only safe* means that could be employed.

Dr. Hering, above all men in our ranks, best understood the art of acquiring wealth, that real wealth which far transcends the value of such material dross as gold or silver. Look at his Lachesis! Is not this alone a work worth living a lifetime to accomplish? Surely it would be a sufficient consolation at the close of any one's life to be able to say, "I have done thus much for the good of humanity."

Dr. Hering's note book was always at hand, and ever and anon, wherever he might be or with whomsoever conversing, he jotted down observations, precious "nuggets" as it were, to be deposited in his big strong box so soon as he had retired to his private study. As yet, only a few peeps into that box have been granted to his heirs,—for, are not *we* his heirs, and are *we* not to receive our respective shares of his valuable legacy, *pro bono publico?* And we trust this will all be dealt out to us, in good time, by the publication of his invaluable work, "THE GUIDING SYMPTOMS."

Never did the slightest feeling of jealousy cross his mind. If any of his patients became restive and called upon other physicians, his first inquiry, on missing them, was, "Where have they gone? If to another *homœopathic* physician, then I am satisfied;

there is no loss, but rather a gain to our cause." He was large-hearted and liberal, seeming to take in the whole profession as one man and considered himself as one of the least.

As an observer, none equalled him. On entering the sick room, for instance, his all-seeing eyes took in at once the condition of things and his mind had often decided upon the proper course to pursue before a question had been asked; his interrogations, later, were often more to confirm and place on record than to elicit facts for decision. Intuition was a powerful element in his mind, and this was cultivated to a high degree by his truthfulness of character, and his good thoughts and feelings toward every one he knew. He never plotted evil and never sought revenge, but was as innocent minded as a child. He reached out in all directions for truth, and wherever his investigations extended, all Nature seemed to yield up her treasures to him, for she found no corrupt or opposing influences in his mind to operate against her. Truth ever responds to the true-minded truth seeker; and never was she better treated, never less perverted, than by Constantine Hering.

But his race is run and he has left us. He was almost the last one of Samuel Hahnemann's pupils who remained upon this earth. Hahnemann and his faithful cotemporaries are now reunited in a nearly completed phalanx, to stand enshrined in our memories as the noblest representatives of the cause they lived for in this world. It was a needful and an orderly step that our good doctor should go to the end, that he might become more fully conjoined to, and continue and labor with those faithful and powerful allies on the other side. And he departed, was almost translated, in the Lord's own good time, and now we may reasonably expect a fuller, a more powerful and a more general display of the real Hahnemannian principles than ever before.

Let us profit by his example and cherish in our memories the truths which came worded from his tongue.

Dr. Robert J. McClatchey being called upon spoke as follows:

If I have a proper understanding of the object and scope of this meeting, it is to afford an opportunity to those who loved and who revere the memory of Dr. Constantine Hering, to testify their respect for his memory, and, at the same time, to give evidence in some way of their appreciation of his character as a man and as a physician; so that by the contributions thus made the world may be able to know what was thought of our departed friend, by those who knew him best, and who are most capable of estimating him at a proper value.

Upwards of thirty years ago, Dr. Hering wrote as follows, in an article entitled, "Requisites for a Correct Estimation of Hahnemann," published in the *Hygea*:* "If we would form an estimate of a man who belongs to history, an estimate which shall itself lay claim to a place in history, and rise above the fleeting interest of ephemeral productions, we must found it upon a full consideration of the whole life and labors of him to whom it relates."

"Thus should the historian accompany his hero to the time when a friendly beckoning hand withdraws him from things without, his senses close to page and speech, unfold to sources of joy and hope, and he departs, at peace with himself, with God and with the mantled world.

"Then let the estimate follow—not in the work—not penned by the laborious biographer, but formed in the inmost soul of him who shall have read and weighed the whole."

It has seemed to me that there was no more marked traits of Dr. Hering's remarkably pronounced character than his *steadfastness* of purpose, in his endeavor to carry out to the utmost every task laid before him; and there is, in my opinion, a unity of purpose distinguishable through all his work, and characterizing it in a marked degree as well as exhibiting this steadfastness.

---

* *Hygea*, v. 22, p. 296.

Those of us who had the privilege and pleasure of personal intercourse with Dr. Hering, know well what an instructive and even fascinating conversationalist he was. And we know how that, while pursuing a subject in this way, his vast learning would often lead him away from the path that led directly to the subject under consideration, into what at a superficial glance, seemed mere no-thoroughfares of thought, that led no whither, it would soon prove that these were instead pleasant and beautiful conversational by-paths, which led directly into the main pathway, and which had served simply as an agreeable and momentary diversion, but not in any way distracting attention from the end in view. Even in such matters as these, of every day occurrence, and coming up in the way of chance and every day conversation he exhibited the utmost steadfastness of purpose. How much more marked then might we expect to find this steadfastness in his life's work.

I can liken Dr. Hering's life to nothing more appropriately, I think, than by comparing it to a magnificent and grand piece of music by a Bach, a Handel, a Mendelssohn, a Haydn, in which, whatever variations are introduced the original theme is recognizable throughout and at all times, and which gives to the variations their tone, their key, their character and their power.

The theme of Dr. Hering's life-music consisted in his desire and striving for the elevation of his beloved Homœopathy to a position among the sciences; to place it upon a scientific basis and to make its workings those of an exact science. Refer to this great man's life and labors. Consult his writings as I have done, from his earliest to his latest, and you will see, as I have seen, that he had this constantly in view, and was steadfast in his wish for its accomplishment; and no matter into what no-thoroughfare or byways he may have strayed, he never lost sight of his great goal.

There was nothing meretricious about Dr. Hering. Whatever work he did was for Homœopathy and the truth, and without reference to pay or reward. He was always accessible and always willing to teach all who wished to learn what he considered to be the better way, but he never indulged in that very agreeable, but by no means useful pastime, of "damning those he had no mind to." He afforded the fullest respect to the opinions of others, and largely for that reason he and his opinions always commanded respect.

The amount of work he did was simply enormous. He was an earnest and a patient toiler, who, as we are informed, died almost with his working harness on.

In his work, whether in verbal communications, through books, or through journals, he supplied enough of wisdom, of learning, and of other requisites to make first-class reputations for a score or more of doctors. His works were grandly conceived and as grandly executed, and of course there was surplusage. To him and his works are applicable the words of Schiller:

"How many starvelings a rich man can nourish!
When monarchs build - the rubbish-carriers flourish."

"So then our Greatest has departed. That melody of life, with its cunning tones, which took captive ear and heart, has gone silent; the heavenly force that dwelt here victorious over so much, is here no longer; thus far, not farther, by speech and by act, shall the wise man utter himself forth. The End! What solemn meaning lies in that sound, as it peals mournfully through the soul, when a living friend has passed away! All now is closed, irrevocable; the changeful life-picture, growing daily into new coherence, under new touches and hues, has suddenly become completed and unchangeable; there as it lay, it is dipped, from this moment, in the æther of the heavens, and shines transfigured, to endure even so—forever. The week-day man, who was one of us, has put on the garments of Eternity and become radiant and triumphant. * * * * *

"The man whom we loved lies in his grave; but glorious, worthy; and his spirit yet lives in us with an authentic life. Could each here vow to do his little task, even as the departed did his great one, in the manner of a true man; not for a Day, but for Eternity! To live, as he counselled and commanded, not commodiously in the Reputable, the Plausible, the Half, but resolutely in the Whole, the Good, the True:

'*Im Ganzen, Guten, Wahren resolut zu leben!*'"*

Dr. Bushrod W. James next made the following remarks:

Fellow-Members of the Profession:

We, the intimate associates and friends of Constantine Hering, M.D., and residents of the city of his adoption, assemble together to-night, as do his friends in other cities all over the land and the homœopathic world, to say a few words of meed in honor and to the memory of a great and good man.

We are not here to erect a monument, for that his life has done for us, in his works, and writings, and teachings.

His labors are known, his virtues need no further inscription, his good qualities of heart are impressed upon all he conversed with, his professional skill was undoubted, his steadfast purpose of benefiting mankind was always a guiding star in his life; he was always at his post of duty, and he filled the post allotted to him by the Great Architect of the Universe with faithfulness and cheerfulness of disposition.

His mission was first that of a standard-bearer of the new system, and later he was acknowledged a superior officer in the warfare of the medical systems of the age.

He lived an eventful and useful life, and died with honors and glories surrounding him.

Every age has its progressive spirits; men that are born to leave a name inscribed upon the scroll of time deeply cut in letters of gold, and whose acts stand out in plain relief and beauty

---

* On the Death of Gœthe, by Thomas Carlyle.

among the good deeds of others around them; our fallen companion was truly one of these.

He was a liberal man in his prescribing, and was not bound to any excrescent ideas; he read Hahnemann's works as he did his Bible, and he tested all that was there advanced, and he held firmly to all that was valuable and useful in the Organon of Homœopathy, as written by Dr. Samuel Hahnemann, and like him was not afraid to stand boldly up for its truths at all times.

He was not one to fetter the dose or limit the repetition or size of the same; he allowed every physician his own judgment in such matters, and he unswervingly exercised his own. But while thus liberal he always adhered strictly to the law "Similia Similibus Curantur," and also to the selection of the remedy according to the totality of the symptoms.

He was most careful in the proper and thorough examination of all the symptoms of his patients, no matter how much time and trouble was involved in the questioning, knowing that success depended on obtaining a true picture of the disease.

He believed in a general knowledge of all the branches of medicine of both schools, for he says: "No one can be a successful disciple of Hahnemann who is not well versed, as Hahnemann himself was, in the learning of the medical schools, and it would be just as impossible for him to act judiciously without a knowledge of anatomy, physiology, pathology, surgery and materia medica, together with chemistry, and botany, as for a man ignorant of navigation and seamanship, to carry a vessel with safety into port."

He was free in giving advice to learners, and would sit by the hour and converse with any member of the profession who desired to have the benefit of his wide experience with our homœopathic remedies, and his mature judgment in the proper selection of the remedy in complicated and obscure cases was often thus sought. Even when I was a student, I, with a number of others, paid frequent visits to his house, at his request, to hear from his lips (without any desire of recompense), the unfoldings of the materia medica, and the clinical experiences of this large-hearted, generous disciple of Hahnemann.

No toil was too arduous, no time thus spent was considered lost, no research on his part was thought burdensome, no careful study was left undone that would enable him to present to students of Homœopathy in or out of the profession clearly the doctrines of the homœopathic practice.

He was a constant student and an arduous laborer in the cause. He fought for a higher medical education all his medical life: he directed many a battle; he passed through the life-work campaign; he was on the upper outlook of the mountain peak of knowledge himself, and saw the desire of his heart realized, the victory won, the world acknowledging the truths of Homœopathy and its educating influence upon the profession and people: and to-day we place the laurels upon the brow of one of Hahnemann's most trusty and worthy generals.

Dr. John C. Morgan pronounced the following eulogy:

Ripe, full of days, and rich in worthy doing, so departed our friend, our teacher, our patriarch, Dr. Constantine Hering; and to-day, we would speak of the loved and lost.

Deep in the human soul, to-day, as ever, survives that earliest idea of worship—the homage of the Past—overlaid and encrusted, indeed, with the material glory of the Present, but warm and vital, ever awaiting the artistic touch, the seer's interpretation, or the tension of public or private grief, or triumph, for occasion to glow, bright and beautiful, in the sunlight of the human affections.

Are the Fathers in honor? Then do the children rejoice, with front erect, bold, forceful. Are they in contempt? Then do the children cringe, falter and fail.

Time was, when ancestors' manes were household gods; time was, when citizens, blameless, devoted, venerable, invincible, departed life for the land of shades, only to be deified—we know better now, do we not? But in the grand old days, the heroes lived evermore, caring for the commonwealth, guiding counsel, directing war, upbuilding the state; as demigods adored, with sacrificial honors. Insult offered, even to the statue of the hero, was insult inflicted upon the state; nay, more—whoso refused homage was the enemy of the state and of his people. In the Christian ages, the church has ever done likewise by her saints, revered, even when unadored.

Hero-worship! is it commendable? Ancestral glory! is it nothing worth? Antiquity! is it venerable? Let the potent conservatism of "the medical profession" answer. Let the large and respectable clientèle of that old guild, reply; that army of devotees who bend the ear to hear, and the knee in devotion, as *medical antiquity* is exalted, and its heroes named; justly exalted —truly named. The heroes and their deeds—their thoughts, their words—these are indeed immortal! 'Twere but a bootless venture, were we, their legatees, to turn the ungrateful back upon those mighty dead.

But the long, long past stretches forward unto this day. Homœopathy writes beneath that noble galaxy, the name of a new constellation—a group of heroes as glorious as they; few in number, but of imperishable fame. Antiquity overtakes us. Hahnemann, Gram, Jahr, Bœnninghausen, Buchner, Hausmann, Grauvogl, Henderson, Quin, Jeanes, Beebe, Temple, Williamson, Dunham, Gardiner, Payne, Hempel, Hering; these have gone over to the reunion of the great. One by one has the heroic Past inscribed them upon her scroll. We, too, are acquiring a history—short, it may be, in time; but long, in all that makes time venerable; ages old, in the truth spoken, and in deeds performed.

Ye homœopaths, behold these, your heroes! measure the territory, glory in the fame they have won for you; emulate their exalted worth. Mark well, too, the noble souls who yet remain with us, to pile still loftier mountains of grand doing upon the heights attained by them. Behold our fast rising

Olympus, our moving Pelion, our trembling Ossa, upheaved by their giant shoulders, and say, if we live not in the heroic age ourselves—the age of the pioneers—the age of laborious sowing—the age of iron, of the power of LAW, in the history of medicine, as of universal progress! Let us know what is our birthright—recognize the heavenly afflatus inspiring our own heroes—erect our own Palladium—build our own Pantheon—perceive the vision of our Olympian court—cherish worshipfully our own hastening antiquity—and condemn the threatened oncoming of an untimely age of brass; of an early and slovenly reaping; of glib and lively egotism, and, it may be, of reaction.

What care we for that—or for them? That is the mete-yard of our own domain. They fought and labored to win it; their posterity enter in and possess it. Homely and trite is the proverb—and true as trite—" 'Tis but an unclean bird who befouleth his own nest." He is but an unworthy homœopath who would asperse his own professional ancestry. And for what? To conciliate the medically ungodly? To win opponents, never generous, never just? (I except individuals). Rather let us learn their politic wisdom. *Fas est ab hoste doceri.* The compulsion of history alone can win them; each full-mailed warrior, like the ancient Spartan, must fix the boundary of his estate, only with the point of his spear! Each man must be a hero, each hero panoplied in the armor of truth, sent down from heaven at the prayer of Samuel Hahnemann; claiming the whole continent, moving forward—forward—upward, evermore!

Constantine Hering thus fought the good fight, and has conquered. The hero has taken his Olympian seat. The glory of the ancients is his. His deeds and his memory remain to us. Thus he fought, and thus he won. By that same sign may all we prevail!

And as we look backward upon the more than half a century of his struggle, may the lesson of his life be to each of us, at once an inspiration and a new point of departure; may each emulate the courage, the patience, the industry, the truth, the faith, of those grand fifty years of his doctorate; remembering ever, that for us, as for all, the path of true honor lies oftenest through valleys of obloquy, to hills of difficulty, mountain-high; our only sustenance, ofttimes, the soul-power within; ofttimes unresting, ofttimes alone.

> "The heights by great men won, and kept,
>   Were not attained by sudden flight;
> But they, while their companions slept,
>   Were toiling upward in the night.
>
> We have not wings, we cannot soar,
>   But we have feet to scale and climb
> By slow degrees, by more and more,
>   The sunlit summits of our time."

The life of our departed friend was the realization of this song of our national poet; for

> Thus did our Hering toil and climb—
> Thus proved his life-work true, sublime—
> Thus wrought, thus fought, thus won; then died,
>   Nay, lived anew, and Death defied.
>
> Sage! teacher! hero unexcelled!
>   Thy name shall be in homage held—
> Thy work endure, while time shall be;
>   Thy praise befits Eternity.

Dr. Martin Deschére, of New York, was the next speaker, who said:

I, too, was permitted to press his hand once in my life. My longing for that moment to come was more than compensated by the happy hours which I spent in his sacred study. Those few hours were blessed. They truly belong to the happiest ones in my life.

Many of you who knew Dr. Hering intimately are better able to speak of his personal traits than I am.

To my mind the object of this memorial meeting should be the collection of those thoughts which characterized the man for whom we mourn to-night. For within us he planted the seed of his wisdom; unto us he left the great work of his life as a sacred inheritance—the search after truth. Therefore we can honor him no more than by following his footsteps, by marching onward from where he stopped, by fighting with his weapons for our beloved art. And here we must ask the important question: What was the mission of Constantine Hering? It was to make Homœopathy universal; to proclaim its truth to all mankind!

The history of his life tells us how far he has succeeded. He has spread Homœopathy over nearly one-half of the globe. But is Homœopathy universal? It is not. And here begins the work which he left for us to do, which we must do, as far as our power permits, with all energy and force, just as he did himself. This is the inheritance which he has left us and which we must hold sacred.

If we look to-day at the number of homœopathic physicians in the United States, with its flourishing colleges, its numerous societies, its well-conducted hospitals and dispensaries, we might be inclined to think that nothing remains to be done, that all is good and working for itself. We might be inclined to think that Homœopathy is really becoming universal.

But look at Europe. Look in particular to Germany, where stood Hahnemann's cradle, where Homœopathy itself was born, where Constantine Hering was consecrated to the cause.

I hold in my hand a letter addressed to Dr. Hering by a man who, from pure devotion to Homœopathy, begs a few articles, written in defense of Homœopathy, for a German periodical. In this letter the position of Homœopathy in Germany is painted in the most pitiful colors, and Dr. Hering is requested to write a treatise on the success of our cause in America, that it may open the eyes of the public across the Atlantic.

The one who wrote the letter is not a physician. He is a man who has witnessed the great blessings of Homœopathy among his friends, and who cries for help in behalf of his fellow-men throughout his country.

The letter never reached him to whom it was addressed. It arrived in Philadelphia a few days too late and was sent to me, with the request that I should fulfil the demands expressed in it, for it certainly carries a plea of great significance.

Just at the moment when our great counsellor parted from us, this voice calls from abroad for help—help in our good cause.

Homœopathy is not yet universal. The iron chains of prejudice, of scientific idolatry, of despotism, hold it in their tight grip.

From this country of freedom alone, liberty must come to Homœopathy throughout the world. In the name of Constantine Hering let me beg of those gentlemen who will visit the World's Convention, to be held abroad next summer, to remember this meeting, to keep sacred Hering's inheritance, and to fight for Homœopathy in Europe.

I trust to their wise counsel that by some means they may plant a nucleus containing sufficient life from which to develop a giant in aid of Homœopathy abroad. The World's Convention here, which Dr. Hering instituted, was a great step toward the universality of Homœopathy. And in working thus with the true spirit of progress we shall honor our immortal Hering.

It is a sacred debt we owe, and we must pay it.

Dr. Constantine Lippe, of New York, followed with the following remarks:

Allow me to offer my tribute of respect to the memory of my name-father. As an individual loss, his departure leaves a great void.

It was my custom on my visits to Philadelphia, to call upon our friend and spend some very profitable hours with him. His uncompromising adherence to the strict principles of Homœopathy, as taught by Hahnemann, helped me in a great measure to be more certain that these principles were true, for in his long and successful practice he, by adhering to those principles, could and did cure cases of disease, entirely unmanageable by any other course of treatment.

Dr. Hering was one of the best friends I ever had, genial, cordial; and never was a visit paid him by me but he was ready and willing to share his great knowledge on any subject inquired upon. He took great pleasure in imparting his information, gained by his close studies and long experience. But he completed his life, full, long, and useful, and dropped to sleep to wake without the worn-out frame which had become enfeebled.

"That bodies should be lent to us while they can afford us pleasure, assist us in acquiring knowledge, or in doing good to our fellow-beings, is a kind and benevolent act of God. When they become unfit for their purposes, and afford us pain instead of pleasure, instead of an aid becoming an incumbrance, and answer none of the intentions for which they were given, it is equally kind and benevolent that a way is provided by which we may get rid of them. This way is death." So wrote Benjamin Franklin in 1756.

Our friend has departed from the earth sphere, but his memory will be held in dear remembrance.

Dr. Charles B. Gilbert, of Washington, D. C., expressed himself in this wise:

Having been a member of Dr. Hering's household for some months, and having had some opportunities for observing the inner life of that great and good man, there is one quality to which I wish to refer. As I was hurrying across the country from the West to attend the funeral, to relieve somewhat the sadness of my thoughts, I took up a little book that had been put into my hand by a friend just before I started; it was the little story by Edward Everett Hale, of the "Poor Men of Lyons"—as they were called—how they had given up wealth and position to spread the gospel; their appeal to each other was—" For the love of Christ" and the answer was—" In his name." " Verily," I said, Doctor Hering was a " Poor Man of Lyons," indeed, and a prophet among them.

On the day of the funeral, as I stood by the door receiving the hundreds who came to view the face of their benefactor, and saw among them scores who could, in their poverty, only have called on him "For the love of Christ," I could not help thinking— these are the " Poor Men of Lyons;" the tears that rolled down their cheeks told louder than words that the answer to their appeal had been—" In his name."

I cannot find words to express my individual sorrow and indebtedness to him on whose monument no fitter motto could be engraved than this—" He loved his neighbor as himself."

On behalf of Dr. C. W. Boyce, of Auburn, N. Y., the secretary presented the following reminiscences of Dr. Hering, prepared and read before the Central New York Homœopathic Medical Society, October 17th, 1880, by Dr. Boyce, who desired the contribution to be made a part of the proceedings of the Philadelphia Memorial Meeting:

We speak to-day in memory of the late Dr. Constantine Hering, of, I cannot say Philadelphia, because he belonged to the world. You have selected me to say something in regard to him, not because I am more competent to do it than the rest of you, but from the accident that I had been thrown more into his society. In order to explain how my acquaintance with him began, and why it continued, I must commence several years before I first saw him.

The name of Dr. Hering is so closely associated with Lachesis, in my mind, that when one is mentioned the other is almost sure to come up with it, and to a great extent, with me, Homœopathy depends upon Lachesis for its glory. It was by Homœopathy that I became acquainted with Lachesis, and it was by Lachesis that I came to know Dr. Hering. In 1846 I first became practically acquainted with Homœopathy, and began to practice it in preference to the ordinary method. It was not until several years after that, that the wonderful healing powers of Homœopathy were fully revealed to me. I had a case of typhoid fever which had continued for twenty-one days unchecked. At this time there seemed no chance for the patient to recover. Hope had been abandoned, when, during the night following the twenty-first day, Lachesis was given every two hours. Next morning there was a complete change. The tongue was moist and the delirium was greatly lessened. From this time on convalescence commenced and progressed until health was restored. This case was never forgotten, but in my daily rounds it was a long time before I saw another such result. It came, however, in a case of gangrene. A woman discovered a small black spot on the calf of her leg, which gave her a great deal of uneasiness, and it rapidly increased in size. When I saw it she was in bed, and the spot measured three inches in diameter. It was rapidly increasing, in size, and she grew sicker and sicker. Lachesis was given, and in a few hours the progress of the disease was checked. In a few days the entire piece of flesh which was affected fell out, leaving a hole reaching to the sheath of the muscles. This healed kindly in a very short time. These cases were treasured up in memory. Soon after this, a case of aneurism of the aorta, where the patient was obliged to sit by the open window day and night, in order to get all the fresh air she could, was wonderfully relieved by Lachesis.

Again followed a time of professional drudgery without striking results, when I was startled. A woman who was nursing a child was aroused at midnight by the cry of fire. She had only time to grasp her child and rush out of the house in her night dress. It was winter time, and she went into snow up to her knees. She stood about in this undress until the house was consumed before seeking shelter. The result was that she did not get out of bed until the next summer, and then only by the help of Lachesis, which in nine days not only took her out of bed, but set her doing her housework.

Now to me, Homœopathy was fast coming to mean Lachesis, but I was soon to be aroused from any security I felt in the practice of even Homœopathy. A great grief came upon me. My only son sickened and died in a few days. During his sickness I could not see that anything given medicinally produced any effect. The disease went on unchecked until he died. On the day of the funeral the twin sister was taken sick with the same disease, and only after a severe struggle was saved. Disheartened I asked whether there was any remedial virtue in medicine? My cases treated by Lachesis answered this question. Then came another question: has my practice of medicine been a success? On comparing results with other physicians whose death-roll I knew, I found that my success or failure, whichever it might be called, was, perhaps, a fair average. But this did not satisfy me; I asked myself another question. If I could occasionally get such results as I did from Lachesis, why could I not get them from other remedies? where should I seek for the answer? I had been for several years practicing Homœopathy, and preferred it to Allopathy, from which I had turned. During these years of practicing medicine I had not seen in either practice any such results as came from the administration of Lachesis. Two steps had been taken; I had found Homœopathy; I had found Lachesis; I knew or believed that Dr. Hering was the one who introduced this remedy into use. The next and third step in progress was to seek Dr. Hering. I wrote to Dr. Hering, asking him whether I could call upon him and hope to find him unoccupied long enough for me to get some information which would help me in the practice of Homœopathy? I was impressed with the idea that by seeing and talking with Dr. Hering I should be able to go on and acquire what I wanted. I did not wait for an answer to my letter, but went at once to Philadelphia and called at his house on the same evening of my arrival. I found him entertaining a large number of physicians in his garden, which for the occasion was lighted by tapers in the trees. The garden was full of little tables, which held refreshments, and which were served after the German style. On announcing myself at the door as a physician, I was ushered into the garden, along with the rest. After being there a short time I learned which Dr. Hering was. I saw a large man with long grey hair which fell down upon his shoulders, and with a beard, likewise grey, which reached to his breast. As I watched him, first talking to one and then to another, I almost wondered why I had ventured there. He was always the centre of a group of interested doctors. Presently he turned to one of the tables, which fortunately was near where I stood, and took some bread and cheese. Now was my opportunity; I stepped before him and announced my name. I wondered how I should be received. All at once he laid down his bread and cheese and taking both my hands he said; "O, Dr. Boyce, I am glad to see you," and calling his daughter, cried. "Here, Odelia, is Dr. Boyce; keep him until all these go away; I want to talk with him." Odelia fulfilled her father's desire, and gave me my first introduction to limburger cheese. I have always thought that she and Mrs. Conrad Wesselhœft, who was her companion for that evening, must have enjoyed the scene when I first essayed the eating of some of this cheese. It was made up into the most inviting little balls, ornamented with greens. Dr. Hering again took up his bread and cheese and began to eat, and following his example I took one of these beautiful little balls and a piece of bread. The balls looked so nice and withal so small, that I put the whole of one into my mouth and began to chew. Imagine me standing before Dr. Hering with this in my mouth, trying to hold it and at the same time wishing to keep him from turning to some one else, and you can have some faint idea of my first experience with limburger cheese. I was finally obliged to turn away from him behind the neighboring bushes and spit it out. On turning back again I caught a glimpse of two pairs of eyes set in countenances convulsed with laughter. This was my first introduction to Dr. Hering and limburger cheese. I was with him until late in the night and nearly all the next day, and the next, and so on until I was ashamed to take up any more of his time, and excused myself on the plea that I must go home. In about one month another great calamity seemed impending. My eldest daughter was taken with diphtheria. It went on to the croupy stage. This was when I had never seen a case recover in which the larynx had become invaded. The disease first showed itself on November 1. You all know how the disease progresses, and how anxious we all are when we have such cases to treat. This case progressed until the eleventh day, slowly but surely getting worse, when I wrote to Dr. Hering, giving minutely the symptoms and condition, saying that on the thirteenth day, when I knew he would have my letter, I would telegraph him how the case was, if alive. This I did, and soon had the reply, "give Lachesis." The case began to mend from this time, and finally recovered entirely.

In December, 1863, another claim came to me in my immediate family. To give a correct account of this case I must copy it as reported at the time: "A child of twenty-one months, with light hair, blue eyes and light complexion, took cold on Christmas day. During the night of the 26th there was fever and rapid respiration. At 11 A.M. December the 27th, the child had a spasm lasting fifteen minutes. From this time until January 8th there was continued fever, greatly increased at night, with a pulse of 150. The respirations were 70 per minute on actual count, and at no time were they less. Generally there was a red spot on one cheek, which frequently changed sides. When one cheek was red the other was generally pale. All this time the left lung was impervious to air. Auscultation revealed slight bronchial respiration but no vesicular murmur. The right lung was not implicated; there was constant cough, yet much increased at night. The case had gradually but surely got worse, until the

8th of January, when the right lung began to be affected. This day the child became uneasy and restless, throwing itself in all directions and into all positions in its efforts to get breath. The face grew dark; there was constant spasmodic cough with labored breathing; the little thing in its agony striking its mother for controlling it at all. When it fell asleep for a few seconds the throat became so dry that a condition resembling croup came on, and all the sufferings were increased. This fearful condition was rapidly hurrying the little sufferer to its grave. All the prominent remedies for the condition had been given, including Lachesis 200th, with no result. At this juncture Lachesis 12th (three pellets) was given dry on the tongue; immediately (the pellets had not entirely dissolved on the tongue) the cough stopped and the breathing was relieved for four hours. At the end of this time the cough gradually returned with all the sufferings (in a diminished degree) when another dose of Lachesis 12th produced the same decided relief, which lasted sixteen hours. Four doses in twelve hours so changed the condition that the child slept nearly all night, and the air again passed freely to all parts of the before obstructed lung."

During the autumn of 1863, and up to January, 1864, there seemed to have been some severe sickness nearly all the time in my own family, and twice during that time had Lachesis helped me out. In the summer of 1864 I again visited Dr. Hering. I was received with the same cordiality, and made at home at his house. At this time the old faculty of the Homœopathic Medical College of Pennsylvania, had become tired of bearing the burden imposed upon it. The trustees of the college offered this charge to Dr. Hering, or at least so that Dr. Hering associated with his friends, might have control and direction of it. They accepted the offer, and associated themselves together and formed a new faculty, which gave its first course of lectures during the winter of 1864–65. Drs. Hering, Lippe, Guernsey and Raue were professors in the college, and Dr. Hering invited me to attend the course of lectures given that winter. This I accepted. When in

October I presented myself at his door, ready to follow his instructions, he said to me, "Now, here you are at home; come every day at three o'clock in the afternoon and take coffee with me. At this hour I have my noonday rest and I allow no one to disturb me." Every day at three o'clock found me at his house where I spent this hour with him. All this time he did the talking, and spoke of Homœopathy, and almost everything else. It finally came about that every evening found me at Dr. Hering's house, where I always met some one or more of the above-named professors, and often all of them. There I spent the winter, virtually in association with Drs. Hering, Lippe, Raue, and Guernsey. These four were like school-boys learning their lessons. Every night they met at Dr. Hering's house and related the experiences of the day, and when any new result was reached they all noted it, and Dr. Hering recorded it in his manuscripts.

A close friendship with these men was begun in consequence of the publication in May and June in the *American Homœopathic Review*, a periodical which all these were interested in maintaining, of a minute account of all the results I had obtained by the administration of Lachesis as a curative agent, up to this time. Those of you who remember the controversy which was at that time going on as to whether there was any remedial virtue in Lachesis, can appreciate the pleasure with which this publication was received by these men, all of whom were positive, both from having helped prove it and from using it in practice, that it was a great curative agent. Hempel had fulminated his anathemas against it, declaring it inert. Others had condemned it in every respect. This report detailed cases in actual experience, where such wonderful results were obtained that no one could make any answer to them except he said, "I don't believe him." I stood ready to prove every case and bring the witnesses, before any court, and take their sworn statements to the truth of what I had written. Dr. Hering felt and always said that this was the turning point with Lachesis, and at once called me the man who saved it. Often, as I came into his house, he would cry out,

"Here comes the man who saved Lachesis." He loved to tell me about the capture of the snake, and how he took the poison and how he had proved it. We were to go to the Academy of Natural Sciences together and see the original snake.

What great results often follow small affairs. In this case the publication of what seemed to me only an ordinary report of cases cured, was followed by the life-long friendship and even gratitude of one of the greatest benefactors of the human race, for so I consider the discoverer of a remedy which will produce such wonderful curative results as Lachesis does.

During this winter which I spent in Philadelphia, and so much of the time at his house, just at Christmas, I received a message from home that Mrs. Boyce was severely sick, and that I must go home at once. On my arrival I found a case of typhoid-pneumonia of a serious nature. After studying the case carefully I gave Phosphorus, but feeling anxious I telegraphed to Dr. Hering the condition, and again received help from him. He was ever ready to do anything in his power for any one who suffered. In about ten days I was able to return and finish the winter.

Another circumstance shows the constancy of Dr. Hering's friendship. Sometime before the commencement of the college I wished to go home, but this Dr. Hering did not want. He said, "You have been here so far, now stay to the commencement." On commencement day Dr. Hering invited me to accompany the faculty and sit on the platform. When the ceremony of conferring the degree of the college was concluded by the president, and each recipient of a diploma had been given a bouquet of flowers, I noticed that Mrs. Hering had another bouquet and wondered why it had not been given to some one. I also noticed that the dean of the faculty had another sheep-skin, but had no idea that this had any significance for me. But soon the dean stepped out upon the platform and began to speak. I heard my name called, and in the confusion which followed, I managed to stand up and hear whatever of his speech I could. The purport of it was that the faculty of the Homœopathic Medical College of Pennsylvania had unanimously voted me the special degree of the college, and that the association with me through the winter had been such as to give them great pleasure at this time in conferring the degree upon me. Then Mrs. Hering gave me the bouquet which I had noticed in her hand, and then came the congratulations of the different members of the faculty, and then I was glad to get out of the Hall.

Altogether this was the happiest and most instructive winter I ever passed. So many memories cluster about these men and those whom I met at Dr. Hering's, that I must stop and think of them. There was our noble Dunham, our Damascene P. P. Wells, our loving Jeanes, our lion-hearted Lippe, our beloved Raue, and our accurate Guernsey. Drs. Dunham, Gardner, Jeanes, and now Father Hering are gone. Those who are left of the old guard are well worthy of our love and respect, and as we drop a tear upon the graves of those who are gone, let us not fail to cherish a warm love for those who are left to bear aloft the standard of pure Homœopathy. Many times since 1865 I have visited Dr. Hering, and was always received with the same warmhearted welcome. These interviews were always full of instruction and friendship. I wish I could describe the many reminiscences I retain of him as I remember them, but this I cannot do. I can only do the best I can, and with your patience and indulgence I will give you a few of the incidents which occurred during these visits subsequent to 1865.

For several years after 1865 every summer I visited Dr. Hering, and was always as warmly welcomed as before. In his home, (a double house, Nos. 112 and 114 North Twelfth St.) on the first floor, beside the kitchen and the laundry, were four rooms. The two front rooms were his reception rooms. The north room was the ladies room and the south his ordinary business room. This last was merely evenly divided across from between the two windows by a couple of desks, behind one of which he stood with pen in hand ready to note down the symptoms or to look up the remedy, the other desk was for his secretary. Many a time I have seen the space in front of these desks full of patients and then even extending out into the hall, and, in fact, all over the lower part of the house. Then behind his desk he stood passing upon one and then another until all were served, then he would go out and see patients until all these were seen. The other two rooms on the first floor were respectively a dining room and his reception room for visitors. This room was about 20x30 feet; on two sides were shelves full of books; on the west end were windows; at the east end were folding doors separating it from the ladies' reception room. Over these doors was a portrait of the original serpent from which was taken the Lachesis. As I remember it, half erect, with its body coiled and mouth open, it seemed a formidable reptile. I have often wished that I had a photograph of it. In my office is a representation of the South American lance-headed viper which a water-color artist made for me from the description in Jahr's "Pharmacopœia," but it does not resemble this portrait which Dr. Hering had painted. People often come into my office and, after looking at my picture with a shudder, say: "How can you bear to have that ugly thing here?" Ah! that, to them ugly thing is to me a thing of beauty. I never tire of looking at it. As I look at it I seem to see one of my children, if not two, who were saved by Lachesis, and as I continue to look I see here one and there one who only for this serpent would have passed over to the majority. I went there almost daily, and rejoice that Dr. Hering lived to introduce this remedy into practice. Once when I visited him there was a stranger who answered the bell when I called and who ushered me into his reception room. There were several patients there when I entered. He took no notice of me whatever, but went on with his examinations and prescriptions until he got through. During all this time I sat there watching him, but he did not show that he had ever known me. But when the last patient passed out and my turn came, he said, "come in our room, I can't see you here." He wanted to hear something about Lachesis. During the time I sat in his reception room he would not allow himself to be diverted from his purpose, even so far as to recognize me, but kept steadily on until he had made his prescription for the last one, when he immediately dismissed all from his mind, and gave himself up to friendship. I really thought he had forgotten me and said so. "No," he said, "I never let one thing interfere with another." At one time when I had called early in the morning I found him in his room where the manuscripts are kept. This room is on the second floor over his business room. It was here that he shut himself up and generally admitted no visitors. This room was full of books and articles which he wished for his own private study. At one end was an iron safe for special manuscripts, and this was full. Dr. Dunham was a prized friend and a frequent visitor in this room. He once said that his highest ambition would be gratified if he could but edit Dr. Hering's manuscripts. I am not sure whether I heard Dr. Dunham say this, but, if not, it came direct from him to me through his next friend, Dr. H. M. Smith. It was in this room where Dr. Hering went in the morning to write and study. As soon as he waked he would hurry on his pantaloons, and maybe a vest or not, just as he happened to be in a hurry or not, and here he would sit until Mrs. Hering came in to advise him to get ready to see his patients. He never seemed to know when it was time to get ready for the day's business. On this particular morning when I was in this room Mrs. Hering came with a bowl of water and some towels for his toilet. When he came to change his night-dress for his day-shirt I thought it time for me to retire, and was about to pass out of the room. "O don't go," he said, "I am not a woman." I remained until his toilet was completed and then we went down to his business office. He had an apparatus with which he could prepare coffee in this room and sometimes did so. I have supposed that he often did this, but do not know. His mind was constantly occupied, and he was either talking, writing or listening. He was a good listener if one had anything to say of any value. I well remember the first time I saw him to have any conversation with him. I happened to speak of an effect produced by *Euphrasia* on the nasal mucous membrane and some use of this remedy in measles. At once out came his pencil and paper and down it went, subsequently to appear in his portfolios, if finally approved. He always carried with him tablets of paper, about three by four inches in size, on which he wrote all he observed or heard. On these tablets he also noted his cases. I don't think I ever saw him when he felt too weary to tell something which would help others in Homœopathy. I don't remember that he was ever the first to say good-night.

The great desire of his heart, through all the time I knew him, was to publish a complete Materia Medica. During the winter I spent with him he tried to consummate this wish and issued a prospectus for publishing the work, both in German and English, in the same book. He offered it at the exact cost of printing and paper for five thousand copies. Some money was raised for this purpose, how much I do not know Although this project fell to the ground, I know that he was happy in making the effort. Those who sent the first instalment of five dollars had their choice either to take the money back or a copy of Gross' Comparative Materia Medica, a work which he translated; I presume they all took the book. Later he made another attempt to get out his Materia Medica, in a periodical, and through this he issued several pathogeneses in the *Am. Journal of Hom. Materia Medica*. This came to an end all too soon. At last the desire of his heart was about to be gratified, and his "Guiding Symptoms" began to make its appearance under such auspices that a certainty had been reached. And now, instead of the enterprise falling through and thus disappointing him, he passed away. Like Moses on the mount viewing the promised land which he was not to enter, Dr. Hering at last had a view of the consummation of that which he had been looking for for so many years. This work is in loving hands, and it will be completed, I hope, before long. His expression to me about this work was full of enthusiasm, and was, "when this comes out what a grand thing it will be. Nothing which has ever been published can compare with it." What a life his was! A life of desire to benefit others. Laboring on even up to the last hour of his life. If I were to be asked what was the chief trait in his character, I should say that it was a desire to aid his fellows, and with this a perfect confidence in those whom he trusted. It will seem presumptuous in me to attempt to give an estimate of how much Dr. Hering knew, since this will be told so much better than I can do it by his many associates. I only knew that there seemed to be no subject which he did not appear to understand, and frequently when with him he would start out to talk upon his favorite theme, Homœopathy, and from this he would pass to some other—perhaps music—where he seemed equally at home. Once, I met at his home a celebrated opera bass singer, Carl Formes, I think, and as I listened to their conversation I could see that Dr. Hering was as conversant with operas and opera music as was this professional singer. I well remember this meeting, for I was surprised to hear Dr. Hering talk and to hear Carl Formes listen to him. Afterwards, when I was listening to the singing, in opera, of this artist, I found myself wondering whether Dr. Hering might not have been a success as an opera singer if his pathway had led him to it. That same evening when we were alone together, he gave me, as I now see it, about all the information I possess in regard to opera. He knew the history of all the artists who were successes in their line. At times he would talk of the future life and what he expected in it. It was, to him, only a step in progress. We are to take up our life and go on in the future just where we lay it down here. Our pursuits are to be the same, only the incumbrances will be removed. I don't think I ever heard him hesitate in this regard. He seemed to have reflected upon this subject, and to have settled it in his mind just as definitely as he had any other subject which he undertook to study out. He believed that we carry with us our preferences and our distastes, and that we will exercise them there as here. I have no doubt he expected to gather his students about him and to go on increasing in knowledge forever.

In 1876, at the time of the World's Convention, there was a large number of physicians present from all the States and from abroad. Dr. Hering's time was very much taken up by calls from a great many of these strangers, all of whom wished to see Dr. Hering. I began to fear that I should not enjoy a visit to him, when, on the day of Dr. Lippe's dinner at the Union League Club House, Dr. Hering said to me, "Come here this afternoon and go with me to the dinner, I shall not go unless you go with me." I was told that he seldom went out alone now, and as he desired me to go with him for fear that he should fail to see me at any other time, I did not fail to go. We took the cars on Twelfth St., at his door, and rode to Walnut St., where we took other cars and rode to Broad St. near the Club House. It rained hard all the time, but this did not disturb him. He talked all the way about the first winter when the new faculty lectured and of the class, all of whom he seemed to look upon as his children. Some of these he met at the dinner table. He seemed very happy all the evening but was glad to get home again. When I left him he said, "Now when you come to Philadelphia again we will call on Dr. Lippe together, and I shall not go until you go with me." I saw him but once more at this time and then only for a few minutes. He said, "There are so many here now to see me that I have no time for you, but I am hungry to see you just the same." There was always a chair at the table for me, where I afterwards learned to like cheese, but I did not want it in two ounce doses without bread. I can vouch for the flavor of limburger cheese when taken in small quantities and as a flavor to bread or crackers.

In 1877 I was at his house again, when he invited several of his friends to supper with me in the garden. He seemed more fond than ever to call around him the younger members of the profession, and on this afternoon I think there were at least ten or twelve. He was particularly pleased that so many came to see him. When he invited me to come to this supper he said, "I want them to see the man who saved Lachesis." After they were gone he talked about the first time we met in this same garden and how unexpected the meeting was. He had received my letter asking to be allowed to call on him for instruction in Homœopathy, only a day or two before. He said that this had been his chief pleasure in life, meaning the imparting to others whatever he knew. We expected then to make our call on Dr. Lippe but were prevented. This called up the time when Dr. Lippe was very sick with typhoid fever and his visit to see him, when he took down the Materia Medica and looked it through and found the remedy in Silicea, which soon changed the whole condition, and Dr. Lippe was saved to Homœopathy. When I left him he said, "Come again next year." I said yes, and I fully expected to have done so but I did not, and I never saw him again. In writing these reminiscences I have given our association as it recurred to me. On reading it over I am forced to wonder whether his friendship for me was any closer than for others. I sometimes feel that I was more than ordinarily a favorite, but when I recall the memory of those whom I have met at his house I can not pride myself on it. I will not undertake to name these others, but as I remember what Dr. Hering said of them I can but think that had I not wanted instruction in Homœopathy I should never have found the way to his heart, and so must give the honor to Homœopathy instead of to myself.

This morning a postman brought me a letter with the postmark Philadelphia. On opening it I read, "Enclosed I send you a lock of father's hair." How glad I was to get it I will not undertake to tell, but I will say that I shall cherish it as a memento of that dear old man who for so many years honored me with his warm friendship.

Dr. John K. Lee surrendered the chair at this stage of the proceedings to Dr. Henry N. Guernsey and addressed the meeting as follows:

We have listened with intense interest to the naration of the personal reminiscences of Dr. Hering and been touched by the glowing eulogies upon his life, and it may seem superfluous and redundant to pay a further tribute to his revered memory. But whilst he has been extolled for the greatness of his intellect, his profound erudition, his untiring research and his devotion to his profession, still the portraiture is incomplete because it does not include a delineation of his moral qualities. And these, according to their development, either add grace and dignity to intellectual endowments and link man to his Creator, or else dim the splendor of his achievements, tarnish the lustre of his fame and spread a pall of darkness over his grave.

In this respect, I am happy to affirm, that it is not necessary to prevaricate or enfold Dr. Hering in the mantle of charity, since his moral nature expanded in beautiful harmony with his mind, and blending, they reflected each the glory of the other and formed a well rounded and symmetrical character, always grand, because it was underlaid by simplicity and fidelity to truth.

A single instance in his history, related to me by one who was admitted to his confidence and privacy, will illustrate the elevation of his moral sentiments, his magnanimity and his abhorrence of the least departure from the path of rectitude and honor. Some years ago, says the relator, during a conversation with Dr. Hering, he remarked, "J—— is stopping with me. He is a man of wonderful ability, but I have lost all regard for him. At supper last evening, in a burst of feeling, he said, 'O how badly it makes one feel to be convinced of error!' I felt indignated at such a sentiment and replied, No! not if he be moved by proper motives. The only feeling of an honest man should be, how glad I am to learn the truth; and from that moment I lost all regard for the man." The thought here expressed is so lofty, grand and pure, that I will not impair its force by verbal comments, but leave it to penetrate your minds and influence your lives.

Dr. Joseph C. Guernsey here arose and addressed the chair as follows:

Mr. President:—I do not rise to eulogize Dr. Hering, or to recount his many good works in the advancement of our cause. There are many here to-night who can do, and have already done, more justice to that than I.

I merely wish to present an interesting memento relative to his medical graduation. It is a translation from the Latin of the subjects of his Thesis, which he defended in public disputation before graduating at the University of Würzburg, in the year 1826.

The following preamble is printed in Latin on the cover of the Dissertation:

Johann Lucas Schœnlein, Dean *pro tempore* of the gracious order of physicians, Doctor of Philosophy, Medicine and Surgery, and public professor in ordinary, etc., etc., with all due courtesy, invites the noble vice-rector of the Academy, the senate fathers, the professors of all grades, the academic citizens, finally men of letters and the patrons of letters, to a public disputation, to be held March 22d, 1826, at 9 A.M., by the very noble, illustrious and learned man, Mr. Constantine Hering, Saxon, under the presidency of Caritanus Textor, Doctor of Philosophy, Medicine and Surgery, Aulic Councillor to the August King of Bavaria, and public professor in ordinary, etc., etc., for the purpose of duly obtaining the highest honors in Medicine, Surgery and Obstetrics.

Inaugural Dissertation.

On Psychic Remedies.

Theses.

I.
Springs are living fossils.

II.
I hold that there are nerves in the placenta.

III.
The "ganglion petrosum" is to the ear what the "ganglion ophthalmicum" is to the eye.

IV.
The olfactory, optic and acoustic nerves are apophyses of the cerebrum and cerebellum, not nerves.

V.
The old man is the perfect man.

VI.
Materia Medica is to Hahnemann what Pathology was to Hippocrates.

VII.
Such as life is, is disease.

VIII.
The rational system is not merely the better, but the only one in pathology.

IX.
I deny psychical diseases.

X.
Any disease may be removed at any stage.

XI.

No one has yet appeared to refute Hahnemann.

XII.

Homœopathy is heterostheny, and its fundamental law: *Contraria contrariis.*

XIII.

In the struggle of vital forces as a foundation rests every vital effect.

XIV.

There is only one normal position for the fœtus.

XV.

The resurrection of the dead is the highest ideal of medical art.

XVI.

Not to deliver individual men from particular diseases, but to deliver the whole human race from the cause of disease, is the ultimate goal of medical science.

INAUGURAL SUBJECTS.

I.—*President's Question.*

The checking of traumatic hemorrhages.

II.—*Candidate's Subject.*

THE MEDICINE OF THE FUTURE.

Dr. Charles Mohr then rose and made the following remarks:

"I approach the subject of anything relating to the life and work of Dr. Hering with a great deal of diffidence. But on this occasion I cannot, consistently with my sense of duty, neglect saying a word or two in regard to the manner in which Dr. Hering treated the stranger student and younger practitioner of Homœopathy. I remember the first time I ever saw Dr. Hering. It was one evening after I had attended a lecture in this room and I was somewhat perplexed about a case I was treating and I thought I would like to hear what he had to say in relation to what had best be done. I rang his door bell, was shown into his office, and when I told him what my purpose was in seeing him he at once extended his hand and gave mine a hearty shake and said "sit down," and after he had waited upon two or three patients he was ready to hear my story, which I related. I think it was more than an hour before I was able to leave him. He gave me his opinion as to the nature of the case and what I might expect and what in his judgment was the proper remedy, and I wondered that the man, without the least idea of receiving any remuneration, should take so much time and trouble to give me, an utter stranger, the knowledge I desired; and when I rose to say my good-bye and express my thanks he extended his hand again and, shaking mine with a hearty grip, he said in that tone which after that became very familiar to me, "Well, come again!" And I did go again and again, and I never saw Dr. Hering in my life that I did not learn something which has profited me and profited those who came within the influence of my professional life.

I saw Dr. Hering for the last time just two days before his death. He was reclining on his couch in his study with books and papers piled about him, showing that he had been hard at work before he lay down to take a needed rest. My business then was to see him in relation to a new subscriber to "The Guiding Symptoms," his life-work. When I told him that it was necessary for him to sign a paper, as president of the Society that was publishing his work, he got up like a new man to affix his signature, apparently delighted that one other man in the Homœopathic profession appreciated his work sufficiently to assist in supplying the means to further its publication. As was his wont on such occasions he began to talk about his *Magnum opus* and about the prospects of the American Homœopathic Publishing Society; and inasmuch as several of the speakers this evening have referred to that work, and of its completion, I feel impelled as one of the editors to state here that it is the purpose of Drs. Raue, Knerr and myself to give the profession the GUIDING SYMPTOMS just as Dr. Hering would have given it had he lived to complete it.

On this occasion we may naturally ask, what can be done to perpetuate the memory of Dr. Hering? We may publish a memorial volume; we may build a monument of the finest marble; but neither of these would be so grateful to our departed friend—if things transpiring here are known in the higher life—as the publication of the whole of the work on which he was engaged almost hourly for the last fifty years. In the GUIDING SYMPTOMS Dr. Hering has perpetuated his own memory; but the great bulk of the work is in manuscript, and I think this a fitting time to appeal to the profession in the United States and the world by generous subscriptions to help the editors to publish the work as Dr. Hering would have been pleased to complete it. I do not know what more fitting thing the profession could do than that; and besides that it must be remembered that the work is a legacy to the Doctor's family.

He said to me one day: "Before the tenth volume is out I shall not be with you. I do not know whether I shall live to see the completion of another volume, but I feel that the GUIDING SYMPTOMS will be finished, and, perhaps, from my place in heaven, I may peep through a little hole and see that my work is well done."

Now even such an expression as that, so simple and childlike, shows that his whole heart and soul were wrapped up in the completion of that work, and I ask again, what thing can we do better than to get out of the shelves of his study the materials he has collected for the last fifty years, and give them to the profession and the world, for the benefit of suffering humanity.

There being no other speakers, a motion made on behalf of the Memorial Committee, that they be discharged, was duly carried.

It was next resolved to appoint a Committee to solicit subscriptions to defray the expenses of publishing a Memorial Volume, to contain a biographical sketch of Dr. Hering, and the transactions of the meetings held in all parts of the world in his memory. On motion the literary executors of Dr. Hering, namely, Drs. C. G. Raue, C. B. Knerr, and C. Mohr, were appointed to constitute this Committee, and they were given full power to edit and publish the volume as to them seemed best.

On motion the meeting then adjourned.

ST. LOUIS MEMORIAL SERVICES.

In compliance with the request of the Memorial Committee, and under the inspiration of such an appropriate and beautiful thought, something over four hundred of the best people of St. Louis met at Pickwick Hall on Sunday evening, October 10th, 1880, to listen to the Hering Memorial Services given under the auspices of the St. Louis Society of Homœopathic Physicians and Surgeons.

Music softened and sweetened the air. The hush of prayer pervaded every heart; the muses sang in lyric and heroic verse, and oratory, in all the luxuriant finish of classic diction, hung garlands of immortelles all along the wondrous career of the hero whose memory it was meet to honor.

The meeting was called to order by W. A. Edmonds, M.D., President of the St. Louis Society of Homœopathic Physicians and Surgeons, when a Quartette: "Come Gracious Spirit" (E. Marzo), was sung by Mrs. O. Girard, Mrs. J. E. Mills, Prof. Allman, and H. Blickhan. Miss Lizzie Garriott, accompanist.

After an invocation by Rev. John Snyder, Dr. Charles Gundelach read the following biographical sketch:

Constantine Hering was born in Oschatz, Saxony, on the first day of January, 1800. From his earliest age he exhibited an insatiable thirst for knowledge, and many of his boyhood's earliest hours were spent in wandering over his native hills exploring the works of nature. From 1811 to 1817, while attending the classical school at Zittau, he made a large and valuable collection of minerals, herbs, skulls and bones of animals. His medical studies were pursued at the Surgical Academy of Dresden. Later he entered the University of Leipzig. Here the celebrated surgeon, T. Henry Robbi, who was his preceptor, made him, in 1820, his assistant. While thus employed, Dr. Robbi was requested by the founder of a publishing house to prepare a work that in its thorough exposure of the system, should utterly uproot Homœopathy from the land. Dr. Robbi declined the enterprise, but referred to young Hering as one perfectly competent for the task. Hering accepted, and in preparing himself was compelled to consult the works of Hahnemann, which, after a diligent research and study, convinced him of the truth of the law, "*Similia Similibus Curantur.*" He pursued this new study with characteristic ardor against the counsels of his teachers and the entreaties of his friends. An incident which occurred about this time contributed largely to the decision at which he had arrived. He had received a dissecting wound which resisted the utmost efforts of the best physicians and surgeons. His hand was in such a condition that amputation was advised as the only hope of saving his life. In this exigency the treatment with *Arsenicum*, administered by a homœopathic friend, proved eminently successful and saved the limb. Dr. Hering then determined to devote his life to Homœopathy. In 1825 he was enabled to prosecute his studies at the University of Würzburg, where he graduated the next year on the 23d day of March, with honor, defending at the same time his chosen thesis, "*De medicina futura*," thus showing no concealment of his sympathy with the views of Hahnemann.

In the following year he was appointed instructor in mathematics and natural science in Blochmann's Institute in Dresden, and after remaining there for several months he was appointed a member of the royal commission to make researches and collections in zoology in Surinam, South America. During his stay there he continued his study of Homœopathy and practiced it to some extent, besides writing some articles for the "Homœopathic Archives." This latter proceeding was brought to the notice of the King, who directed Dr. Hering to confine himself to the duties of his appointment and let outside matters alone. By return mail Dr. Hering sent in a report of his accounts in full, and resigning his official position, began the practice of medicine in Paramaribo. A few years later he sailed for home, and on the way landed in Philadelphia, in 1833. Here he found that a good introduction of Homœopathy had been made by the late Dr. George H. Bute in the previous year, during the epidemic of cholera. He was persuaded to stay, and soon acquired a large and lucrative practice. Dr. Wm. Wesselhœft, who had established Homœopathy on a firm footing in several counties in Pennsylvania, made Dr. Hering's acquaintance and proposed the establishment of a homœopathic school at Allentown, which was to be supported by a stock company. Dr. Hering agreed to remove to Allentown and to assist in the school whenever a salary was "guaranteed to him equal to that of any first-class clergyman in Allentown."

The stock company was formed and the small salary provided, and Dr. Hering went to Allentown, where he remained two or three years. He was made president of the Homœopathic School, which was the first of its kind in the world, and from which the Homœopathic Medical College of Pennsylvania afterwards sprung. Dr. Hering returned to Philadelphia and has resided there ever since. He published a pamphlet on "The Rise and Progress of Homœopathy," which had a very extensive circulation. In 1846 the Homœopathic Medical College of Pennsylvania was founded, and Dr. Hering was elected Professor of Institutes and Materia Medica, which he held at intervals until 1867, when he assisted in founding the Hahnemann Medical College of Philadelphia, in which he held the same chair until 1869, when he resigned and was made Emeritus Professor.

Dr. Hering was a member of the Academy of Natural Sciences of Philadelphia, to which institution he presented his large zoological collection. He was one of the founders of the American Institute of Homœopathy, and was its first president. He was also one of the originators of the American Provers' Union, instituted August 10th, 1853.

Dr. Hering's life work was Materia Medica. He made physiological provings of the most of our remedies, introduced many new and very valuable drugs, and published his remedies and experiences in different works, and was during all his years of practice a very diligent contributor to the periodical medical literature in America, as well as in Germany. Of his publications should be mentioned his "Domestic Physician," published in 1835. This work passed through seven editions in America, two in England, thirteen in Germany, and has also been translated into the French, Spanish, Italian, Danish, Hungarian, Russian and Swedish languages;

The Effects of Snake Poison, 1837;

Suggestions for the Provings of Drugs, 1853;

Amerikanische Arzneipruefungen, 1853–1857;

Translation of Gross' Comparative Materia Medica, 1866;

Analytical Therapeutics, first volume, 1875;

Condensed Materia Medica, two editions, 1877–1879; and

Guiding Symptoms, the third volume of which he began just prior to his death. This, his life-work, proposed to give the characteristics of every drug used by the homœopathic profession. The manuscript is in such shape that the work can be completed.

In person, Dr. Hering had an imposing and dignified appearance. He was tall and wore spectacles; beard full and hair long and curling. Dr. Hering was married three times. His first wife he married in South America, where she died, leaving one son, who now resides in Paramaribo. While living in Allentown he married a Philadelphia lady, by whom he had three children, only one surviving, a daughter, married and living in Boston. His second wife died, and during a visit to Germany in 1845 he married the daughter of Dr. Buchheim, a celebrated allopathic physician, by whom he had eight children, six of whom and their mother survive him.

Dr. Hering enjoyed good health until about ten years ago, when, at the ripe age of seventy, he occasionally suffered from attacks of asthma. Even to the last day of his life he was in comparative good health, having attended to his patients during the day, had retired later in the evening to his library and was engaged in his literary study, when suddenly he was attacked with paralysis of the heart and died, surrounded by his sorrowing family, on Friday evening, July 23d, 1880, in the 81st year of his age.

Dr. W. A. Edmonds followed with these remarks:

We are here, saddened and subdued by bereavement in the death of our distinguished friend, to condole with each other in our severe loss, and to pay the last sad tribute to his blessed memory.

In surveying a great and noble life, like that of Dr. Hering, we very naturally incline to be inquisitive as to the peculiar point or quality of character which may have resulted in so much usefulness and prominence.

Undoubtedly the great beacon light of his life-work and charm of his character, was his enthusiasm; the enthusiasm of conviction, and especially his conviction as to the theoretical and practical truth of Homœopathy.

By enthusiasm, we understand that particular emotional glow and warmth of delight experienced upon the attainment of a new knowledge or new idea.

All of us have greater or less experience of such emotion; but so soon do we turn aside into the avenues of sordidness and selfishness, to see what of gain or position may be made out of the newly gotten idea, that the sensation, like the sparkle and aroma of the recently uncorked vintage, wastes with the touch of early use.

A pure and unalloyed enthusiasm is not found in companionship with avarice, ambition and untruthfulness. The purely selfish intriguer may be impelled by his desires, to heroic efforts and deeds of daring, but is ever a stranger to that holy poetic fire which warmed and illumined the pathway in the life of our distinguished comrade. To say, then, that he was enthusiastic, is to say that he was truthful and loyal to his convictions.

Peculiarities of organization and modes of life, as before intimated, render enthusiasm with most of us an ephemeral affair. With our dear departed friend, this activity was in ceaseless motion ever present. He loved the truth for itself, and for its usefulness to humanity; he loved it as the young mother loves her newly first-born; and as the love grew older, it grew stronger and warmer, until in the very last days of a long and eventful life, it shone with a phosphorescent glow and undimmed splendor. His unselfish love of the truth and devotion to conviction was "a thing of beauty, a joy forever." With all my soul I bow with reverence and adoration in presence of a life so resplendent with loyalty to truth, or at least that which he believed to be true. Hundreds of practitioners, the country over, evince much of his brain power and industry, but for want of his mental warmth never approached his eminence. There seemed to be a charm and magnetism about this element of his character, which sent him at a bound away ahead of all competition. When a new knowledge, or a new truth had set his head and heart fairly aglow, he never halted to inquire what might be the consequence of its adoption; whether it would bring gain and position or loss and disparagement. In the earlier years of his life, he was requested by his preceptor, to furnish a paper in refutation of Homœopathy. Most young men under such circumstances would have set to work in quest of material to furnish the desired refutation and thereby receive the approbation of his superior. But he, with a true nobility of soul, went straight to the side of Homœopathy to ascertain what might be said in its favor, with the result of his immediate conviction and conversion, instead of the contemplated refutation.

At a later period of his life he, with others, was sent abroad by his government for scientific purposes. Very soon he was detected by one of his medical associates in the promulgation and practice of Homœopathy, who at once reported his conduct to his superiors. He was ordered to confine his attention to special objects of his appointment.

Promptly he closed his portfolio, set his papers and accounts in order, tendered his resignation, entered upon his life-work in the teaching and practice of his profession; and so continued to teach and practice, through good or evil report, praise or disparagement; living long enough to see the hated heresy a power in the civilized world, and a boon to humanity, in the ills to which flesh is heir.

In tracing his life and character, we find a striking parallel to that of the dramatic life of the illustrious Apostle Paul, who had but to know the truth of his convictions in any given premise, and he was ready to brave all the perils and hardships of fire, famine, stripes, imprisonments, shipwreck and martyrdom in its vindication. The trials of our friend were less literal and corporeal, but the social and official ostracism of his early days were scarcely less trying to a sensitive and noble nature.

Who shall estimate the results of such a life as its benign influence radiates and ramifies down the chambers and corridors of time, through ceaseless future ages, until our efforts at comprehension are paled and wearied as in an attempt to grasp an infinity.

"If a man die, shall he live again?" Let us, our friends, in this, our hour of bereavement, accept such a life and character as a great and mighty revelation in behalf of the soul's immortality. The good Father never made such a life to go down in one eternal night of annihilation. In the matter of what we call his death, we recognize the breaking up of the casket in order that the jewel may have a new setting, to fit it for the glories and splendor of the great beyond, where it is destined to glow and sparkle with an ever increasing brilliancy, through the countless cycles of an eternity, of which we may talk and write, but of which our present finite powers can have but a poverty of expression or appreciation.

Our friend in the flesh has gone; we shall see his face here no more forever.

For eighty long winters and summers did he continue the voyage of life, and when his mortality went down in the Jordan of death, he went down as some gallant ship, with sails unfurled and banners flying, with the inscription high over all: "Homœopathy as a truth once, always and forever."

Dr. S. B. Parsons prefaced the reading of the following poem by saying:

The theme of this poem was suggested by an incident in the life of Dr. Hering, which was that, in the early part of his professional career in Philadelphia, he was called to attend a little girl, an only child, who had been given up to die by all the physicians that had seen her. Dr. Hering was summoned to the case, not because the parents had any faith in the homœopathic mode of practice, but because they had heard of him as a gentleman of culture, a man of scientific attainments, and hoped there might something be found in his treatment that would restore their loved one to health. Dr. Hering's treatment was successful, and when his little patient was out of danger and able to talk and laugh with her mother, the parents overwhelmed him with expressions of gratitude, complimenting him in the warmest terms on his skill and ability, and drew a bright picture of his future life and the high eminence he would some day attain in his profession. When they had ceased, he thanked them kindly, and replied: "I am nothing, God is great!"

    Could we draw the veil aside
      From the night of infant state,
    Mortal eyes would see the guide—
      "I am nothing! God is great!"

    Happy childhood—morn of life—
      Chasing shadows drawn by fate,
    Knows but faintly in the strife—
      "I am nothing! God is great!"

    Ever smiling, sunny youth,
      Weaving webs to captivate,
    Then unfolds the spirit's truth—
      "I am nothing! God is great!"

    Resting on the fair mid-land
      'Tween the in and outer gate,
    Budding manhood's thoughts expand—
      "I am nothing! God is great!"

    In the bloom of life's bright day,
      Lurid storms may devastate;
    Through the darkness beams a ray—
      "I am nothing! God is great!"

    Nearer draws futurity,
      Nor asks the penitent to wait:
    Clearer sees maturity—
      "I am nothing! God is great!"

    Gently comes life's winter day,
      When the heart seems desolate;
    In true faith will be its lay—
      "I am nothing! God is great!"

The following tribute was paid by Dr. J. Martin Kershaw:

As the majestic river passes to the far-off sea beyond, so has the life of him we have come to honor, gone to the unknown country. Like the grand old oak, ever erect and noble, he bore alike the storms of adversity and the clouds of sunshine, throughout the scores of years that were his to work and be faithful. Towering above his fellows, working and waiting for what he knew was truth, he was rightfully and indeed a king among men in his God-like work for humanity. The truth, the pure, snow-white, spotless truth was that for which he labored and toiled, from the early spring-time of life, until the frosty winter of old age had come upon him, and then, full of years and full of honors, he crossed over to that land the Deity has given to those who work faithfully and well. His priceless treasures he has bequeathed to us and to the multitudes of God's sick and suffering creatures, in every clime and country, and the world is richer and better to-day, because Constantine Hering lived and worked in it. In the quiet city of the dead, where countless weary toilers sleep, the sad song of the autumn winds is heard above the resting place of him for whom we mourn to-night; but the earnest life-work, and more than human deeds of the great departed, still live for us and the coming worlds of people.

Dr. C. W. Spalding next addressed the meeting as follows:

Mr. President: There are epochs in human history that are occasioned by the discovery and introduction of new principles or laws, which in their operation have a direct relation to human happiness and the welfare of society. Not that there is anything absolutely new; for all things exist potentially, in the Creator from eternity; and are called new, when they come into actual existence in the material universe.

The discovery and announcement of the law "similia similibus curantur," constitutes such an epoch. Upon this great basal verity, has now been founded a school of medicine differing from all previous schools, in the adoption, and application to practice, of this therapeutic law. The fundamental principles of medical science are the same in all schools of medicine; the differences being chiefly in their systems of therapeutics.

In order that the beneficent effects of a new therapeutic system should be made available for the alleviation of human suffering by the removal of diseases, it became necessary to develop and establish by study and experiment, a system of medication in agreement therewith. Homœopathic Materia Medica has arisen from this necessity. The proper presentation, and the ultimate establishment of new ideas in the minds of men, or of new methods in their habits of life, call into activity the labors of a class of minds peculiarly fitted for the performance of their definite tasks. As the knowledge of the discovery of this new therapeutic law was disseminated, it arrested the attention of such medical minds as were endowed with sufficient independence of thought to allow them to be open to conviction; and prominently among these was the man whose life, and not whose death, we are now assembled to commemorate. His first study of the new system was occasioned, we are told, by his being assigned to the duty of refuting it. This is not the first time that the individual chosen by his fellows as the one most capable among them of disproving the new ideas, has become an able instrument in establishing them upon surer foundations and of spreading among mankind a better knowledge of their transcendent merits.

In reducing the new law to practice, the great problem to be worked out was the ascertainment by trial of the specific action of drugs upon the human system, and subsequently the orderly arrangement of the great mass of experimental knowledge thus obtained, into such form as to render it readily available in the practice of medicine. For the successful accomplishment of this important task, it was requisite that individuals peculiarly qualified by nature and education for this particular work should devote their lives to its development and perfection. In this arduous labor, Dr. Hering has spent the best years of his life. To him, in very large degree, the homœopathic physician is indebted for the completeness of our system of medication. Patience, industry and untiring perseverance have been brought to the work, and if any man is more than any other, entitled to be called the apostle of Homœopathic Materia Medica, that man is Constantine Hering.

Dr. J. P. Frohne then spoke as follows:

The gentlemen who spoke before me, have eloquently dwelt on the merits of the departed as propagator of Homœopathy in this country. Therefore, allow me to also remember his love for his native country, of which especially during the Franco-German war he bore brilliant testimony; celebrating the victory of the German arms most solemnly at his own house. He thus manifested that he was proud of being a native of Germany, of that country which sent many a great man over the ocean to sow the seeds of German thought and German art among distant nations.

The departed has shown his love for his native country, and his interest in science by multitudes of articles in homœopathic journals.

His essays are as genial as they are instructive, and his memory is, in due appreciation of his merits, this day celebrated in the cities of all Germany. And, wherever upon the face of the world Homœopathy has gained permanent ground, the name of Constantine Hering will be known and be ever memorable, since he has by his works secured for himself an immortal name!

To but very few of us mortals is it granted to do as much for suffering humanity as he has done, for Providence had laid in him the talents of a true therapeutist as well as of an author, of which during his long life he has made the most salutary use, saving the lives of thousands who in the sense of gratitude now lament his loss.

The life and works of our Hering ought to be a shining model for us younger physicians, and may his memory be everlasting!

The following remarks were then made by Dr. Chas. L. Carriere:

Grand is the celebration of to-day! The fact that all homœopathists of the world join in a Memorial Service of one so universally known, esteemed and beloved as Dr. Constantine Hering makes this celebration one of the grandest of the kind. It is proper, therefore, that on this occasion everything should be thought of which may add to the honor of our departed friend.

I have chosen to occupy the few minutes allotted to me, to draw your attention to the fact that Dr. Hering was not only a man of great culture and a most successful practitioner of the Healing Art, but in addition to his excellent qualities and his superiority, he was also on the progressive path as a christian; not a christian by name only, but one who did believe and trust in Jesus Christ, our Saviour. Still, his faith differed from the generally acknowledged doctrines of the church of the past. As he left the old school of medicine and adopted the doctrine of "similia," and became one of the founders of Homœopathy, so he also left the old church and became a receiver of the doctrines of the New Jerusalem. Thus he was one of the beginners and promoters of the New Era, both in Medicine and Religion. A German paper, referring to his departure from this world, says: "Dr. Hering was made acquainted with the doctrines of the New Church soon after his arrival in the United States; he received them with warmth and zeal; he was of the opinion that the action of the homœopathic remedies would at some time be established by the doctrine of correspondence." It may be proper here to state that the doctrine of correspondence is a doctrine of the New Church. The paper referred to, also states: "He occasionally mentioned that in his house the first German Christmas tree, in the whole large city of Philadelphia, spread its brilliancy." The words, "German Christmas tree," were probably used because it is claimed that the Germans have introduced that custom in this country.

In looking at Dr. Hering as a medical man and as a religious man, we see that he was not led by a blind faith, he was not bound to the doctrines of his predecessors, because they were believed by them, or for the reason that they were the old and acknowledged doctrines of the world; he would investigate for himself, and be a rational believer of that which he accepted as truth. His religious belief differed as much, and even more, from the generally accepted doctrine of the Church, as his homœopathic theory and practice differed from the old school of medicine.

The difficulty of three persons in the Godhead, and how to make one of the three, did not trouble his mind, for he knew and fully understood that the Trinity was embodied in the Divine Humanity of Christ, and that there is but one God in but one person. Nor was it difficult for him to solve the apparent contradiction of the literal sense of the sacred Scripture, neither the apparent contradictions of scriptural statements with the developed facts of this age; for he well knew that the Word of God is infinitely higher than human thought or language, and that in the inner life of these literal forms we find an inexhaustible fountain of the Divine Wisdom from which we may drink and never thirst.

From his knowledge of the spiritual world, and the relation between this life and the life to come, he knew that man as a spiritual being continues to live, that death is only the departure from one world to another; that it is but the material body that dies, and returns to the earth from which it was taken, there to remain and to rise no more, but man himself will never die.

When he, therefore, at the last moments of his earthly life, spoke the words: "I am dying," he knew that it was but the material form that had fulfilled its mission and would cease to exist, but that he, who had for many years, in and through that body, accomplished great good to this world, would not go from this land of the living to the silent repose of the dead, but from the land of first development and preparation to that of eternal perfection.

Dr. C. W. Taylor expressed himself next in these words:

"The air is filled with farewells to the dying, and mournings for the dead." Hourly, in some graveyard, the yawning earth is closing around the inanimate forms of loved ones. We are summoned but once to join the innumerable caravan moving on into the "silent land."

When the summons came to Constantine Hering, it found him ripe in years and intellect—four score years replete with benefits to his brother man.

Quietly, as a child, he sank into that last dreamless sleep and was borne to the "garden of the slumberers."

He whose soul panted for communion with the great and good, and reached forward with eager struggle to the guerdon in the distance, has passed away.

A flower is plucked from one sunny bower, a breach made in one happy circle, a jewel stolen from one treasury of love. A harvester has disappeared from the summer field of life, and his funeral winds like a wintry shadow along the street. A sentinel has fallen from his post, and is thrown from the ramparts of time into the surging waters of eternity!

His heart was hopeful and generous, his life a perpetual litany —a May-time crowned with passion flowers that never fade.

> Deck not his couch with sombre shrouds,
>   It is not death, but only sleep,
> That kisses down his eyelids now;
>   Then why should we in sadness weep?
> He has but gained the needed rest
>   From weary toil, from care and strife:
> His fittest meed of praise will be
>   The grandeur of an earnest life.
> Take each the lesson to his heart,
>   And in his earnest struggles know
> That he strives best, who strives for truth,
>   Though faint and weary he may grow.
> You may not reach your highest aim,
>   Nor tread the heights that Hering trod,
> But do your duty—in that lies
>   The path that leads you nearer God.

Dr. C. H. Goodman related the following incidents:

My relations with Dr. Hering were only those of pupil to teacher, for it was my privilege to sit under his instruction during the medical season of 1868-69 in the Hahnemann Medical College of Philadelphia. I can see him now as he hurried into the lecture room, his long hair flowing over his shoulders, and his eye aflame with zeal and enthusiasm. What scrupulous attention to detail; how minutely and analytically he dwelt on the symptomatology of each drug, carefully weighing and balancing every expression and utterance! His mind was so full, so teeming with facts and information, the hour was too short to impart them to his hearers. During my calls at his residence, I was particularly impressed with his having recourse to his Materia Medica at every prescription. My examination hour with him was one of the pleasantest I have ever passed. The subject of my thesis being of some interest to him, he discussed it fully and took occasion to enlarge upon his own peculiar views of what constituted Health and Disease, and of the analogy between the effects of the latter and drug provings. He narrated to me at the same time his experience in curing with *Antimonium crudum* a large corn on the sole of the foot of a sea captain. "Why," he remarked with a merry look, "in a short time I was consulted by all the captains in the navy, and they all had corns on the soles of their feet, and I nearly lost my reputation because I couldn't cure them all."

My last sight of him was on graduation day, as he sat on the stage of the Academy of Music beside Dr. Raue, to whom he was especially devoted, completely wrapped up in the orchestra, which was rendering an air from the opera of "Der Freischütz." He was nodding and bending his head in unison with the music, apparently oblivious to all his surroundings, smiles of pleasure brightening up his venerable face as the harmonious strains fell on his ear.

So was he completely attuned to and in harmony with the world and profession to which he devoted his life and best energies, and he fell like the ripe fruit from the tree and was gathered into the garner of the faithful.

Dr. Philo G. Valentine next recited the following original verses:

> In a far-off land—toward the rising sun,
> In a Saxon village there was begun
> The story of a life, I shall unfold,
> As the lyric muse shall render me bold.
> 'Twas *New Year's* day, on the century's morn,
> That this child of genius, *so rare*, was born.
> Of Christian descent and imperial mien,
> He received the prenomen of Constantine.
>
> He grew and thrived like that great emperor,
> Tho' in different fields was *he* conqueror.
> He fought battles, 'tis true, but no blood was spilled,
> 'Twas with love of learning *his* soul was filled.
> 'Twas hard to find such a *searcher for truth*,
> Such a *lover of lore*, as this promising youth.

In classic schools, he made reputation
Beyond his fellows, or expectation.
In Leipzig and Dresden he did pursue,
His surgical studies, and medicine too.
At length, though young, he a *leader* became,
And carved his name high on the roll of fame.

Now, some learned doctors, self-styled orthodox,
Desired the uprooting of heterodox,
Which doctors, *like clergy*, are prone to hate,
Despise and abhor and *abominate:*
A philosopher, sage, or *any man*
Was searched for to conquer *one Hahnemann*,
To write down *his* heresy, the *worst of all*,
This curing the sick with *no medicine at all*.

Young Hering knew University men,
And they knew *he* yielded a trenchant pen;
They tossed him the glove, he accepted the banter,
To crush out *similia similibus curantur*.
To post himself for th' annihilation,
He sought *every* book, *every* compilation.
Consulted great volumes, high-shelved and low,
This new medical creed to overthrow.
In hot pursuit of his line of attack,
Numerous libraries he did ransack,
Never omitting to make quotation
Of *every* phrase at all in relation
To the subject matter taken in hand—
To drive Homœopathy *from the land*.

Such was the feeling in Hahnemann's day,
The public arose in hostile array,
And, denouncing him as a *frenzied fraud*,
Compelled him to seek a residence abroad;
In a land where learning and science advance,
In a land of sunshine, *liberty-loving France*.

But Hering *softened* in the presence of truth,
And with the ardor of genius and youth,
Saw, as light shone in from the other side,
It was *with error* he had been allied.

Our honest hero *now*, convinced of his wrong,
Retraces his steps, and sings a new song;
The *creed* that was to be shown a *disgrace*,
He clasps to his bosom in fond embrace;
It became his solace, his pleasure, his pride,
And *he* its champion till the day he died.

He soon thereafter obtained his degree,
In an old German university.
His researches in science were so well known,
His name and fame reached the ears of the throne,
And with the King's commission in his hand
He sought his fortune in a foreign land.
'Twas *now* his intention, his theme, his boast,
To study nature on a tropical coast,
Beyond the sea he was destined to roam,
And *South America* became his home.

By the King he was especially sent,
To the southern half of this continent,
To learn *in the woods* of the Torrid Zone,
The *flora and fauna* till then unknown.
To natural history he gave his time,
Of all researches, none more sublime.
He gathered specimens, some of them *grand*,
And shipped them homeward to the Fatherland.

For *seven* long years was he thus occupied,
Garnering knowledge from every side,
Selecting and classing whatever found,
Then, set sail in a good ship *homeward-bound*.

He sailed from the tropics to a northern sea,
In the year eighteen hundred and *thirty-three*.

His voyage came to an unexpected end,
By disembarking in the land of Penn,
A stranger he came, altogether unknown,
And *Philadelphia* claimed him as her own.

Inspired with great thoughts in this new found field,
And new beauties that nature here revealed,
In the realm of letters gained he quick position,
Which later in life gave him full fruition.

A return to Europe was in contemplation,
And arrangements were made for embarkation,
But, an *affaire du cœur* brought *that* to a close,
And our country henceforth was *couleur de rose.*

Near fifty years have rolled around *since then,*
While gifted Hering rose exalted among men.
In Materia Medica *without a peer,*
He won laurels *all along a brilliant* career;
As husband, father, professor and friend,
I have nothing to say, except to commend.

But, there's an ending to *everything here,*
And *he's gone higher* to a brighter sphere.
'Twas a *midsummer night* he passed away,
And *climbed the heights* of the "golden stairway."
His evening like his morning in beauty gleams;
His death, but the lying down to pleasant dreams,
He's now in Elysium forever to dwell,
"After life's fitful fever he sleeps well."

Dr. G. S. Walker then delivered the following oration:

Constantine Hering is dead. The great Healer has passed from the realm of wounds and diseases. The Antagonist of Death, and his Conqueror on a thousand hard-fought fields, has yielded at last, when the issue of the struggle was but his own life. Invincible in his conflicts for others, he was mortal only when he struck in his own behalf. And death has gained a splendid prize. If the old chivalric theory be true, that all the honors of the defeated belong of right to the victor, Immortal Death has seldom, in all the ages, from the issue of a single fight, won so large a spoil. The mighty Physician, whose visits to the couch of suffering were as the Angel of Heaven's mercy, and whose prescription was Healing's potent spell; the calm, all-furnished schoolman—the Champion of the Old School—who laid his boyish lance in rest against the Black Knight of Medical Heresy, and, doomed to dismemberment by his Client, was saved by his Adversary, and thence consecrated all the energies of his redeemed strength to the new banner of "Similia"—bearing it, in triumph, through both Hemispheres and in every clime, under the southern Cross and Northern Pleiad, and planting it, with his dying hand, on the very citadel of the Enemy; the great Teacher, whose graduation thesis was "*De Medicina Futura*," and who founded the first College of our Order in the world; whose name lies at the foundation of our Medical Literature, side by side with that of the immortal Hahnemann; the Poet, whose creative genius found and grasped, and whose sense of harmony set in eternal order and beauty, the great original truths of our system; the Seer, whose prophetic vision pierced the sullen shadows of the Infinite, and brought within the apprehension of common men a revelation of the Divine; the Laborer, whose untiring energies knew no pause or recreation, save in added and deeper toil; the Hercules, who cleansed the fouler than Augean Stables of Medical Science, and encountered and slew the Nemean Lion of Medical Orthodoxy; the gentle, generous, brave, great-hearted, whole-souled Man, whose qualities were more simply great than his attributes were sublimely splendid: all these have gone down in that last desperate struggle, in closed lists, where his only second was a woman, whose loving hand and tender strength were all unable to hold back from his heart the icy grasp of Death. Constantine Hering is dead, and all the orphaned Children of Affliction weep, and all the generous and noble of earth have sympathy in their sorrow and are partakers of their grief.

In the effulgence of his larger and brighter fame, we are sometimes inclined to forget that Hering was pre-eminently the Physician. Let us tenderly and gratefully, in sympathy with the wide circle of his bereaved patients, remember this fact tonight. Nature and education combined to render him the great Healer. His temper was generous, ardent, tender, affectionate and high. The pathematic was among the strongest forces of his grand nature; and it was always a wisely regulated and perfectly governed force. High over all that wealth of sympathy, delicate, and susceptible as ideal woman's, sat the intelligent and regal Will, rendering it subservient to the great end of his presence in the sick-room. And what a presence there! His stately form—his curling locks and flowing beard—the pure white light of cultured intellect shining on his lofty forehead, and flashing in his earnest eye, but mellowed and softened by the roseate hue of deep and hearty kindness—his mere appearance was the Harbinger of Hope to the Couch of Despair. And then his manner! Quiet, not soft; gentle, not weak; firm, not hard; confident, not rash; serious, not solemn; the gravity of simple earnestness, combined with the assurance of abundant resources and an armed disciplined Intelligence: it was the finished perfection of the bearing of the Typical Physician, and had, in itself, some healing power.

His Method of Diagnosis was the analysis of exclusion. He ascertained with the utmost care, and minuted with the greatest exactness, every characteristic symptom. This group of hostile appearances he attacked with all the energies of his powerful mind. One after another, he cast out and trampled under foot every false and specious probability, until he stood, at the last, face to face with his great enemy—the actual, the imminent and the dangerous Dynamic Force; and against this, when found, his Arsenal of Provings rendered him almost invincible. He was never hasty or empirical in practice. He cared nothing for the man—whether rich or poor, or high or low—but everything for the patient. It was a hand-to-hand fight with Disease; in which, once engaged, he thought only of his Antagonist, and would neither surrender nor be beaten. Of course, his success was great, if not unexampled. By his own personal and individual prescriptions, he snatched from the hand of Disease and Death unnumbered and innumerable thousands; and indirectly, by the influence of his discoveries, suggestions and teachings, he was undoubtedly the most valuable factor of his age in the grand multiple of Health and Life. His patients venerated, trusted, loved, idolized, and almost worshiped him. No other man or men could supply his place to them. He was their favorite and all-powerful Apostle of the Gospel of Health; and when they could not secure his visits, they would fain, like them of old to Peter, have brought forth their sick into the streets, that at least his shadow, in passing, might fall upon and bless them. And this great Physician is dead!

Hering was the unrivaled champion and advocate of the Eternal Law of *Similia Similibus Curantur*. Sincere, intelligent, high-cultured, profound, original, bold and eloquent, he lifted its banner from the dust of popular contempt, and challenged, for its insignia, the admiration and gratitude of the nations. All his interests, all his prejudices, the bent of his education, the pride of championship, the heat of conflict, the hopes of his friends and admirers—all forbade him to embrace the new and despised Heresy. Yet embrace it he would and did, with all the fervor of his hero-heart, simply because upon investigation, not impartial but prejudiced, he found it true. The wave of conviction which rolled into his mind, from the vast Ocean of Truth, washed every stain of prejudice from its shores, and left them shining with the calm light of certainty.

And his was no emotional conversion, born of a moment's frenzy and destined to perish with the passing furor. It was not because the New School saved that right arm which the Old had doomed to excision, that he devoted its energies, with such consistent and efficient fidelity, to the redemption of a pledge wrung from him in an hour of insupportable anguish. It was because, with all the exhaustive thoroughness of his grand and luminous intelligence, he had previously investigated, tested and proved, until his whole nature was rife with conviction, that the healing touch of Homœopathy had power to kindle the long-prepared train and dedicate him, in an explosion of feeling, to the perpetual championship of its incomparable merits. Thenceforth, all his previous attainments became but the stepping-stones by which he ascended to the serene heights of Culture, and stood on their loftiest professional pinnacle, alone.

Hahnemann became his friend, intimate, and teacher; and from this Sage the hungry Neophyte drew all the accumulated treasures of his lore. Thence, girt with the commission of Royalty, under the stellar light of the Magellan Clouds, he sought the secrets of nature in her most affluent home, and, fast as they accumulated, turned these treasures to the light of public advocacy of the cause he had so earnestly espoused. Far-seeing, patient and profound, as broadly and highly cultured, he rested not on any yielding soil, but digged, and digged, until he reached the rock of ultimate truth ; so that he may be said to have stood, with his head among the stars, catching the earliest and latest gleam of heaven's light, and with his feet planted upon the immovable foundations which support the world. With this gigantic reach and grasp of truth, he could not but be original. With the constituents of sincerity, earnestness, and self-sacrifice, he could not but be bold. With the freshness and enthusiasm of the youth, joined to the knowledge and culture of the philosopher and the sage, he could not but be eloquent. All these he was. And this invincible Champion is dead!

Hering was *par eminence* the inspired Teacher. "*Poeta nascitur non fit*," had never truer application than to him. He was born for the vocation. And this high and incomparable gift of original genius he supplemented by the most careful training. Always he taught *con amore*. At home, on the street, in the sick-room, in his study, in the clinique, from the chair of the lecturer or the rostrum of the orator—wherever auditors could be found—he was their wise, patient, and delighted instructor. This was the purpose of all his learning. He gained but to impart. His whole capital of mental wealth was free to all comers. Of his illimitable gains he hoarded nothing. The fountain of his instruction was perennial, and had its source in the everlasting springs of Genius, Labor and Love. And, though he sought not this end, the paradox of Scripture was fulfilled to him : all his gifts were gains. By the operation of a changeless law, what he gave to others was doubled to his own bosom. This was the secret of his unfailing readiness and fulness. Knowledge, he deemed a universal heritage, to which every willing and capable mind had an indefeasible right; and wherever he found such minds, it was more blessed for him to give than for them to receive. Yet these gifts, widely and lavishly as he flung them forth, were but the small change of his thought; and his mind was rich in massive ore, in ingots and gems. And with all this priceless wealth he dowered Humanity by his pen.

He was the father and maker of our Medical Literature; for what he did not produce, he inspired. His own thought-products, completed, begun and designed, are so many and so intrinsically great, that admiration loses its flippant eloquence, and sinks into wonder and awe before the processes of so vast a mind. No such writer on Popular Medicine has ever lived. No such writer on Scientific Medicine has ever lived. His "Domestic Physician" still teaches the multitudes, in many languages and editions, the secret of health at home; and his "Analytical Therapeutics" and "Guiding Symptoms" are of a quality which might satisfy the aspirations after fame of many first-class minds, and will require the labors of many such to complete them, with the materials already gathered and prepared by their great Author. All these precious instructions to the world are couched in terms the most simple and direct, and distinguished by an entire absence of *style*. He wrote but to expound his thought; and his words are that thought's simplest and strongest vehicle. Of him it may be said, with truth and emphasis, that, not only to our own school, but to the whole world of Medical Thought and Culture, "He was a Teacher sent from God." And this matchless Teacher is dead!

Hering was an unexampled Laborer. In boyhood, his sport was toil. In maturity, his recreation was creation. In age, his repose was application. He took no rest, and needed none. Work was his pleasure and his passion. Each day of his life was too brief for the busy ends he assigned it; each hour of every day, though beginning with the third after midnight and ending only with the tenth after midday, too short for his toilful purpose. To the very last day, and almost the last hour of his life, his unresting exertions never ceased. And yet, his energies never flagged. He did not toil on doggedly and dully, the reluctant slave of a cruel purpose; but with such warm, earnest, and cheerful interest as made him dread the hour of necessary suspension of his task. The sustained fire of his energy was simply marvelous. There is nothing in the correlation and conservation of material forces which can at all account for it. It did not lie in the food he ate, or the sleep he took. Rather, it would seem to have been the result of such an uncommon affluence, in the original endowment of his vital forces, as the world has seldom if ever seen. Instead of losing, as is the case with other men, this rare mind seemed rather to accumulate fire and force by its own progress. And it was no unregulated and disorderly energy, which thus found its necessary expression in ceaseless action. Every mental impulse had a method—every intellectual ebullition poured its forces into a prescribed channel—every molten thought settled into its previously prepared mould, and hardened into the shape which it was predestined to take and wear forever. It was labor with such method as economized and utilized every particle of mental energy; as if the worker had been the poorest of the poor, instead of the wealthiest of earth, in intellectual endowments. And the method was no clumsy, fanciful or grotesque contrivance of idle revery, perverted taste, or passionate prejudice, but the highest and most finished product of original genius, guided by intelligent and cultivated skill. It was such a method as one may see a sample of in the "Analytical Therapeutics;" a method to fill the mind with wonder and joy, and to fall upon the world of Medical Thought and Culture like the benediction of the Most High.

And all this measureless strength, indicated by such unrivaled labors, was dedicated to the grandest objects, and justified by the highest results. Its products, crystallized in print, admirable and wonderful as they are, are but a small part of these results. The walls of Hering's study, from floor to ceiling, are filled with manuscripts, in his own handwriting, all perfectly arranged and methodized, to carry on and complete the incomparable works which he began and designed. Thus the matchless Worker, standing in his study, built up around him that pearly palace of his thought, which shall never know decay. Alas! our Ulysses has departed on his travels, and there is none left at Ithaca strong enough to bend his bow! Atlas has gone to the Hesperides, and there is none to bear up the skies. And this incomparable Laborer is dead!

Above all, Constantine Hering was a Man. All the constituents of manly character were his. Strength, courage, force, and constancy distinguished him above other men. In ability to grasp, and firmness to hold, all that he recognized as truth, he had no peer. In adventurous daring, supported and justified by the tremendous momentum of his mind, he was simply sublime. His principles were pure, unselfish, and high, and his loyalty to conviction unwavering. A better or truer man never lived. And this strong base of noblest manhood was overlaid with the fine gold of all gentle and attractive qualities. He was susceptible, appreciative, affectionate, constant, tender, and forbearing. His heart was open as his hand, and the clasp of the one was warm with the pulse of the other. His tastes were cultivated and refined to that degree, that his house was the home of Art and Culture, and the refuge of struggling Genius. His friends were statesmen, artists, scientists, of world-wide reputation and renown; and of these, once gained, he never lost one. All who loved him, loved him to the end, either of their own lives or his. He was gentle as a child, pure as a snowflake, and warm as a sunbeam. In a word, the "grand old name of Gentleman" was his by right of eminence in the essential qualities which constitute that character. In the words of one of our sweetest modern poets,

"To him were all men heroes, every race noble,
All women virgins, and each place a temple:
He *knew* nothing that was base."

And this peerless Gentleman is dead!

Dead! Aye, even as the mollusk, the builder of the sea-shell dies, leaving his soul crystallized in forms of imperishable beauty, which still ring with the sound of life's eternal sea. Hering is not dead. He doth not even sleep. His waking spirit walks abroad, through all the realms of thought. For such as he there is no death. He lives, and must ever live, in Memory, in Blessing, and in Hope. In the hearts of many, rich and poor, high and low, his deeds have built a shrine whereon Gratitude will lay her morning and her evening sacrifices, until the hearts which cherished him as a Physician have ceased to beat; and even in dying, they will bequeath his memory as a rich legacy to their children. The disciples and lovers of the cause he espoused and defended will never cease to hear the all-eloquent Champion of Homœopathy. The Student of Medicine, in the remotest future, will bless and revere the name of Hering, as the great Bringer of Order out of the chaos of the Materia Medica. The immediate and remote beneficiaries of his life-work will join hearts and hands, in gratitude for his benefactions and emulation of his industry. And, ennobled by his name and fame, ever and forever, "his children, and his children's children, will rise up and call him BLESSED."

After the eulogy the following ode was sung:

> How sleep the brave who sink to rest,
> By all their Country's wishes blessed!
> When Spring, with dewy fingers cold,
> Returns to deck their hallowed mold,
> She there shall dress a sweeter sod
> Than fancy's feet have ever trod.
>
> By fairy hands their knell is rung;
> By forms unseen their dirge is sung,
> There Honor comes, a pilgrim gray,
> To bless the turf that wraps their clay,
> And Freedom shall awhile repair,
> To dwell a weeping hermit there!

A benediction was asked by the Rev. John Snyder, and the meeting adjourned.

MEETING IN KANSAS CITY, MISSOURI.

At a meeting of homœopathic physicians held at Kansas City, State of Missouri, October 10th, 1880, to take action on the death of Dr. Constantine Hering, the subjoined preamble and resolutions were presented and approved:

WHEREAS, We have learned with sincere sorrow of the decease of our venerable colleague, Dr. Constantine Hering, whose splendid attainments in science, varied experience in practice, and long service to humanity, we now recall with transport and shall remember with gratitude; therefore, be it

Resolved, That in the late Dr. Hering we recognized our ideal of a man, a scholar, and a physician. His early struggles for the establishment of homœopathic medicine, and his later triumphs in the security of the same, are masterly and imperishable achievements.

Resolved, That in the death of Dr. Hering the cause of Homœopathy has lost its ablest worker, the family of homœopathic physicians its dearest member, and homœopathic literature its most honored name. As we revere his memory let us emulate his character, and the great and good of our school whom he has joined in the world of spirits, who "rest from their labors though their works do follow them."

UNIVERSITY OF MICHIGAN MEETING.

At a meeting of the faculty and students of the Homœopathic Department of the University of Michigan, Ann Arbor, held on Sunday evening, October 10th, 1880, W. P. Polhemus, the president of the class, called the meeting to order and briefly stated the object of the gathering.

He then introduced Prof. E. C. Franklin, who spoke as follows:

Mr. President, Ladies and Gentlemen:

At a meeting of the homœopathic physicians of the city of Philadelphia, called together on the 25th day of July last, for the purpose of expressing their views and sentiments touching the history, position and connection of the late Dr. Constantine Hering with the cause of Homœopathy, it was resolved "that a memorial meeting be held in honor of the deceased, at which physicians from all parts of the world should be invited to participate in person or by letter." In compliance with this resolution, we, the Faculty and Students of the Homœopathic Department of the University of Michigan, with such friends of our system that feel an interest in the present occasion, have assembled together as earnest memorialists, to express our profound regret at the loss of this truly great man, our condolence with his family, and to convey to distant friends our appreciation of the distinguished services Dr. Hering has given to the cause of Homœopathy during the last half century.

The early history of Dr. Hering finds him a bitter opponent of Homœopathy. Born with the beginning of the century in Oschatz, Saxony, we find little in early life to interest us, until the period when he began his student life under the immediate charge of his father. Here we observe him as a diligent and faithful pupil, developing those sterling qualities of head and heart that made him so attractive to his teachers while pursuing his studies in the gymnasium at Zittau, then under the rectorship of his father. His remarkable powers of observation and analysis, his centering application, marked him out as no ordinary individual. In his twentieth year he matriculated as a student of medicine at the University of Leipzig, and during his pupilage here was singled out by his preceptor, on account of his superior literary attainments, to prepare a monograph in opposition to that medical heresy that was at this time agitating and unhinging the medical mind in Germany and other parts of the Continent. Elated with the prospect of a scientific tilt with the sage of Coethen, he began a review of Hahnemann's writings, hoping to obtain an easy victory in his medical contest; but his readings only impressed him the stronger with the doctrine of Hahnemann, and scientist as he was, he became so thoroughly convicted with the depth of reason and glow of genius of the great medical reformer, that his criticisms were turned into laudation of the teachings of the author, and he became a convert to their strongly impressed truths. About this time, and while pursuing his anatomical demonstrations, he inflicted upon his hand a poison wound from the keen edge of the dissector's knife, which subsequently gave him no little solicitude and anxiety. He sought medical counsel of his old friends, and in spite of their best directed efforts he grew daily worse, and the gloomy alternative was given him of amputation of the hand. Chagrined and discomfitted, he accepted the proffered aid of a friend, a disciple of Hahnemann, and had the proud satisfaction of seeing his hand daily grow better, and finally saved from the dreaded prognosis pronounced by his attending physicians. With this his conversion to Homœopathy was secured, and he left Leipzig strong in the faith of Similia and entered the University at Würzburg. After attending lectures here, he graduated in 1826, and returned to Saxony to practice his profession on his native soil. He accepted the position as teacher of natural sciences and house physician in a prominent school under the charge of Director Blochmann. Wearied with continued application along the old groove of medical thought, disgusted with the endless jargon of medical theories and changing dogmas, and soured with the intolerant bigotry of that old school, that is "broken down in council and in fight, in hospital and in camp, yet brokenly lives on," his active and restless spirit, imprisoned no longer by the bonds of state medicine, sought new and unpent fields for its scientific longings. He saw in the profession of medicine a system of castes of corporations, not of individual, but of collective castes. He saw that a man may be anything he can, but no man can be anything out of the caste. He longed to be free, and like the imprisoned bird sought freedom in the boundless continent of beautiful fruits and flowers. An opportunity was soon presented, and he eagerly accepted the position that was the fulfillment of his day-dream of usefulness, and which gave us the bright realization of his long-cherished hopes and made him a hero in the new world of progressive knowledge. A distant relative had just returned from South America, whose vivid descriptions of the beauty and splendor of the natural curiosities of that far-off tropical region, where "nature wears her sweetest smile and sings her loveliest notes," inspired his young heart to woo fickle fortune in the distant lands of the occident. By the aid of influential friends he procured an appointment from the King of Saxony to accompany the accomplished naturalist Weigel, and in 1827, with rosy hopes and elated spirit, he set sail for his far-off western home, and arrived in Dutch Guiana soon after. Hopeful and buoyant, and with a soul full of ardor for his cherished work, he entered upon his new field of labor and made many friends and converts to the faith that animated all his labors. Still keeping up his medical studies, *pari passu* with his zoological enquiries, he attracted considerable attention both to himself and the system of medicine by which he was continually bequeathing rich legacies to suffering humanity. While upon the very tiptoe of encouragement and merited commendation from those who were the almost daily recipients of his kindly care and thoughtful consideration, and while pursuing with diligence and earnestness his chosen field of study, a message was handed him from the Fatherland reprimanding him for daring to extend and popularize the hated science of Homœopathy, afar off though it be, in the lands beyond the sea. His noble spirit, no longer fettered by the chains of that medical despotism that had bound him to the care of a hated propagandism during the earlier period of his student life, was stung to the quick, and chagrined at the unlooked-for result of his chosen mission, he resigned his office and devoted himself to the practice of medicine in the city of Paramaribo. Soon after this he accepted an invitation to come to Philadelphia, where he arrived in January, 1833. From here

> "Out of his self-drawing web he gives us note,
> The force of his own merit makes his way;
> A gift that Heaven gives for him,"

we see him always intent upon his grand mission and entering upon his new work with renewed purpose. His enthusiasm for the theme of his chosen life-work overcame every opposition, and we see him ere the mantle of citizenship draped his manly form, lecturing in his native tongue to the few but earnest disciples of the new system gathered together to do homage to their distinguished countryman. From that time to the day of his death, animated by the noble purpose of improving as far as he could his cherished science, he labored constantly and enthusiastically for its advancement. He was the first physician who taught Homœopathy publicly, at Allentown, Pa., and in 1835, in conjunction with Dr. Wesselhœft and others, he organized "The North American Academy of the Homœopathic Healing Art," which flourished for a season and accomplished a great amount of good to those interested in its work. This institution temporarily succumbed to the pressure of pecuniary embarrassment, but soon after was revived on a larger and more extended scale as "The Homœopathic Medical College of Pennsylvania." It was the master spirit of Dr. Hering, the liberal, energetic and enthusiastic admirer of a broad and liberal education in the arts and sciences, that gave birth to our own American Institute, the first national medical organization in the United States. His contributions to the homœopathic literature coeval with "*The Archives*," even at that early day, secured for him an honorable position in the world of letters and established him as a worthy standard-bearer of our exclusive law of cure. I will not speak of his many and interesting contributions to our Materia Medica in which he was, of all others in this country, its most diligent and faithful contributor. I will leave that with one more competent to do the subject justice. He was truly the pioneer of our school of medicine in the United States, and by his labors on our Materia Medica he has added more wealth to our school of practice than any other man living since the days of the immortal founder of our school. "The great joy of his late days," says a distinguished scholar and contemporary, " was the reading of the address delivered by the President of the American Institute of Homœopathy in which the methods of Hahnemann and the immutable principles governing our school were so earnestly laid before our National Institute, as were also the proceedings of its members." A close student, an able teacher and an indefatigable worker for more than half a century, he furnished valuable and often brilliant articles to the periodical literature of America and Germany. In his social life he posessed a fund of anecdote and humor that made him a genial companion and an agreeable friend. He enjoyed in turn a good joke, and laughed heartily at its recital. Of late years his bodily vigor gradually failed, in consequence of his mature years and frequent asthmatic attacks which prostrated him severely. I remember him well at the Centennial meeting, during my visit to Philadelphia at that time. I was invited to his house and became one of his few guests at a supper given in honor of that memorable occasion. He died as he lived, a firm friend, a devoted student and an uncompromising disciple of the truths taught by the immortal Hahnemann. He was borne to his last resting place at Laurel Hill by friends and colleagues who had shared his toil, and who gave him " Tears for his love, joy for his fortune, and honor for his valor."

At the conclusion of Prof. Franklin's remarks, the

chairman introduced Prof. T. P. Wilson, who spoke as follows:

Ladies and Gentlemen:

The glory of the Roman Empire and the name of Julius Cæsar are inseparably connected. The grandeur of the American Republic and the name of George Washington are almost one and the same thing. And so I turn to the name of Dr. Constantine Hering, but I need not ask to what system of philosophy, to what department of knowledge or to what great enterprise that name is indissolubly joined. Constantine Hering and American Homœopathy have grown together, the one from infancy to old age, crowned at last by the laurels of death, and the other, from infancy toward a matured youth; and so closely have they been joined that nothing but the searching hand of death could put them asunder. Yet, in a certain sense, Hering is not dead. In the highest sense in which he lived, he still lives; and will continue to live; and his acts will be repeated,

"In states unborn and accents yet unknown."

When Hering was born, medical science and art were "without form and void, and darkness was upon the face of the deep." As night upon the seas enfolds the boundless waters in her jetty wings, so in those days, chaos covered and clouded all. Scarce one department of our present system of medicine had more than "a local habitation and a name." Anatomy had achieved some progress, and the human body had itself undergone some rude and imperfect explorations—no more; but physiology was as a dream to the human mind, and its beauties had not reached the point of conception, much less had they been born. Pathology was an inextricable mass of facts and fancies, and upon these sat superstition enthroned, threatening divine vengeance to all who had the temerity to question their real character. Surgery, with its rude implements, was staining the earth with human gore; and while ignorantly striving to relieve, it added indefinitely to the sum total of human misery. As for the general practice of medicine, it was "confusion worse confounded." Empiricism reigned supreme, and being without law, it was without order; and being without law or order, it was without success. It was then that the great Frenchman Bichat, said of medical practice, it "is an incoherent assemblage of incoherent ideas, and is perhaps of all the sciences, that which best shows the caprice of the human mind. It is a shapeless assemblage of inaccurate ideas, of observations often puerile, of deceptive remedies, and of formulæ as fantastically conceived as they are tediously arranged."

It was into this age that Constantine Hering was born. And when he had come to mature life, it must have been a strange infatuation that led him to select medicine for his life's work. Perhaps it was in the vain hope that he might amend its broken ways. Perhaps it was under the delusive teachings of his preceptors, who taught him that

1st. Medicine was a great and perfect art.

2d. It had some few minor imperfections which might be improved; and

3d. That he who would attempt to improve it would in all human probability be eternally damned.

Passing out of the deleterious influences of the schools into a wider arena of thought, young Hering heard of the writings of one of his fellow countrymen, a distinguished German physician, by the name of Samuel Hahnemann. He went to the store and bought his books. He took them home to read them and to try to understand them.

Like another, in later years, he might have used those books for wadding to load a rusty ancient gun, and leaving to others to fire the train, he might have escaped across the seas to await the result of the explosion—and he might have returned to find no damage done worth speaking about. Hering did sincerely expect to overthrow Hahnemann's argument; but alas! he was himself overthrown. He had read Hahnemann's writings, caught such glimpses of the truth, that thenceforth, like the children of Israel wandering in the desert, he had ever before his eager gaze the divine Shekinah which led him out of darkness and out of bondage into the land that flowed with milk and honey.

For more than fifty years he was a faithful follower of Hahnemann's teachings. If he had a creed, it was a short one and to the purpose: "I believe in the one great law of cure."

With him this was not a blind faith. He brought that declaration to the test of his experience, applying it with infinite patience to multitudes of suffering men, women and children—for let me say here that Constantine Hering was no idle dreamer. He never attempted to evolve truth out of his own consciousness; but he gave to this new doctrine the only test by which it may be proven, namely, demonstration. I do not think his mental constitution led him far into the rationale of the law. He was no speculator. He looked upon this truth as thoroughly a practical one; and it was his life's labor to increase the facility of its application. And in that life there was wrought the labors of two score of the ordinary men of the profession. I think I may safely say that Constantine Hering was chiefly great because he was an incessant toiler. I do not think he ever grew weary of his task.

If you will go back to the time when he landed on the shores of this new country, with this new truth burning like a sacred fire on the altar of his heart, you will see him, an alien and a stranger, looking in vain amid a people whose language he did not understand, for kindred spirits, with whom he might commune, and for temples of science to whose altars he might bring his spotless offering. There were medical schools and journals and societies, and there were thousands of medical men, but they had no sympathy with his thought. But, ah, his was a heroic soul! He knew the truth; he loved and worshiped it, and he resolved to give it to the world.

In a little town in Pennsylvania he laid the foundations of his work. I have never been at Allentown, but I would walk its streets to-day, if I could, with reverence. The rostrum and the press were the agencies he chose for his instruments. And how well they did their work, let the record of the last half century testify.

But another great secret of Hering's success lay in the masterly power of his inspiration. Himself endued with inexhaustable inspiration, he seldom failed to inspire all with whom he came into contact.

It was no more idle to think of touching fire without being burned, than of meeting Hering and not catching some of the enthusiasm that warned his breast. Nay, believe me, it was an inspiration which made his face radiant with light, and caused his halting tongue to adorn the English language, which he never quite mastered, with new beauty.

It was not my privilege to know him intimately, but I have known many of his scholars; I have met many men who have sat at his feet, and God bless his memory, I do not know that he ever sent out a halting or a doubting disciple. However some of them may have become broken pitchers in subsequent years, they came from Hering's hands without flaw or blemish.

Constantine Hering was a true Homœopath. With his whole heart and mind he believed the truth as expressed in *Similia*. The power to demonstrate its universal application to all forms of disease, was greatly limited in his earlier days. The needed agencies were few. There were no medical schools to teach Hahnemann's doctrines. There were no books to promulgate this new-born truth. There were no journals in which to show the results of experience, and there was as good a chance of finding paintings by the old masters on this new continent as of finding drugs of any sort fit for homœopathic prescribing. In some obscure corner of Philadelphia, in some hidden recess in New York, there might, perchance, be found a few remedies prepared after the formula laid down by Hahnemann; and these, when found, were mostly in the 30th centesimal attenuation.

But in those days they knew no better than to give such things to people who were sick. They had not heard of the Milwaukee Academy or of the revelations of the Boston microscope. And so the 30ths were given, and as the sick recovered, the name and fame of Homœopathy were spread abroad.

From Allentown, Hering went to Philadelphia, and on a broader stage, surrounded and aided by ardent and able disciples, he found his cause growing with great rapidity.

It is not too much to say that the sceptre of command which he first took upon coming to America, did not fall from his hand until he was stricken by death. He fell at his post of duty, and upon the day of his death he was no less ardent and devoted to the truth of Homœopathy than when he first espoused the cause.

We have seen some attempted changes in our school within the past few years. Our fabric has been rocked by the baleful influence of the spirit of reaction toward the chaos of eclecticism and the discarded errors of Allopathy; and while our future may be in this respect, clouded in doubt, we have the proud satisfaction of knowing that, upon the fair escutcheon of Hering's name, this cloud can never rest, for never did he bow the knee to Baal.

The heroic old man is dead. Here ends one of the grandest epochs of medical history. Henceforth on her fair pages shall stand four score years marking the life and labors of Constantine Hering. What a magnificent spectacle is the production and completion of such a man! What a crown of glory it places upon the brow of humanity! What a priceless gift is such a life to the human race! What a harvest of intellectual wealth is now gathered in by the death of this great man! Like some choice ceramic he passed unharmed through the fires and became more and more beautiful as the flames of adversity burned deeply into his moral and mental nature, the immortal colors of a deathless life. Constantine Hering was a born leader of men because of his high intellectual endowments and his whole-souled devotion to truth. Tradition tells us that, in the far east, and in ages long since gone by, an elder Constantine, while at the head of his imperial army, saw in the clouds a vision of the cross and over it these words: "*In hoc signo vinces,*" and that by that sign he went forth to conquer, and laid the foundations of a great and lasting empire.

So in later times this young Constantine, saw in his imagination, the fair temple of medical science rising till its golden spires were kissed by the clouds of heaven, and over its fair portals he saw deeply graven by the Divine hand these trenchant words, "*Similia similibus curantur,*" and he exclaimed, " by that sign we shall conquer," and like a true prophet he prophesied and then fulfilled his own prophesies. It is a supreme happiness to us who live to-day, that we have seen such a spotless life completed. He lived and worshiped at the shrine of nature; and when his days were numbered, he fell into the mighty arms of the All-Natura which had cradled him in his infancy, and in that great bosom, the love and power of which no man knows, Constantine Hering sleeps the sleep of the just.

The chairman next introduced Prof. H. C. Allen, who said:

It is a remarkable fact that the efforts of the opponents of our system of practice to prove the law of similia a "humbug," by the writing of a work that should thoroughly expose it, completely uproot the heresy, and thus prevent its dissemination, should have resulted in giving our school two of its strongest defenders and ablest champions—Dr. Quin in Great Britain and Dr. Hering in America. Commissioned to strike the budding truth a death blow in its infancy, they were themselves convicted and became enthusiastic converts.

The former, as President and one of the founders of the British Homœopathic Society, has done yeoman service in his native land—the land of Harvey, Jenner and Sydenham; while the latter, as one of the founders of the oldest medical society in

America, and its first President—the American Institute—as one of the founders of the first Homœopathic College in the world and its first Professor of Materia Medica, has not only rendered heroic service to the Homœopathic School, but has left a name honored and revered wherever scientific medicine is known.

Hering's labors in the field of Materia Medica have been of a two-fold character, viz., *his personal contributions*—second only to those of Hahnemann in number—and the contributions which through his magnetic enthusiasm, that brilliant coterie of co-laborers by whom he was surrounded, were induced to make. To Hering, more than to any other man, are we indebted for the Materia Medica contributions of Carroll Dunham—some of the clearest expositions and ablest differentiations of the mode of action of some of the remedies to be found in our literature. Dunham has said that "in Constantine Hering I gained the most helpful, generous and genial friend I have ever made;" and few men were more capable of judging than Carroll Dunham.

But it is not so much the number of remedies which he has added to the Materia Medica, great as they are, as the *manner* in which they are added, for which we should be most thankful. Like Hahnemann, Hering grasped the basic principle upon which alone an enduring Materia Medica can be constructed, viz., that the positive facts of the prover shall be recorded in plain, untechnical language, free from theoretical speculations. Provings thus made are of the nature of lasting observations, and are as fixed and unchangeable as the law of cure. This is the reason why the simple pure record of observed facts, which Hahnemann and his disciples recorded in the Materia Medica Pura fifty years ago, free from theories and speculations of a physiological and pathological character, are to-day as intelligible, as available, as well adapted to meet our wants in practice as when they left the Master's hand. Hering, in our day, had the same material from which to construct a physiological theory of the action of a drug that Hahnemann and his disciples had; in fact, the great advances made by the progressive sciences of physiology and pathology in the last fifty years, gave him a vast advantage over Hahnemann. But, like Hahnemann, he confined himself simply to the recording of the fact, thus leaving each observer free to place his own construction upon the action of the drug. This is a work which cannot be delegated to another; because, as Dunham says: "*The significance of a fact is measured by the capacity of the observer.*"

Next to his tireless, never-flagging industry, "the capacity to measure the significance of a fact" has been equalled by but few men our school has yet produced, and excelled by none, save Hahnemann himself. That rare quality of the student of Materia Medica, possessed by Hering in such a remarkable degree, viz., the ability to detect the individual characteristics of a drug—those finer points of difference not to be found in the provings of any other—is what has rendered his labors of such lasting benefit to his fellows. It is this quality which has made his Condensed Materia Medica the best work of ready reference yet produced in the Homœopathic School for the busy practitioner. This is also the first work of a standard character, in which the general anatomical divisions in our Materia Medica adopted by Hahnemann as a basis for the classification of symptoms, has been departed from. The rubrics, it is true, are increased in number, but they are admirably arranged to meet a two-fold object: the condensation of numerous provings, and the classification of symptomatology for ready reference, a want long felt in practice.

The introduction of the serpent poisons, in the magnificent proving of Lachesis, marked an era of advance in our Materia Medica. It was violently assailed by the pathologico-physiological branch of the school, both in this country and in Germany, and the author accused of "manufacturing the symptoms," etc. The old view entertained by toxicologists "that the poison of serpents is digested by the gastric fluids, and cannot manifest any poisonous properties when introduced into the living organism through this channel," was first disproved by the proving of the attenuated poison of Lachesis, and abundantly verified since.

Hempel's Materia Medica, first edition, page 1143, says: "The provings of the Lachesis virus have been instituted with very small quantities of the poison, mostly with the hundredth up to the infinitesimal portion of a drop. It has, therefore, become questionable with a great many, and indeed, so far as Germany is concerned, with almost all thinking homœopathic practitioners, whether the almost interminable array of symptoms which Dr. Hering alleges to have been produced by the Lachesis poison, is not the work of fancy rather than of actual observation. In spite of every effort to the contrary, the conviction has gradually forced itself upon my mind that the pretended pathogenesis of Lachesis, which has emanated from Dr. Hering's otherwise meritorious and highly praiseworthy efforts, is a great delusion, and that, with the exception of the poisonous effects with which this publication is abundantly mingled, the balance of the symptoms is unreliable."

The above was written in 1859, and it certainly was some gratification to Dr. Hering to have seen the verification of his proving in the succeeding twenty years, and his character for accuracy maintained. The verifications of the provings of Lachesis opened the door for all the other serpent as well as insect poisons; the principle involved being the same. Hence Crotalus, Naja, Apium virus, etc., have been accepted as proven.

As Hering was far in advance of his colleagues and cotemporaries in the demonstration of the power of the attenuated remedy to produce genuine and reliable pathogeneses, so he was in practical therapeutics when he published his "Analytical Therapeutics" and "The Guiding Symptoms." He lived long enough to see his Lachesis proving verified in practice; and from Pisgah's height he viewed the Canaan which the general profession may see in the next generation, when there may be a demand for those two works. Let us emulate his virtues and practice his never-tiring industry, so that we may be able to contribute our mite to the common stock of knowledge.

After the remarks of the faculty, the following resolutions were presented and unanimously adopted:

WHEREAS, We learn with sorrow of the death of Dr. Constantine Hering; therefore,

Resolved, That we recognize in his death the termination of a great and useful life.

Resolved, That to Dr. Hering belongs rightfully the title of "The Father of American Homœopathy."

Resolved, That to his life and labors medical science will be forever under obligations.

Resolved, That we unite in an earnest request, that a fitting memorial, monumental or otherwise, be made to his memory by the medical profession of America.

MEETING IN CLEVELAND, OHIO.

The Cleveland Academy of Medicine and Surgery met on October 10th, 1880, pursuant to call; Dr. H. F. Biggar, President, Dr. A. C. Buell, Secretary. The object of the meeting was explained by reading the call for the Hering Memorial.

The Rev. Dr. Bolles, who had been requested to open the meeting with prayer, prefaced the devotions with some remarks, of which the following is an outline:

But why commemorate the faithful departed?

Why think of them at all? Why not rather let them be forgotten as a dream of the night—buried forever in oblivion—never more to come as ghosts to disturb our slumbers—or why not, if we *must* sometimes think of them, let it be only as gone, lost, dead, buried, annihilated, absolutely extinct—never more to live in thought or memory?

Alas! alas! an impossibility. As well might we endeavor to annihilate ourselves—as well might we try to extinguish the light of the universe, as to quench the embers of an undying memory of the dead.

But if we *must* think of them—*how ?*

God be praised, we have an answer to this momentous question in Holy Scripture, as plain as the sun in the heavens.

How then must we think of them? How commemorate them? Let the Bible answer.

1st. We must think of them *as still alive*—that "Death hath no more dominion over them;" that "in that they died, they died unto sin once; but in that they lived, they live unto God;" "delivered from the burden of the flesh and are in joy and felicity," for which we love and praise, and magnify His glorious name!

What said our Saviour of the departed faithful of old—of Abraham, of Isaac and Jacob?

Expressly that they are alive, awaiting the resurrection; for "God is not the God of the dead, but of the living"—and if they are alive, much more "the faithful departed," from their time to ours, who "have fallen asleep in Christ."

2d. We must think of them as "witnesses" ever living, and ever testifying—"an innumerable cloud" or multitude, as when the Apostle wrote his Epistle to the Hebrews—and yet then only skirting, as it were, the horizon, but now covering the whole heavens; and what they see and what they testify, no tongue could begin to mention.

3d. We must think of them as part of ourselves, our own members, already rescued, saved, housed, and yet still holding on to us, our hands clasped together in theirs, in Christ; our hearts knit together with theirs, as in one common bond of love and peace and joy—their song of praise must be ours—theirs in triumph, ours in hope—theirs for us as well as for themselves, and ours for them as well as for ourselves; remembering always that the same almighty power, and love, and mercy which have carried them safely through the trials and conflicts of this mortal life, and made them victorious, are pledged to us, and will make us victorious, provided only we let not go our grasp, and "be faithful even unto death."

> "Men once like us with suffering tried,
> But now with glory crowned."

4th. We must think of the faithful departed not as lost, not as dead, not *only* as still living; not only as our witnesses; not only as our members with us of the same mystical body; but as still our friends, our companions, our associates, our brethren, our "well beloved in Christ," bone of our bone, flesh of our flesh, soul of our soul, from whom it is impossible for Death to separate us, or to break the sacred ties of our common humanity.

Drs. J. C. Sanders and H. H. Baxter were then appointed a committee to report the expression of the meeting, and reported as follows:

The death of Dr. Constantine Hering, which occurred in Philadelphia, on the 23d of July last, impresses us with mingled rejoicing, sorrow, and sense of loss.

We are constrained to rejoice that in Divine compassion by which his death was unheralded, and sudden, he was spared the painful consciousness of decrepit powers, usually inseparable from the frosty age into which his years were mercifully lengthened, and the sense of suffering and anguish, so common to mortal life and death. We rejoice that to him were vouchsafed such extraordinary physical strength and endurance, such splendid mental endowments, and such an evident Divine calling to the profession to which he gave his life.

We rejoice that in the great diversity and range of his study and work, he always proved loyal to the great Master whose disciple he was, and whom he faithfully followed.

And we rejoice that all his great powers, and distinguished

study and work were consecrated to the discovery, and determining the best and surest means of relief and cure of human sickness and suffering, and that he unselfishly and freely gave to the profession at large whatever he regarded valuable in the products of his study and thought, and therefore that his name is written imperishably,

"Where they who have loved their fellow-men, have names,
Whom the love of God has blessed."

But we sorrow with his kin that we shall see his genial face no more, or hear his winsome voice, or feel his inspiring presence, or have our paths lighted by another thought from his earnest, hallowed mind.

And this is the great and irreparable loss we personally, and as a profession deplore, a loss which leaves an ineffaceable shadow upon all who knew him, all who loved him, all to whom his name is dear.

Dr. D. H. Beckwith then made the following remarks:

Mr. President:—I desire to say a few words in regard to the event which has caused this Society to assemble here to-night, in grief, in sorrow, in honor, and respect. A few years since we mourned the loss of John Wheeler, M.D., who died in this city, ripe in years and full of honor. Our next call was to the memory of William E. Saunders, M.D., who passed away in the spring-time of life, with brilliant prospects for the future before him.

We are called once more to bow with submission to the inscrutable will of Him, in whose hands are the issues of life and death, to mourn the loss of one who, during a long career, has distinguished himself in our profession as a writer, a translator, a teacher, a practitioner of medicine, and a prover of remedies. That mysterious roll of human fate slowly unfolds her book, page after page, guided by the unerring hand of time, and calls us, one by one, to a sphere of higher existence. It would be a strange neglect on the part of the medical profession if we should give no formal expression of our grief and sorrow at the death of one who has done so much for us all, and, while we mourn the loss of this great man, we may also rejoice that such a man lived in our day. No future can rob him of his history, and for many years his name shall be cherished and his works be emulated. Like the falling leaves of this beautiful October day, many of our physicians pass off from the stage of existence, and no public record is made of them, while, on the other hand, history takes up our great men and holds them as precious jewels on her pages, embalms them in her records, and perpetuates their memory to generations yet unborn.

The profession will agree with me, without a dissenting voice, that Constantine Hering was a man of application to that science he loved so well. In his writings he had a keenness of vision, a power of observation accorded but to few. He was devoted to his profession for over half a century, studying it always as a science, and practicing Homœopathy as taught by Samuel Hahnemann.

When I call up the name of him whom we eulogize to-night, it seems to me that he was an old good friend of mine, that he was one of my teachers of Homœopathy thirty years ago. At that time his name was familiar to all the homœopathic physicians of the West. In the year 1850 and 1851 there were but few homœopathic publications and books in the English language.

Among those in my library were:

1st. "Hering's Domestic Physician."

2d. "Samuel Hahnemann's Organon of Homœopathic Medicine," translated in the year 1849 from the last German edition, with suggestions and additional introductory remarks, by Constantine Hering, M.D.

3d. "How to Study Materia Medica, and the Effects of the Poison of Serpents."

4th. "Chronic Diseases, their Specific Nature and Homœopathic Treatment," with a preface written by Constantine Hering.

5th. "Jahr's Manual of Homœopathic Medicine," in two volumes, with improvements and additions by C. Hering.

Also "Jahr's New Manuel of Symptomen Codex," of over 2000 pages, in two volumes, with a preface from Hering written in 1848. (I regard this work of great value to the practitioner, as well as to the student of medicine.)

In February, 1851, the first number was issued of the *North American Homœopathic Journal*, a quarterly magazine of 148 pages, devoted to practical and scientific articles. Constantine Hering was the editor-in-chief, and each number contained several articles from his pen.

From book acquaintance I had formed an exalted idea of Hering as a writer and teacher of Homœopathy. He was regarded, as a practitioner of medicine, second to none. In the year 1863 I formed his personal acquaintance, and since that date have often met him. He was a ripe scholar, refined by study, cultivated by extensive foreign travel, and familiar with most of the leading homœopathists of the Old World. He was at most times able and willing to instruct those who were thrown in contact with him.

I regarded him as a man of positive qualities, untiring in his labors for his profession and true to the principles of Homœopathy. I well recollect a call at his office several years ago; he was not in his usual social mood, but seemed very indignant that so many homœopathic practitioners in Philadelphia had deviated from the teachings of Hahnemann and were practicing a mongrel system of medicine.

He exhibited to me a list of homœopaths on one page and the other class on the opposite one. He was so positive in his remarks in regard to their practice, that I yet recollect the names as they appeared on the different pages. It was a source of deep regret to him that so much eclecticism was practiced by those who were so intimately associated with him in college and other work.

Mr. President, we all might have asked that a man so intellectual, so gifted in character, so true to his profession, might have been spared a little longer to have finished the work he was engaged in and so near completed, but the Great Physician called him to a nobler and higher sphere for his future labors.

Waiving on this occasion all utterances of private sorrow, we unite this evening with our brethren in other cities, at this hour assembled, in placing high on the roll of professional honor the name of Constantine Hering.

Dr. Clausen moved the adoption of the resolutions, which motion was carried, and the meeting adjourned.

MEETING IN DENVER, COLORADO.

The Hering Memorial meeting was held in Denver at the residence of Dr. Ambrose S. Everett, Drs. Burnham, Cole, Everett, Eastman, Hart, Smythe and Wheeler, of Denver, and Dr. Piepgras, of Loveland, being present.

The meeting was called to order by Dr. Everett, who read the circular letter of the Hering Memorial Committee, and stated the object of the meeting. He then nominated Dr. Smythe, who was elected chairman of the meeting. On motion of Dr. Wheeler, Dr. A. L. Cole was elected secretary.

Dr. Everett then read letters of regret from Drs. Aaron Walker, of Denver, C. C. Brace, of Boulder, L. E. Marsh, of Greeley, and W. R. Owens, of Pueblo.

On motion of Dr. Everett, a committee was appointed to draft resolutions in honor of and respect for the deceased. As such committee the chair then appointed

Drs. Everett, Wheeler, and Hart, who reported the following resolutions, which were unanimously adopted:

WHEREAS, After a very long and useful life, and at a ripe old age, it has pleased Almighty God to remove from the scenes of his earthly toils and labors that venerable father of homœopathic medicine on this side of the Atlantic, that kind-hearted and genuine friend, that excellent citizen and devoted husband and father, Dr. Constantine Hering; therefore, be it

Resolved, That we return thanks to the Father of us all for the great measure of his days, and for the blessings which we have inherited by reason of his long and useful life; and be it

Resolved, That the void we feel and the loss we sustain shall but stimulate us to renewed industry for and devotion to that school of medicine to which he was so much attached, and for which he gave all the years of his manhood; and be it

Resolved, That we pledge ourselves to keep his grave green and his memory fresh in the hearts of his medical brethren where the lofty mountains and the broad plains meet; and be it

Resolved, That we, as the representatives of Homœopathy in this, the Centennial State, tender to the family of our deceased brother all the sympathy and consolation that it is possible for those imbued with human impulses to bestow.

Pending the adoption of the foregoing resolutions, the following addresses in honor of the late Dr. Hering were made. Dr. Burnham spoke as follows:

Fourteen years ago last August I first met Dr. Hering in his home in Philadelphia. I found him a genial, generous-hearted, painstaking man, whose ambition and highest aspirations pointed to the present and future growth of the principles and practice of Homœopathy.

As a man, one of the noblest types of his nationality by birth, and whose life career has adorned and made illustrious the nationality of his adoption.

As a scientist, the genius of his superior abilities numbered him among those of the largest attainments.

As a theorist, he largely possessed the ability to prove and practically apply in science and medicine.

As a writer and author on medical subjects, he was one of the ablest and most industrious of his time.

As a practitioner of the healing art, his eminent success gave him a world-wide reputation.

As a pioneer of Homœopathy in America, he has lived to see it rise from small beginnings, when its practitioners could be counted upon his fingers' ends, to be numbered by thousands, and whose patrons are found among the most cultured, refined, and wealthy of the land, and whose literature, limited though it was in the primitive days of Homœopathy, yet founded upon a principle as fixed and as potent as the fiat of its creation, has grown with its growth and strengthened with its strength, until it occupies no inferior place in the annals of medical science; whose institutions of learning, started first by his enterprise, nurtured by his care, as a lone representative for the teaching of the principles of the new science and art in medicine, are now to be found in nearly all of the large cities of the continent.

Of all the names of the worthy few of the pioneers, none have contributed to render the literature and practice of Homœopathy more illustrious than Constantine Hering.

I consulted him on one occasion with reference to a patient in whom I had an especial interest (it being my other and better half), and, after making a careful and critical examination, he invited me to his private study to review the case further, and proceeded to make an exhaustive investigation. His manner of study, his thoroughness in analyzing a case (so in contrast with many whom I have met in the profession, possessed of more assumption than wisdom, who would deign to study a case only as a marked exception), impressed my mind most forcibly as to the necessity of a thorough and accurate knowledge of pathological conditions, symptoms, and remedy, before prescribing. In the course of that investigation he remarked to me, "Let us apply the triangular test, and if we can find three important or characteristic symptoms pointing to one remedy, let me assure you that we can prescribe it with almost unerring certainty." I have tested its application in hundreds of cases, and when clearly defined, it seldom fails to fulfil its mission. As an aid in my investigations, I have kept faithfully in view the illustration of the triangle, the trinity of symptoms, in the selection of a remedy, with the motto inscribed within the boundaries of its lines and angles so appropriately expressed: "By this sign we conquer."

And now, fellow-members of the profession, let us one and all strive more fully to emulate the example of him in whose memory we have assembled here to-night, illustrious in not only a few, but in many things; working so faithfully in the cause so self-sacrificingly espoused, even to the very day and hour when his spirit was summoned to leave this earthly tabernacle, to come up higher; inscribing his name among the highest on the triangular pyramid of fame, wreathed with a galaxy of time-honored achievements, whose lustre shall brighten as the days wear on and the years roll by, to be crowned with an immortal inheritance.

While thousands are assembled in their respective places of abode, on this day and this hour, throughout the length and breadth of the land, to do honor to his name—fitting tribute to one so noble and so worthy—I will gladly express, in the language of another, a sentiment: "May his memory grow green with years, and blossom through the flight of ages."

Dr. A. L. Cole then arose and made the following remarks:

The spirit of man takes its departure from the body, the lifeless tissues return to the elements from which they originated; the atomic re-arrangement of these elements convert them again into living organisms, and man once dead again lives.

The transitory stage from life to death is not one of fear, pain, or agony; not of anguish or regret, but calmly the vital forces ebb away, the combination of vital organs cease to perform their functions, the vitalizing fluid ceases to circulate, respiration is suspended, and all that was once a living animate being is transformed to a lifeless structure.

Man is but a mass of matter, the feeblest in nature; yet how mighty when compared with all else of the animal creation. This element we see in men like Hering, feeble in muscular development as compared with others, yet yielding an intellectual power which commands the respect, love, and admiration of their strongest brothers. He will live in the minds of men; although literally dead, his memory is always fresh, his career bright, beautiful and pure, like the rich, sparkling diamond.

He lived for the good of man, in order that this world might be beautiful from his having lived in it, and to this end a greater portion of his valuable life was given up to the work for the benefit of others. He lived an honest, upright, modest life, temperate in his habits, pleasant and gentlemanly to those who sought his acquaintance, and aiding many without remuneration, to the great detriment of himself.

His home was in his study, the ornaments of which were volumes of manuscript; there he loved to devote his hours in gathering the products of thinking minds the world over, of ascertaining their accuracy, and arranging them into convenient form for us to digest.

And so he succeeded admirably, the products which from the result of his great mind are to be found in the library of his fellow-laborers of every land, cherished by their possessors as only the works of Hering can be cherished, and more valued than the wealth of gold and jewels.

For the noble work performed by him we this day assemble to commemorate his life, and may his memory be cherished by all. May we spare one moment in thought for him, and when in our library we ponder over his master-work in search of knowledge that will enable us to save the life of some poor creature entrusted to our care, let us praise Hering for his great work.

Dr. Emma Eastman followed with the following remarks:

Examining a placer mine and hearing a miner say that he wanted its gold, but it would not pay to work it, reminds one of American scholars who bend all their energies to the test question —will it pay? If it pays, they burn the midnight oil and use their brain power without stint or measure; but if not, the Yankee seizes upon the results of others and often robs the laborious student of his hardly won honors.

It is not so with the Germans. They are willing to delve for the grains of golden truth until their accumulations are the envy of all nations.

Pre-eminent among such miners was Dr. Constantine Hering. While a student he became so renowned for his profound scholarship and for his bitter hostility to Homœopathy, that he was appointed to expose the fallacy of the doctrine of "Similia similibus curantur." Like a true scholar he investigated and experimented for himself, until he was won over to the new theory of medicine and wrote a thesis, "De Medicina Futura," in which he expounded and maintained the doctrine of Hahnemann in the great University of Würzburg, where he graduated.

Thus was the seed sown which will make the name of Hering go down to the ages growing brighter and brighter unto the perfect day.

Dr. L. J. Ingersoll addressed the meeting in the following words:

A great and a good man has fallen. Dr. Hering was great as a student, as a scientist, and as a benefactor. He was great as a leader of a most beneficent profession; great as an organizer of a comparatively new school of medicine; great because he made few mistakes; great because, while he excelled others in breadth and in an exactness of knowledge, he was held as an enemy by none. He was great by nature and great by culture.

Dr. Hering was good because, while "cultivating earnestly the best gifts" for himself, he strove "through good and through evil report" to lead all men up into a higher and a better life; good because, while he acquired all the knowledge he could that would relieve the suffering and keep the well from sickness, he used his skill not for self, but for the good of all who would receive.

And now that Dr. Constantine Hering has gone from among us, we shall do well to gather up what of wisdom he has left us, remembering he has written nothing that ought to be forgotten.

While we lament that one so great and good should have been called up higher from so needful a work, I am most thankful that he lived so long and did so much for his race—how much, we can never know. As physicians we can never cease to cherish his memory, or forget the gracious heritage he has left us in his unsurpassable Materia Medica.

Hering is dead, but his works and words live to bless mankind. The stream that rose among the hills of Germany so many years ago, and which for half a century blessed our Western continent, has peacefully found its way back to its source. That life that sent sunshine and joy into so many sick-rooms, and brought health to so many aching hearts, has at last gone out in the still brighter glory of the redeemed. He, who saved so many from the destroyer, could not save himself. Hering cheerfully passed away as one conscious of having dried many tears and of having turned sighs into joy.

Who of all the thousands that remain will take the place of this fallen chief, this great and good "Master of Homœopathy" in America? I can say to every brother physician and to every patient, "I have lost a teacher to-day."

Dr. Ambrose S. Everett then said:

I have known Dr. Constantine Hering, whose genius and whose life-work they meet to-night all over the world to commemorate, personally for nearly fifteen years, and since my first acquaintance with this Hercules of our school of medicine, I have never allowed myself to visit Philadelphia without calling upon him.

While I do not now realize that he has gone from the scenes of his earthly labors, and that the places that once knew him shall know him no more forever, yet I have no doubt, when I come to visit Philadelphia again, I shall miss him, and his absence from the field of battle and the bivouac of professional life will come home to me in language far more eloquent and pathetic than I can now conceive or express. Of this I can assure you, that I never called upon him that I did not find him the same affable, courteous, and hospitable gentleman. He always addressed me in terms of respect, and in language that showed that I was not only a welcome guest at his house, but that he bore for me an affection born of a true and lofty manhood. I have also seen him entertain others, and can say for and of him that he always made his visitors feel at home, and all that he had in the way of entertainment was theirs. No matter how young or humble his visitor in professional rank, that visitor was made to feel before he left that in Dr. Hering's character and make-up there was no such thing as caste or rank. In manner he was simple and unostentatious. He never paraded his knowledge or displayed his learning for the mere sake of show, nor did he try to impress one with the greatness of his character or genius.

He spared no pains or expense in showing his admiration for and his attachment to his medical confrères.

While there is much in his life and character to respect, admire, and venerate, yet there is one trait that strikes me with peculiar interest, and that is his life-long devotion to a single object and a single purpose. This trait stands out more boldly and more pronounced than all others.

What he accomplished in the field of Materia Medica by this oneness of aim proves that the first great law of success is concentration. He bent all his energies to one point, went directly to that point, and looked neither to the right nor left. He showed great wisdom in daring to leave many things unknown, and practical common sense in leaving other things untouched. If I study this trait of his character aright, he was impressed with the fact that life was too short and art too long and too valuable for universal scholarship. The range of medical thought and knowledge is so vast and extensive that no one brain can encompass it or grapple with it as an entirety. Therefore, if we would know one department of medicine well we must have the courage to be ignorant of some others, however attractive or inviting they may appear. If we would succeed as did Hering, we must single out our specialty and pour the whole stream of our life into it. No name has been longer or more intimately connected with homœopathic interests and homœopathic literature than that of our deceased brother, Dr. Constantine Hering. Certainly none is more widely known, more generally honored, or more universally beloved.

For nearly the whole period of his life he has devoted and consecrated all the energies of his mind and body to the unfolding of homœopathic truth, and to the dissemination and elevation of its principles.

Even in old age he did not seek the rest and retirement which his years justified and his health demanded. But he, full of love for and devotion to his chosen school of medicine, worked on with such well-directed zeal as to merit the highest respect and admiration of all succeeding generations. Although dead, he still lives in the books and works which he has left, and which are ours to inherit and enjoy. These are his voice, coming to us from out of the grave of the past, floating on the tide of time, and breathing forth the fire of his youth and the wisdom of his riper and more matured years.

Dr. Piepgras, of Loveland, then made the following address:

Providence has called one of our dearest and greatest members to eternity, and we wish to express the deep grief which wells up from the depth of our heart.

The name of Constantine Hering will be spoken with reverence by every true homœopath down to remotest time, as he was a champion of truth in medicine, and one of the chief pillars of our school in Europe as well as in America. I am sure every advocate of the truths of Homœopathy will love his memory until he joins him above.

I never enjoyed the honor of his personal acquaintance, but knew much about him through my master, Dr. Arthur Lutze, now deceased, and also by his writings.

I may be permitted to mention a little anecdote, which may be new to you, and will give a pleasant remembrance of our dear departed.

"Whilst traveling in Germany," says Dr. Hering, "I one day came to a village, the proprietor of which invited me to spend the night at his house, in place of putting up at the inn. He was a rich old gentleman, a great original, always an invalid, having ennui and good wine to a great extent. Learning that I was a young medical man, about to commence my travels, he told me he would sooner make his son a hangman than a doctor. On my expressing surprise at the observation, he produced a large book, saying that it was now twenty years since he first became ill in body but not in mind; that two doctors of celebrity, whom he then consulted, had quarrelled about his disease, and that, consequently, he had employed neither of them nor their medicines, but that he had registered the affair in his book. Then, after finding that the disease did not get better, he set out on his travels, resolved, *if he could find three doctors who perfectly agreed upon his case without any hesitation,* to allow himself to be treated by them, but never by any other. For this purpose he had consulted at first all physicians of any reputation, and afterwards others whose names were less known, but having, in spite of all his sufferings, never abandoned his first resolution, and keeping an exact account of every consultation in a book for the purpose, he never succeeded in finding any who agreed respecting his case. Accordingly, not having followed the advice of any, he still remained an invalid, but he was still alive. As may be well supposed, the book cost him a pretty sum of money.

"This book had the appearance of a ledger in large folio, and was kept in the form of tables. In the first column were the names of the physicians, amounting to 477; in the second, those of the disease, with explanations concerning its nature, of these there were 313, differing radically from each other; in the third column were the remedies proposed, these consisted of 832 prescriptions, containing in all 1097 remedies. The sum total appeared at the end of each page.

"He took up a pen, and said cooly: 'Won't you prescribe something for me?' But having no great inclination to do so, I only asked if Hahnemann was not in his list. With a smile he turned to No. 301, name of the disease O, remedy prescribed O. 'That was the wisest of the lot,' he cried, 'for he said that the *name* of the disease did not concern him, and that the name of the remedy did not concern me, but that the cure was the essential point.' 'But why,' I inquired, 'did you not allow him to treat you?' 'Because,' he replied, 'he was but one, and I must have three who agree.'

"I asked him if he were willing to sacrifice some hundred francs for an experiment, in which case I should be able to mention not *three*, but *thirty-three* physicians living in the neighborhood, and in countries and parts of the world widely separate, who should all be of one opinion. He expressed his doubts, but at the same time resolved to undertake the trial. We then made out a description of his symptoms, and when the copies were finished, we sent them to thirty-three homœopathic practitioners. He inclosed a louis d'or in each letter, begging each physician to name the remedies which were capable of curing, or at least of alleviating his disease.

"A short time since I received a cask of Rhenish, of the vintage of 1822. 'I send you wine of the year 1822,' he wrote, 'because twenty-two physicians agreed respecting my case. I thereby perceive that there is certainty in some things in this world. I have got various works on the subject, in order to gain information upon it. Out of about two hundred medicines, twenty-two physicians have fixed upon the same remedy. One could not expect more. The physician nearest me has got me under his care, and I send you the wine that I may not be tempted to drink too much from joy at seeing my health improving from day to day.'"

Dr. C. N. Hart then spoke as follows:

Colleagues:—There is a beautiful and ancient custom in the land of my ancestors, which causes each person upon the highway to uncover the head as a funeral procession passes, whether the deceased is known or not. This evening we with thousands of our brethren, of all schools, assembled in all parts of the world, have met to pay a tribute to the memory of a great and good man who has passed away—Dr. Constantine Hering.

Let us rejoice that his life upon earth was one of social and intellectual enjoyment, and that upon passing onward he has left us and future generations such works as time cannot destroy.

After a long period of the highest service to his Maker and mankind, both in Germany and America, he has passed onward to a higher and brighter sphere, "*ossa bene qui encant.*"

In the words of the great and lamented Dunham, the study of his life has been "not fabrics, nor wares, nor stocks, the works or machinations of men, but the noblest of God's creation—that which He made in His own image—the body and mind of man." He was to both old and young kind and affectionate, and alike teacher and friend. Envy and malice had no part in his career, but with his one hand as an index pointing onward and his other as a support to those acquiring knowledge, he lived and died. And thus may all strive to emulate this noble man who lived and died in love and honor.

On motion the meeting was adjourned.

MEETING IN MINNEAPOLIS, MINN.

In obedience to the call for the holding of a meeting in memory of the late Constantine Hering, the Hahnemann Society for Hennepin County, Minnesota, held an adjourned session on the evening of October 10th, 1880. Dr. William E. Leonard, a graduate of the Hahnemann Medical College, of Philadelphia, spoke of the last hours of the great man so recently departed, and related many pleasant and touching reminiscences of personal intercourse with him. Subsequent remarks were made by others present, and finally Dr. S. P. Starritt, who had been appointed for this duty, made the following address:

It is customary upon the death of an individual, however humble, to present some form of testimonial, recounting the relations of the deceased to society.

Naturally, the more noted the individual, the more public and demonstrative the tribute.

The idea is primitive and general. We see it among even savage and barbarous peoples, where skill, courage and prowess of the fallen is cited to the surviving for emulation, and as special traits of distinction.

Among the semi-barbarous and semi-civilized, we find these

relations embodied in fervid and glowing apostrophe, the lay of the minstrel, the rude but heroic song.

Among civilized and cultivated nations, witness the sermons, biographies, the finished and studied epic verse, "the towering monument, sculptured bust, and storied urn."

To-night, friends, without pomp, we come in an humbler, but no less sincere way, to pay our tribute to the life and services of one of earth's greatest sons, who has recently been called to another home, to a higher and ampler sphere.

Abraham was accounted worthy to be called the "Father of the Faithful," because at God's call he left country, kindred and home, to go into a strange land, which was yet to be shown him, having *faith* in Him who promised that he was to be the "father of a great nation."

Him whom we honor to-night, God called in no less audible voice, "Get thee out of thy country, and from thy kindred, and from thy father's house, unto a land that I will show thee, and I will make of thee a great nation, and I will bless thee, and make thy name great."

The lives of both these great men have become historic, and history has but proved the truth of prophecy.

Father Hering, as he was truthfully and affectionately called by a great army of co-workers, in his early youth was taught how to think, and no higher encomium, through his long and studious life, could be found, than *he knows how to think*.

Graduating with distinction from one of the great German Universities, he first essayed to teach mathematics, but a fondness or an instinct for medicine led him to acquire what was taught in the schools.

Like all men of great force, profound convictions and energetic will, he espoused the established and so-called "regular" practice with zeal, and was wont to persecute what he afterward with great zeal embraced and advocated.

From the versatility of his acquirements he was selected by his confrères to controvert and annihilate a new and progressive system of healing, which was forcing its way into public recognition and favor. Investigation led to wonder, wonder to admiration, but while still doubting he became a sufferer, and after trying the appliances of the old system without relief, he sought the new and was healed. Thus through suffering did he become a believer, was converted, and, after practically demonstrating the truth of the new art, he became the great apostle of Homœopathy to the Gentiles.

Eminent for his attainments in science, his government appointed him naturalist of a scientific expedition bound for the southern continent of the New World.

Ostracised at home for his new faith, and possessed with the divine instinct of emigration, he eagerly embraced the offer tendered by government, and with the characteristic ardor of young manhood, he discharged the duties to which he was assigned.

Meanwhile, not content with the knowledge already acquired by the New School of Medicine for healing the sick, he began to inquire how he could add to the list of remedial agents, and best disseminate their mode of application.

While rendering signal service to his country, he, perhaps, rendered his greatest service to mankind, by introducing into medicine, with its indications, the virus of the Lachesis trigonocephalus, which, from its healing properties in the hands of our great army of practitioners, has become one of the greatest of our mighty polychrests.

On his return home, while visiting some of the largest cities of the North, it is said that in Philadelphia he received the diviner impulse, which led him to conclude that *there* was indeed the "*promised land.*"

The Old World may boast that it gave us a Hering, but the New World can reply, not so; for his potentiality only became *reality* under the inspiration and progressiveness of the New. Here, cut off from the peculiar bent of the European mind to follow custom and precedent, he strikes out boldly upon a new course, and with the intrepidity of an explorer he never deviates, but so amplifies and gives so many fixed and reliable data, that it makes it comparatively easy for his successors to follow the same route.

There is ever an element of moral courage and greatness in those who discover or follow new truths or paths of which the general mind is ignorant. The investigator is always a brave man, and full of the spirit of sacrifice.

History is full of the sublime examples of men who have breasted the tides of opposition arising from ignorance, superstition, custom, envy and malice, in giving to the world new and progressive ideas and truths. History has also given these men their meed of praise, has placed the laurel upon their brows, and crowned them the *world's heroes*.

The mind sits enchained at the daring and hardihood of the navigator, sailing a new and unknown expanse, from the rugged Norsemen of earlier times down to those of the present, who plow the ice-floe of Arctic seas. The blood is enkindled at Spartan and Roman heroism, and the sanguinary conflict of Dane, and Pict, and Scot. The sublime lessons of patience are taught over the achievements of Galileo, Kepler, Newton, Faraday, Miller, Fulton, Morse, and hosts of others, who, through great toil, have added to the knowledge of Nature and her slumbering forces. What monuments shall we rear to the world's martyrs and reformers, who, in the domain of moral, civil, and religious conflict, have purchased us that *liberty* which has made all the other achievements of men possible?

He whom cardiac paralysis has just stricken down, in the full splendor of his hoary age, is not one whit behind the greatest of those to whom we have just referred, for he possessed their spirit, was actuated by the same motives, and spent his life in the same, or a kindred cause—*the amelioration of his fellow-men.*

Though not the Columbus of Homœopathy, he followed faithfully the chart of the great discoverer. He extended and amplified in almost every particular the boundaries of Hahnemann. He confirmed every fact that Hahnemann had given to the world as such, while the theories of his great Master he tested, and passed upon their validity. He analyzed and systematized where Hahnemann had only generalized; Hahnemann introduced Homœopathy, but it was reserved for the genius of Hering to raise it to the sublime degree of a distinctive science. Both were great and original explorers.

It has been indeed always the pride and boast of Homœopathy, that it is invested with a gift of prevision, that is, given a picture of a certain malady, the remedy is at once forthcoming, already provided. The only limit is one—human incapacity—inability to prove all the medicinal agencies of nature, and to retain their special therapeutic range. So true is this gift, that it matters not whether the disease is obscure or known, or whether it be present or remote. Thus Hahnemann was enabled by *our law of cure*, to point out remedies curative for even the Eastern Plague, and robbed it of its terrors, before he had ever seen a case, or even it had spread to his own country. In like manner could and did Hering for our Southern Plague, the yellow fever. Both these great minds went further than this, they indicated the remedies preventive, so as to render even contagion powerless.

Come now and admire with me the moral courage and greatness of the man who, from adherence to known law and principles, not only called down upon himself the odium of the great minds that had given him his diversified instruction, and from merit has elevated him to confraternity, but also in his emigration to the New World, the same odium precedes and attaches to him, emanating from kindred sources. The Cholera from the distance is advancing, and Hering, true to his convictions, points out a simple and efficacious prophylactic, which only excited ridicule. In the streets of his own chosen city and home, see the rabble and street Arabs pursue him with jeer and scoff, prompted by those holding the same distinguished positions as those who had cast him off in the Fatherland. The quiet shrug, or the curious look of the more cultivated was no less cruel than the open scoff of the slums. But the fatal scourge is come, depopulating the city, and "Sulphur Hering" is remembered, and men now, through fear, began to try the efficacy of wearing a spoonful of the flour of sulphur in their stockings, and received immunity from contagion.

Friends, it requires the highest order of both physical and moral courage, to risk life calmly in trying to succor others. Witness the heroic act of a man alone in a room, whence all the attendants had fled, with a box which he has just opened containing the most venomous serpent, the largest of its species, from whose glands, after the most mature deliberation, he was to abstract the deadly poison. See the nerve of the man, who, alert as is the snake, seizes it just below the head with firm grasp, when with folds uncoiled, with reared head and flaming eye, forked tongue and naked fang, it is poised to strike the intrepid soul who, at the risk of life, seeks from its venom the healing balm for earth's sufferers. Watch him adjust the pointed stick between the opened jaws of the serpent whose bite is certain death, and whose impotent rage secretes the deadly saliva, while he tantalizes it till it can distil no more poison, when into a jar of alcohol he thrusts the monster, nor relaxes his grip of steel till life is extinct. The poison caught in a glass is transferred to the mortar and rubbed with sugar of milk, till his purple and bloated face and swimming brain suspend his eager operation. Observe him toss in his fever, note the loquacious delirium as he flits from subject to subject, note the suffocation, the frantic struggle for breath, while he clutches and tears from throat and breast all clothing; mark his mental condition, the anguish and apprehension, and ask yourselves for whom, for what does he this, and then answer—is he not a hero?

Or friends, can you imagine the sensation of being in a closed room with a rabid dog, bent upon getting the frothy hydrophobinum, for the sole purpose of obtaining a remedy for healing the sick? How would you characterize the act, courageous or not?

Does it not exhibit moral heroism to assert the truth of a scientific fact in face of the denial of the entire scientific world?

Scientists scoffed at the idea, that the poisons he procured and proved at the jeopardy of life, had any remedial efficacy, because, forsooth, they had been preserved in alcohol! "Why," exclaim they, "we drench an individual with whiskey when bitten by the crotalus, and it antidotes and prevents systemic poisoning, and saves the life of the patient!" Alcohol antidotes animal poison, therefore animal poisons preserved in alcohol are rendered harmless and inert, and from the deductions of such logic the world hooted at his provings and cures produced by the alcoholic preparations of his animal poisons, most notably his Lachesis, of which he had asserted much. But he was patient, knowing whereof he had affirmed, and the scientific world, after experimenting, demonstrated that the hypodermic injection of even the third centesimal of Lachesis, and even the still higher dilutions were destructive to animal life, and after many other and varied experiments, it was publicly acknowledged that Hering was right, that animal poisons preserved in alcohol held still their poisonous qualities intact.

Again, think you it required no moral back-bone to stand by the assertion that radiated heat was one of the most efficient agencies to antidote the poison of wounds whatever their origin, when the world denied and disbelieved? Mark the courage of the test! A man with an inoculated arm, swollen, purple, throbbing, painful, threatening the loss of life, will not listen to the voice of friends and the surgeon, but sits quietly down in his kitchen, and thrusts his arm into the heated oven, and holds it there till the poison is extracted or eliminated, and the member is reserved for future usefulness, and again, the world, after experimenting, announces that radiated heat is antidotal to poisonous wounds. Hering was right again.

Still further, witness him walk with quiet dignity into the sick room, where lies a girl in throes of severest agony, after the major operation of lithotomy, and amid the sneers of the operator and other distinguished surgeons summoned in consultation, who had signally failed to mitigate her suffering, and had given her over to the king of terrors—see him solicit symptoms from the sick, and from his inexhaustible fund of knowledge, watch him pour a few pellets of Staphisagria into water and administer it to the sufferer. To the gratification of the sick one and her friends, and to the amazement of the scoffers, the pain is mitigated, finally assuaged, and sleep comes gratefully to restore strength, and a precious life is saved.

These are but a few striking instances which serve to illustrate the timber of the man who, by courage and calm demeanor amid trying scenes and sacrifices, won public and private esteem, when Homœopathy was not to the public what it is to-day, and forced the popular recognition of his system of healing, obtaining for it the sanction and protection of the civic law.

Now it is comparatively easy for the practitioner to dispense the blessings of an enlightened Homœopathy, but what do we not owe to Father Hering, who, by his skill, patience and learning, and above all *moral courage*, overcame the popular ignorance and prejudice, so that it has passed into a proverb, that Homœopathy cannot flourish among the ignorant and unthinking, but numbers its adherents among the cultured, thoughtful and educated.

As a scholar and student Hering stands unrivalled in his time. He was authority in every branch of medicine, and so intimately was he acquainted, not only with medical, but kindred sciences, that his thoughts and utterances became books. His habits and methods were those of the student. Accustomed to rise very early in the morning, at three o'clock, he was wont to take a slice of toast and a cup of coffee, when he would study and write till breakfast, at nine. After breakfast he would pursue his studies further, and attend to his professional duties till evening, when he would either pass the time in continued study or converse with those who desired instruction. I believe it was his custom to retire about nine in the evening. He had pre-eminently the genius for hard and continuous study, and this systematic and arduous course he pursued up to the time of his demise.

The fruit of such labor is, of course, voluminous, and it is by authorship that he will be best known to posterity. He is the author of many books and monographs, and all of them are the acknowledged standards of our school. He devoted the greater portion of his studies to the proving of drugs, and he has enriched our Materia Medica more than any other author, Hahnemann not excepted. His Guiding Symptoms is characteristic, and no such full, complete, and accurate work on Materia Medica was ever published. He esteemed it the crowning effort of his life. It is the fruit of advanced age, the product of a long life of rich and varied experience, united with the most profound research and learning.

One would naturally suppose that he would have fallen in with the prevailing system of German Philosophy, and that his works, like those of Grauvogl, would have been tinctured with theories founded upon philosophical speculation. But not so. He brought everything to the touchstone of scientific experiment, and he was wont to say, "There is no such thing as *belief* in science. A property or thing is, or *is not.*" His method was empirical, perhaps sciential would be the better word. It partook rather of the inductive system of philosophy than transcendentalism. Transcendentalism was to him a horrible word, with a prolonged, rough, guttural roll of the rrs.

Everything was subjected to trial, and if it did not stand the test of experiment, did not prove a literal fact, he never strove to bolster it up with a more plausible theory, but cast it off as one would a useless garment.

Just a year or two previous to death, while the writer with a body of students was sitting at his feet, as sat Paul at the feet of Gamaliel, he remarked: "Well, gentlemen, to-day I have lost one of my best beloved children. For more than twenty years I have been collecting facts and data to establish a pet theory of mine, and I was about to publish and give the results to the world, when to-day I have fully decided that it cannot stand the test of scientific experiment, and so I have buried it out of my sight. Not without a pang, gentlemen, but as my theory is not true, that is the end of it."

His mind was both analytical and synthetical. He was a tall man, sun-crowned in the light of knowledge; a man of capacious soul, gigantic brain, an intellect of colossal proportions. That which seemed veiled to other men was to him luminous with light. In his capacious mind truth alone was sought, discovered, seized upon, made incarnate and disseminated over sea, island and continent, till it became the common heritage.

But it was as an instructor or lecturer that he surpassed himself. Brimful, overflowing with knowledge, he was just as eager to impart as to acquire. Give him respectful attention, and he would forsake every other duty and proceed to talk or lecture without note of time, and I assure you he was as tireless as time itself. He has been known to forget fatigue and rest and sit up all night to instruct some practitioner who wished either to be led into, or receive more light in the sublime degrees of Homœopathy. Even in the last years of his life his eye would kindle in the presence of a body of students, his mind unfold and truth would come forth robed in beauty, and not till the long hours were passed and even not then, unless solicited to cease and rest, would he think of retiring. The *totality* of the symptoms and the *single* remedy corresponding to that totality were his two watchwords.

He was a kind and affectionate father and husband, a good citizen, but a citizen of no particular country. He owed allegiance to the world.

More given to imparting knowledge and ameliorating the sufferings of the race than to the acquirement of wealth, he laid up for himself the true riches. He achieved more than fame—he was great. His kind and beneficent deeds, the truths he discovered and established, the sacrifices he made and his arduous toil, guide us in the divine art of healing.

He died full of years, honored and respected by even his adversaries. A long life of usefulness has been spent. We are fatherless. His sun is but set to us, only to rise and shine with greater and undimmed lustre in a fairer and boundless horizon.

Truly of him it can be said in the language of old: "And thou shalt be a blessing, and in thee shall all the *families* of the earth be blessed."

Friends, the unfolding of the prophetic scroll shall fully establish history, for already has he become the "father of a great nation."

MEMORIAL ADDRESS TO KANSAS PHYSICIANS.

The following address was read at a meeting of the physicians of Kansas, at Topeka, by Dr. Henry W. Roby:

Friends:—There is a pause in our labors; a break in our ranks; a shade on the Stygian river. Constantine Hering, the pupil and intimate friend of Hahnemann; the venerable Nestor of Homœopathy in America; the unrivalled scholar, philosopher and author in the new school of medicine; the most successful practitioner, and the ablest medical counselor of this age, has gone to his final rest at the mature age of eighty-one years. And yet, as was said of the great statesman Thiers, "He died too young by a score of years."

Like Gœthe's, his grandest works were his last. His massive brain and untiring hands had nearly finished the crowning glory of his life-work—the most masterly piece of medical authorship ever given to the world.

Like the immortal Lincoln, he died before God or circumstances had created a successor large enough to fill his place in the world. But nature is rich in compensatory laws. The cause which creates a great leader, like a Luther, a Bonaparte, a Thiers, a Bismarck, a Washington, a Lincoln, or a Hahnemann in one age or generation, will be carried forward through the succeeding ages or generations by their disciples and followers.

A great leader in the cause of the twin-sisters, humanity and Homœopathy, has but recently died in Philadelphia, and to-day physicians by thousands and their patrons by millions, scattered all over the world, sincerely mourn his death. But there is left to us this consolation that the *cause* which he led is strong enough at his death, and well enough officered, to march steadily forward to final and glorious triumph, without the further inspiration of a great *individual* leadership. So, a detachment buries the fallen leader and decorates his grave, while the great army marches on without halting, *for the cause is greater than the leader.*

As inductive philosophy no longer needs a Lord Bacon for leader, or astronomy a Galileo or Copernicus, so Homœopathy no longer needs the personal inspiration of Hahnemann, its original grand master in Europe, or Hering, his co-laborer in America. It now marches steadily onward to the drum-beat of *principle* under the inspiration of a demonstrated and ever demonstrable *truth.* Whenever truth involves enough of human interest to start it on its march around the world, if it does not find in waiting a man sufficiently large for a captain-general, it takes one from the common walks of life and enlarges him sufficiently for the great work of leadership.

And Nature seems to have no regular rule for the choice of men for leaders. She takes a tinker, a printer, a cobbler, a rail-splitter, a tanner, or a student, and so sharpens his vision that he can see the new truth which is marching along through his day and generation, so enlarges his intellect that he can grasp and hold the truth, and so shapes and energizes his tongue and pen that he can show to the world the strength and beauty of the principle he has apprehended, and its correlations to other great truths in the world. In one case she takes a mechanic, puts him into a bath-tub which overflows, and he straightway leaps out and cries "Eureka! Eureka!" In another she leads a dreamer into an orchard and drops an apple at his feet, and in the light of that falling apple he finds *the law of gravity.*

She takes a school-master of Padua, sets him "star-gazing," and his trembling tongue informs an astonished world that all the heavenly bodies, our earth included, are wheeling through immense orbits in immeasurable space and also revolving on their own axes. And thus the science of astronomy is born even under the shame and humiliation of a compulsory recantation. Again, nature takes a poor humble student, leads him along the old paths of knowledge, through the labyrinthine mysteries and utter chaos of old medicine, and then leads him on into that clearer light which gives the world a scientific and perfect guide to the choice of drugs for the cure of disease. And then she crowns him with *leadership* in a grand reformation of a great human *cause*.

And thus, through the long reach of ages, one human interest after another, one great fact or truth or principle after another is developed and established in the minds and lives of men, of communities and races.

But Nature seems to be never in haste. It took twenty-two hundred years of the slow coaching of old medicine to develop a Harvey and establish in the minds of men the fact of the circulation of blood in the human organism. And it took almost two centuries longer to develop and establish nature's law of drug-action on the human system, and to give the world *the law of cure*. The very discovery of that law had to wait for the discovery and development of *inductive philosophy*, for only by its processes could the law of cure be discovered and fully demonstrated. But that law is now incontestably established on an absolutely scientific basis, and to-day it challenges all the scientific tests known to men to disprove its correctness. And Hahnemann, its real discoverer, and Hering, its wise elaborator, can be and are both called from labor to rest. For years the profession has watched with eager eyes the progress of Dr. Hering's life-work almost in fear and trembling, lest he should not live to complete it. But life held on its course, and the indefatigable worker through days and nights and years of incessant study and toil brought the work nearer and nearer to completion. And when at last his work was done, his manuscripts completed and the press began to turn out his volumes, the fiat of "well done" was issued from on high, and he was suddenly called away from his proof-sheets to his everlasting rest. Others could read the proof, and he was spared that labor. *His work* was done. But he had lived to write *the master medical work of the world*, which will soon issue from the press, fitly named "Guiding Symptoms."

Unlike the "Mystery of Edwin Drood," the hand of its creator guided the pen to the end of its last chapter, though proof-readers, pressmen and binders have their work still to perform.

Homœopathy, under the leadership of Hahnemann and Hering, reinforced by an already grand army of coadjutors, has wrought a grand and beneficent reform in medicine, and conferred inestimable blessings on the world. It no longer needs any champion defenders. It is a great and well established fact in the world. It has already become aggressive, has changed the field of conflict and the front of battle, has carried the contest into the enemy's country and put gouty old medicine on the defensive, and compelled it to adopt so many changes and improvements and to abandon so many barbarities and cruel and dangerous devices in its methods, that could Galen, Paracelsus, Hippocrates, Paris, Cullen or Sydenham be called from their graves to-day, they would have a thousand-fold more trouble to recognize their disciples than did Rip Van Winkle to recognize his daughter or his dog after his twenty years of sleep. Hahnemann and his followers have achieved a deeper and broader and sounder knowledge of Materia Medica in the past eighty years than old physic has done in eighteen centuries.

Still the world moves, and even now the sleepy disciples of Galen are waking up and announcing with a great flourish of trumpets to the world as *new discoveries in medicine*, facts which Hahnemann announced over eighty years ago.

Fortunately the world is already astir in all the great camping grounds of philosophy, science, art, theology, law and medicine; it is waking up the Rip Van Winkles all along the line, and demanding of them more intelligent and scientific methods, more light and better results. And when the masses *demand* better lawyers, better preachers, better doctors and more intelligent methods, the demand is sure to be responded to. If the people demand better qualities of books, of food, of raiment, of merchandise, there will not be long wanting live merchants and tradesmen who will find or create a way to supply the demand.

A hundred years ago there went up from an already long-suffering humanity a cry for release from old medical superstitions and barbarities, and for the introduction of a more humane and scientific medicine, one that could give a reason, not only for its existence, but its methods, and already the whole medical world (the most superstitious of all worlds) is revolutionized, and half a million of active brains and busy hands are toiling eagerly to fulfil the demand of humanity. Many of them are among the old sleepers, and we see almost daily some of them rubbing the scales from their eyes, dropping their shackles of prejudice and coming to the front and joining the ranks of Homœopathy. Order is being evolved out of chaos, system out of confusion, light out of darkness, and the cry of the world for a *safe* and *wise* medical system is receiving its answer.

Let the good work go on, and when a veteran and hero finishes his work and is given his eternal leave of absence from our ranks, there will be a hundred willing hands and heroic hearts to take up and carry on the great work. Let us one and all make and hold ourselves competent and ready to take up and carry on successfully any part of the great work that circumstances or Providence may assign to us.

MEETING IN WILMINGTON, DELAWARE.

A memorial meeting in honor of the decease of Dr. Constantine Hering was held in the city of Wilmington, Delaware, on October 10th, 1880, at which Dr. A. Negendank read the following address:

Gentlemen:—While we are here to-day assembled, representing the homœopathic physicians of the State of Delaware, to share in the general respect, and to show our high esteem to the departed master spirit of Constantine Hering, in honoring him I feel that we are conferring honor to ourselves, being followers of the same principle in medicine—"*Similia similibus curantur*"—that our deceased veteran ever defended, and to the elucidation of which he devoted a large portion of a long life of eighty years. Dr. Hering was a man *sui generis*, far above the groveling propensities of ordinary human nature; he forgot in his devotion to science, the entity of worldly existence, for which so many toil. Our profession has always claimed, not for the individual, but for the body collective, a high standard of honor and unselfishness, a position above those who know less of the frailties of humanity. Let every one judge for himself if he deserves such a claim or not, but I say it without hesitation, our departed friend deserved that claim, and I believe him to have been the high priest of his profession.

There are men who seem to be sent into this world for purposes and action only. All their faculties are bent to toil and work: their spirits and their frames alike teem with energy. They pause and slumber like other men, but only to recruit from actual fatigue; they occasionally need quiet, though only as invigoration for renewed exertion; they investigate and reflect; their mission, their enjoyment, the object and condition of their existence, is work; they would not be content to exist here without it, and cannot conceive another life as desirable without it. Their vitality is beyond that of ordinary men; they are never seen idle; in repose they dream of work, and their pleasure is work.

A few years before his death, on a warm summer day, hot enough to lull the energy of the youngest, while sitting in his arm-chair smoking a cigar and sipping his cup of coffee, the venerable old gentleman was overcome by fatigue, and rousing himself from slumber exclaimed: "If it was not for the work begun, and the completion of which rests upon me, the frail and weary body might wish to be at rest." Such a man was our highly esteemed and distinguished Hering.

I had the privilege to live with the doctor for several years, as his assistant, and there is not a day of that time that I cannot recall with pleasant remembrance; at his frugal table he was cheerful, conversational and instructive, never dictatorial, always pleased to receive. If it was upon any subject with which he was not as familiar as the speaker, he would listen with grave attention, and a pleasant sparkle of the eye would indicate his gratification to learn. Humble people were cheerfully entertained at his hospitable table, and the kindest attention and respect were shown them by the doctor, as well as by Mrs. Hering. If friends happened in in the evening, before the doctor retired to his study, he was always ready for a social chat, full of good humor and wit. A cigar, rye bread, a piece of Swiss cheese, a glass of claret, and plenty of time in prospect would furnish material for an enjoyable evening. But if our venerable sage came home overworked and fatigued, he preferred to be undisturbed, and retired to his study where quiet reigned, there to be in company with his books or pen.

To the young man he was full of encouragement; enthusiastic in showing him the way that would be sure to lead him to success; never oppressing him with his store of knowledge or learning, but ready to give to the fullest extent, all that he judged his hearer capable of receiving. A faint smile would probably be all the censure bestowed on a weak effort in literature; but for an able antagonist he had voluminous ammunition for battle, including a fair quantity of grape shot. A good jest, even if it was at his own expense, or even against Homœopathy, he relished, but a cold or wilful expression against the sacred truth of Therapeutics he considered unpardonable. After the death of Dr. Watzke, in 1867, I expressed my regret at losing such an able colleague from our ranks; he knit his brow and answered: "I am not at all sorry; a man who, after finding the truth, can say that he is sorry for it, ought to die."

The patience of Dr. Hering in listening to the endless narration of a patient afflicted with a chronic disorder, was remarkable, and you might have thought the day of our master had no end, or that he had only the one patient to attend. The restlessness of all who were waiting for him in the office, did not in the least disturb him; they might wait, or go home to come back another time. He did not believe in hurry, and often said, "No one is in a hurry but the devil."

Dr. Hering was a power, but what was that power? Was it his learning? no doubt it was a part of it. Was it his industry? no doubt it was a part of it. But the great lever of his power was his character. He was modest, kind and open-hearted. Integrity and honor were his beacon-lights; he was a man in whom there was no guile. I may be asked by some of our friends, did our sage never get out of humor, or could he not scold? I am frank to say, that he could get out of humor and scold too. Tell him that he promised so and so, and you were sure to put him in bad humor; it was specially distasteful to his feelings, as a doubt against his honest character. "No, sir; I never promise, never, never; no one promises but the old Nick, and he never keeps a promise." He had his own fashion of scolding, and it was in full earnest, but never to hurt anyone, as he was always careful not to let its force descend directly upon the subject who had offended.

One stormy winter night, the coachman awaited the doctor at the house of a friend where he was calling, and had become so interested in conversation that driver, horses, and the storm were alike forgotten. About ten o'clock, John, not feeling very comfortable on his box, and perhaps thinking the doctor might have given him the slip by a side door, drove away to the stable. The old gentleman returned shortly after on foot, naturally out of humor, and John was soon hacked to pieces, hundreds, thousands, tens of thousands of pieces, roasted, fried and baked, the pan to be emptied out of the third story window into the dark, cold night. All this time John slept soundly in his warm bed, and never heard anything of these maledictions.

Dr. Hering's standing as a scientist, skilfulness as a physician, his special love and labor as a Therapeutist, I shall pass by in silence, knowing full well that ample justice will be done him this day by our fraternity. Ages to come will appreciate his labor, which was to free medicine and the medical profession from that vortex of endless speculation in Therapeutics which has been a labyrinth as old as the history of medicine. The work of building up a true temple of science kept the tools of our master mason bright. He was industrious to the last breath of his life, when kind Nature's signal called him for retreat.

In love, to the memory of the departed, I give these few outlines of his character.

MEETING IN WASHINGTON, D. C.

The following preamble and resolutions were adopted at a meeting of the Homœopathic Medical Society, held on October 10th, 1880, in commemoration of the death of Constantine Hering, M.D.:

When a man like Constantine Hering is removed from this life, it is fitting that we, his colleagues, should place upon record our appreciation of his eminent qualities as a man and physician; not that it adds anything to the beauty of his memory, but for ourselves, that we may be stimulated anew to follow his example.

Although his investigations of Homœopathy were undertaken for the purpose of destroying the heresy, he accepted fully the truths which were demonstrated by his experiments, though contrary to his preconceived ideas. The truth of the law of similars once proven to him, in spite of all opposition he became a pioneer in the cause, and suffered privations and persecutions such as are measured to all who dare to think in advance of the time. His labors in the cause were unselfish to the sacrifice of all wordly interests, and unceasing. He established the first homœopathic college; the first homœopathic pharmacy was opened through his influence, and to him we owe the first translation of Homœopathic Materia Medica into English. He has made Philadelphia a Mecca from which his influence has extended over the whole world.

While attacking with relentless power what he believed to be error, he was free from professional jealousies and always gave honor where honor was due; his was the fraternal spirit of a gentleman, a Christian, and a scientist. He realized in his devotion to Homœopathy, that with everything to gain in the contest with error, our cause could not afford to be weakened by controversies on non-essential questions. He desired, in the presence of a common enemy, a brotherhood that would ensure at last, a common victory; to this end he contributed much by his charity, kindliness and cheerful disposition, which called out the veneration of young practitioners who were so fortunate as to come in contact with him; his genial spirit gave him a perennial youth which made it impossible that he should die of old age.

He gave most freely of the results of his labors; his heart was open to every one who knocked at its door in the search for truth. Few knew of his labors and sacrifices for the cause. We are greatly indebted for his numerous provings of remedies and especially for the introduction and development of *Apium virus* and *Lachesis*.

But brightest above all, and including all, is the example of his long, noble and active life, devoted to the last moment to the service of his fellow men;—

Therefore, the members of the Washington Homœopathic Medical Society can but express their sorrow for their great loss; and, while bowing to the dispensation of an All-Wise God, would consecrate themselves anew to greater devotion to the cause which was so dear to him, and to the imitation of his shining example.

To his wife and children we extend our deepest sympathy, and the assurance that we mourn with them their loss of husband, father and friend.

MEETING IN SCHLESWIG-HOLSTEIN.

At a meeting of physicians and laymen of Schleswig-Holstein, held October 10th, 1880, at the residence of Herr Billerbeck in Wilster, the exercises consisted of the following:

1. Trauer=Weife von Trauttenfels.
2. Prolog, gesprochen von Frl. Böge.
3. Freunde schmückt des Meisters Haupt, von Dr. Mossa.
4. Prof. Dr. C. Hering's Wirken in Amerika und Deutschland. Vortrag von Dr. Werner.
5. Es wird bereinst die Nachwelt blättern 2c., von L. Frankl.
6. Blau—Weiß—Gold. Vortrag.
7. Der Schmerzensschrei aus allen Ecken. Ein Volkslied mit homöo=pathischen Randzeichnungen. Von Prof. Dr. Hering. Dr. Werner.
8. Schlußwort.

MEETING IN PARIS, FRANCE.

An account of the proceedings of the memorial meeting held in Paris, France, is copied from the *Bibliothèque Homœopathique*:

La fatale nouvelle venait à peine de se répandre dans Philadelphie que le fils de notre confrère, M. Heermann, en informait son père par le télégraphe. Le secrétaire-général de la Société hahnemanienne fédérative comprit aussitôt que les homœopathes français devaient rendre un hommage public et collectif à ce vétéran de l'homœopathie, à celui qui, depuis Hahnemann, avait le plus enrichi la Matière médicale. Aussi il invita sans plus tarder tous nos confrères présents à Paris à se réunir chez lui le 31 juillet 1880, pour aviser au meilleur moyen d'honorer la mémoire de ce grand bienfaiteur de l'humanité. La plupart des membres de la Société hahnemanienne fédérative furent exacts au rendez-vous et la séance fut ouverte à 9 heures du soir, sous la présidence de M. Leboucher. M. Love, vice-président de la Société homœopathique de France, et M. Cramoisy, étaient au nombre des assistants.

M. Heermann, après un court éloge d'Hering, expose l'objet de la réunion. Ensuite chacun émet son avis et l'on adopte à l'unanimité les deux résolutions suivantes:

1. Une lettre de condoléance sera adressée à Mme. veuve Hering et signée non-seulement par tous les membres présents, mais aussi par le plus grand nombre possible de médecins homœopathes actuellement à Paris.

2. M. Heermann, en qualité d'ami d'Hering, est chargé d'écrire son éloge avec tous les développements que comporte l'importance de ses travaux.

Voici le texte de la lettre qui a été rédigée et signée sur-le-champ:

Madame:—

Les médecins homœopathes français soussignés viennent vous dire toute la part qu'ils prennent à votre juste douleur. La mort du Dr. Hering est la plus grande épreuve que l'homœopathie ait éprouvée depuis longues années. Aucun de nous n'oublie les services rendus à notre école par celui que vous pleurez, et qui laisse un si grand vide parmi nous; aucun de nous n'oublie que c'est à lui surtout que nous devons le développement pris en Amérique par les disciples de Hahnemann.

Le Dr. Hering a donné un exemple que chacun tiendra à honneur d'imiter dans la mesure de ses forces. Le plus grand hommage que nous puissions rendre à sa mémoire sera de suivre la tradition de dévouement à la vérité et d'infatigable travail qu'il nous a laissée.

Veuillez agréer, madame, l'assurance de notre très humble respect.

Ont signé : *MM. Boyer, Chancerel* père, *Victor Chancerel*, vice-président de la Société hahnemanienne fédérative, *Claude*, secrétaire général de la Société homœopatique de France ; *Compagnon*, secrétaire adjoint de la Société hahnemanienne ; *Cramoisy, Cretin, Dacher, Dézermeaux, Fournier, Guerin-Meneville,* président de la Société homœopathique de France ; *Heermann*, secrétaire-général de la Société hahnemanienne ; *Leboucher*, président de la Société hahnemanienne ; *Fred. Love, James Love, Monnier, Partenay*, vice-président de la Société homœopathique de France ; *Léon Simon* père, *Vincent-Léon Simon*, secrétaire-adjoint de la Société hahnemanienne ; *Tessier.*

MM. *Placido Diaz*, de Puebla (Mexique), et *Antonio de Mello* de Porto (Portugal), qui assistaient à la dernière séance de la Société hahnemanienne, ont eu la gracieuseté d'ajouter leurs signatures à celles de leurs confrères de Paris.

The following eulogy* was read by Dr. C. Heermann :

On the 23d of July, at half-past 10 o'clock in the evening, Dr. Hering departed this life, having passed his 80th year.

He had for some time before his death suffered from asthma, without, however, ceasing to attend to his daily duties. He retired to his study, on the evening of the 23d, a little after 8 o'clock. About 10 o'clock he called his wife, who found him

---

* Translated from the French by Mrs. M. F. Green and Miss Emily Jones.

suffering from much difficulty in breathing, but in full possession of his faculties. Drs. Raue and Koch were summoned at once, but before they came his soul had passed away.

To one of those around him he said, "Now, I am dying." Upon other occasions, when he had been very ill and given up by his friends, he had always refused to believe that he was dying, feeling sure that his hour had not yet come.

Dr. Constantine Hering was born at Oschatz (Saxony), Germany, January 1st, 1800. From his earliest childhood he evinced a great desire for knowledge, and finished with honor the studies preparatory to entering the college at Zittau, where he devoted himself to classical learning from 1811 to 1817. He excelled in everything, especially in mathematics, and in all branches he went far beyond the average of his time. He had a decided taste for the study of medicine, which he followed first at the Surgical Academy at Dresden, then at the University of Leipzig, where he was a pupil of the celebrated surgeon Robbi. His preceptor having been at that time requested to write an article against Homœopathy, entrusted his pupil with it. The latter threw himself into it with ardor, studied the writings which he was to attack, and there found this expression, "Represent me, but represent me correctly." (*Mach's nach, aber mach's recht nach.*) He decided to make a personal investigation of the matter in order to insure a more complete victory.

Having, with this end in view, applied to a druggist in Leipzig for the bark of "Cinchona," the druggist, who was a friend of his, said to him, after having heard his purpose, "Let that alone, dear Hering, you are treading on dangerous ground," but Hering replied that he did not fear the truth.

The pamphlet against Homœopathy was not written.

About this time a dissecting wound produced on him such serious effects, that not only did amputation seem necessary, but grave fears for his life were felt. One of his friends at this time persuaded him to try against this malady, the power of homœopathic drugs. An entire cure was the result. His conversion to Homœopathy was from that time complete, and his thesis written to obtain his degree contained a masterly defence of the homœopathic law.

After he obtained his degree, March 23d, 1826, at the University of Würzburg, he was appointed by the King of Saxony to go to Guiana, for the purpose of scientific research, and to make a zoölogical collection. There he pursued the study and practice of the new doctrine, and cured the daughter of the governor of the province of a disease which had been pronounced incurable by the resident physicians. Having besides, during his stay in South America, contributed to the *Homœopathic Archives*, thanks to the influence of the court physician, he received "royal notice" to quit the study of medicine and attend only to the duties of his position.

His independent nature rebelled against so much intolerance, and he immediately sent in his resignation, and continued the practice of medicine at Paramaribo. One of his friends and students, Dr. Bute, who had formerly been a missionary there, and who had since then established himself at Philadelphia, represented this city to him as a useful field for his labors. Hering arrived there in January, 1833, but only remained a short time, having been asked by Dr. Wesselhœft, of Allentown, Pa., to assist him in founding there a homœopathic school of medicine, the first which had ever existed. The government of Pennsylvania accorded to the faculty the right to confer the degree of doctor of medicine.

We next find Dr. Hering established in Philadelphia, with a large practice.

So great was the variety of the Doctor's acquaintances, and the charm of intercourse with him, that his society was sought eagerly by statesmen, and the most illustrious representatives of political economy, science and the fine arts.

But the Doctor reserved for the students and younger practitioners his Saturday evenings, during which he taught them from his own experience, and shared with them the boundless treasures of his knowledge. This kind custom was kept up during his entire life, and even the most clever considered it a great honor to be admitted to these intellectual feasts.

What witty nights, where science and manly enjoyment were united to a hearty simplicity and native freshness! What delicious love-feasts under his truly hospitable roof!

As to his works, let us at least give a list of them which will serve to show the boundless activity of this fertile brain. Before leaving the Saxony legation he had proven, *Mezereum, Sabadilla, Sabina, Colchicum, Plumb. ac., Paris quadr., Cantharis, Sodium,* and partly, *Antim. tart., Arg. met., Aristol., Clematis er., Bellad., Caltha palustris, Opium, Ruta, Tanacet., Viola tricolor,* etc.

During his stay in South America his provings extended to *Lachesis, Theridion curass., Askalabotes, Calad. seg., Jambos, Jatropha, Solanum, Spigelia, Vanilla, Alumina, Acid phosph.* and *Psorinum.*

After his arrival in Philadelphia he either proved himself or superintended the experiments and editing of the provings of the following medicines: *Mephitis, Ictodes fœtidus, Crotal., Hydrophobinum, Brucea, Calc. phosph.* (acid and basic), *Hippomanes, Castor equorum, Kalmia, Viburnum, Phytolacca, Gelsemium, Gymnocladus, Chlor., Brom., Ac. fluor, Ac. oxal., Ferr. met., Cobalt., Niccol., Oxigen, Ozone, Thallium, Tellurium, Palladium, Platinum, Osmium, Lithium, Glonoine, Apis, Cepa, Aloes, Millefol., Baryta carb., Nux mos.* and *Formica.*

Besides his contributions to the *Homœopathic News,* 1854, and to the *American Journal of Materia Medica,* 1867–71, and the help which he gave to the translation of Jahr's Manual, we have many of his writings, both large and small:

Rise and Progress of Homœopathy, pamphlet, translated into Dutch and Swedish, 1834.

Necessity and Advantages of Homœopathy, 1835, pamphlet.

Proposition to Suppress Homœopathy, 1846, satire.

Logic of Homœopathy, 1860, pamphlet.

Effects from the Poison of Serpents, 1837.

Suggestions for making Medical Provings.

Domestic Physician, 1835, of which there have been issued seven editions in America, two in England, and fourteen in Germany; it has been translated into French, Spanish, Italian, Danish, Hungarian, Russian and Swedish.

American Drug Provings, 1853-57.

Translation of Gross' Comparative Materia Medica, 1866.

Condensed Materia Medica, two editions, 1877-79.

Analytical Therapeutics, 1875.

Guiding Symptoms, of which the third volume was in press at the time of his death.

The quantity of material gathered together by Dr. Hering, from which are drawn his Analytical Therapeutics and Guiding Symptoms, is a marvel of activity, and the most careful and complete collection which exists upon Materia Medica.

Dr. Hering was an active member of the Academy of Natural Sciences of Philadelphia, to which he gave his large zoölogical collection.

He was one of the founders of the American Institute of Homœopathy, to which he lent his coöperation during his entire life.

He founded the American Homœopathic Publishing Society, whose shareholders obtain his medical works and other publications at greatly reduced rates.

He was a co-founder of the American Provers' Union, co-founder of the Medical Academy at Allentown, co-founder of the Hahnemann College of Philadelphia, where he taught for a long time the doctrine of Homœopathy according to the Organon, which, as a true disciple, he himself honored in interpreting.

The Hahnemann College of Philadelphia was, when in danger of closing, saved and reorganized by Dr. Hering. It numbers ten professors, seven lecturers and demonstrators; contains a large library, a collection of models and pathological specimens, a complete chemical laboratory and rooms for the study of anatomy and practical surgery. Medicine is taught here in all its branches, including toxicology, materia medica, general and special therapeutics, etc. An excellent chance for the allopath who wishes to learn!

At his death Dr. Hering was Emeritus Professor of Institutes and Materia Medica in this institution.

Of medium height and athletic build, nature had fashioned Dr. Hering physically as a wrestler in a struggle, which he sustained during his entire life with ardor and dignity. Upon his broad shoulders was carried a grand head with the resolute look of one who, without any pride, knows how to appreciate his own value, and without affectation, unless one might call such his beautiful hair, which he always wore long, like the Germans of the olden time. He had the well-developed forehead of an observer, heavy eyebrows, shading the black eye of his race, and an expression in which played the anxiety of unwearied thought joined to a boundless kindness of heart. His step, noiseless and elastic in spite of his great weight, prepossessed all in his favor; his presence shed abroad an atmosphere of benevolence, and inspired the young with confidence in a superiority which might have crushed them, the sick with courage and all with sympathy, while to those who were fortunate enough to be able to approach sufficiently near to appreciate him, his presence served to fill them with an admiration of the tenderest nature.

Of a happily tenacious memory, he was at home on all subjects, listening with attention to the young whom he was teaching, and of such affability, that giving, he seemed to receive and learn from them.

His faculties of a superior order, formed upon musical harmonies from his birth, (his father was an organist,) and coordinated by the study of mathematics to a form of reasoning, and by classical learning to the very depths of philosophy, had been enriched by the study of natural science, of which he was a perfect master. His clear, precise enunciation; his sweet voice; his just, candid appreciation, where the severe logic of science was mingled with great goodness of heart, all united in showing a feeling of honest and irresistible conviction at the centre of which resounded like an ever-vibrating echo, these words: Follow me correctly.

Scientifically speaking, his well-moulded hand showed a depth of receptive sensibility capable of analysis, and, by its eastern form, the synthetic power well characterized. Humanly speaking, it was like his heart, which, deeply affected, sympathized with all in the arduous contest of life, giving both of his support and his charity. For it must be said that, slightly negligent of external forms, he seemed to be only the guardian of benefits received, which he scattered round him without any regard for his own interests. He cared nothing for riches; so to him was given the loving title of Father Hering.

To understand him thoroughly one must remember that he was brought up at a time of great effervescence, which accounts for his communicative enthusiasm. Perfectly balanced, his judgment did not allow his imagination to expend itself in any direction, save in the ardor which he lavished upon his studies; and his moral sense or feeling of duty sustained him in his great work, in which he never failed, in spite of the many meannesses of those who were jealous of the great stranger in a country which was not his by an accident of birth, but by adoption, and in spite of the bitterness with which those who, not being able to reach the man, tried to disparage him and the truths to which he had consecrated his life. To these truths he was faithful to a degree which never lessened, neither when pursued by vexations, nor when struggling against the restraints of the age, for, a few days before his death, he returned thanks for all the good that he had received from Homœopathy. He planned even at that time a new Materia Medica, in which the theory and practice should explain each other, to the great joy of the disciples of the school.

The results of his unheard-of work, and of his perseverance, are not only spread through the writings of many periodicals, but are recorded in volumes of extraordinary merit. One is astonished in becoming acquainted with this study, made so deep by comparisons, by parallel quotations, by circumstances of time, of position, of direction, and of sides. And the question arises, why so much care, which no one before him had thought of any use, unless the compilation of Bœnninghausen should be considered as something more than patient statistics. Dr. Hering brought to this work not only the minute exactitude of the naturalist, and the faithfulness of the homœopathic believer, but the ardent perseverance of one who studies the laws of a living pathology. He thought that there should be a reason for the preference of certain remedies for this or that part of the body. Is it the result of medical affinities, of idiosyncracies, or the result of medical action and physical reaction? What law does the circulation of the nervous fluid follow? What reason, what course must be assigned for the vital wave? Through the statistic method to which he was devoted there came to him the suspicion of a law to be discovered. And do not let us criticize too severely this ambition. The measure of intuition and appreciation, which a mind thus exercised makes use of, is not ours. The law of doses, and the law for which Hering sought, will both one day be added, like great luminaries, to the discoveries made for the good of mankind. Hering, himself, knew that the hour of this revelation, a kind of promised land, had not yet come, and he contented himself with erecting a monument of facts and works, so that others might make use of it later on. Then seeing that the Materia Medica, worked in this way, would be almost too colossal a work, he began another, as fine, but much shorter, which the student might, if he wished it, re-work. It is, in fact, more within our reach. Then, to define still more clearly the lines to be followed, in the practical way, he makes a resumé of the whole, and under the name of Analytical Therapeutics gave the result of long years of observation, either by himself or others. A work still incomplete, but, such as it is, of inestimable value.

At the time when Dr. Hering appeared upon the scene, our school but just started, was like a fragile shell upon the waters, ready to be engulfed at the least movement of the waves. Hering came, incomparably eminent, fortified with vast knowledge, an unceasing activity, a boundless kindness, a feeling of duty to be done, equal to every struggle. He started every movement for the good of our school, never allowed himself to be discouraged, was present everywhere upon the scene of action, encouraged and directed the students, stimulated the people to work, adding to his daily practice the work of a large correspondence, of medical provings and of a college professorship. To accomplish this he was often on duty twenty-one hours out of the twenty-four.

Our school has gained in size, in strength, in consideration; it is no longer a shell, a plaything at the mercy of the waves, but a majestic ship, with its flag floating proudly on all shores, the joy of every land. And if we, the contemporaries of Hering, have seen him and known his worth, posterity, on account of the imperishable monument which he has left us as the fruit of his labors, will place him, a worthy competitor, by the side of the Master himself, and bestow upon him the title of "great," which he has so richly deserved.

When Hahnemann attacked the old school at its foundations, by the denial, both of its fundamental principle and the efficacy of its therapeutic power, he did not content himself with a simple denial. For the denial, which may become the starting-point of an argument or a system, is not one in itself. Alone, and without reconstruction, if something has not been rebuilt upon the ruins of that which has been demolished, it is either the return to an unwholesome barbarism foreign to our day, or the paltry confession of weakness of mind. Hahnemann, while making clean work of the old school, determined the rules which should govern the choice of a medicine in a case of sickness, reunited by his system the disavowed ties[1] which exist between the

---

[1] Physiological maxim. The parts of a whole are in the same conditions as the whole, the whole in the same conditions as the parts. All local treatment rests upon a disavowal of this maxim.

maxims of physiology and therapeutics; for the untenable law of opposites[2] substituted the indisputable law[3] of similars, and, by means of provings on the healthy man, initiated us into the complicated study of the psychical[4] and physical man, a close bond, by which in every disease these double beings are united.

Strong in obedience to the law and this science, we entered the arena, physicians of the body, physicians of the soul, apostles of the right, true benefactors, and regenerators of the human race. It was from henceforth a question if the science of medicine should be material or spiritual. By its very constitution Homœopathy is the realization in science of that which the Christian idea has already attained in art and literature, a vital influence which preserves from death.

To deny Homœopathy we must either return to the singularly changeable—some say useless—medicine of the academy, medicine of experiment, of quackery, and which, by the uncertainty of its course, tends to destroy all faith, or else we must invent new principles, the formula of which we do not suspect to-day. And it must be said, during the length of time that we have existed, nearly a century, in spite of the almost febrile mental activity of the times, no one has found this new way. After Hahnemann no denial is possible. In his system the connection

---

[2] Examples of the application of the law of similars. A frozen limb is cured by the application of snow, or the air of a cold room. Inflammation is reduced by the application of warm water. Purgatives are employed in cases of diarrhœa and dysentery. Vomiting is stopped by drinking warm water or by an emetic of mustard, and lastly vaccine, which is not in any respect the opposite, but in every respect like small-pox, is used, indeed legally enforced, by the old school.

[3] This law is deduced from the observation of facts; it is a general one, in so far as no cure is effected without its application.

[4] The study of all our pathogeneses begins by that of the mental, moral, or psychical state in certain physical conditions. One of these conditions being given, the other is necessarily deduced from it. This study, applied to infancy, gives us the means of modifying its psychical tendencies, or of improving the race.

of the different parts is so close and binding that it is not to be wondered at that a mind which sincerely tries to become acquainted with it should be seriously impressed. Hering, the medical student, his knife in his hand, wished lightly to make this acquaintance; but he soon discovered that it was instead a study which one must follow carefully. At a single glance he was struck with the importance of this event in the medical world. He saw not only what we have said, but many other things besides, all the advantages of the position, a victory already acquired, which it was only necessary to organize. This life-work was spread out before him from that very hour.

Armed with the motto, "I can do nothing unless God helps me," he risked his career, and before the faculty which was to decide his fate he dared to throw down the gauntlet in the name of the medicine of the future. This faith never contradicted itself; it inspired him. After a few preliminaries in the way of observations and controversy, he makes his first appearance through the study of *Lachesis*, a production sufficient in itself to insure him the reputation of a master.

For many years he made personal confirmations of the provings made by Hahnemann, verifying them and adding to them new symptoms. His part in the great struggle was determined by the certainty which he thus obtained for the superiority of our Materia Medica, and of the great benefit which our school derives from it. He gave his life to add to the precious discoveries which are comprised in our Materia Medica. If a cure or new symptom was reported to him he made careful note of it, but subjected it to severe examination. When verified, it became new material. He adopted nothing which had not been subjected to positive proof. His horizon, always enlarging, widened by sure degrees. But so great success never caused a single fibre of his heart to contract. Whoever knocked at his door was welcomed kindly upon the threshold, for Dr. Hering joyfully opened to all the doors of the sanctuary of science. And everyone, receiving more than he had hoped to find, went away with his wishes gratified and his heart ennobled by his great example. It is not because the American people were credulous, or lacked a practical spirit, but rather because they were so eminently practical that they listened willingly to this man, who was born a physician of full growth, and that he accomplished under this influence the results which we know. Either as adviser, or associated invisibly with all our struggles, which are crowned with success, Hering, in his turn, did full justice to his numerous fellow-workers, attributing to himself but a small part of the results. And the names of Dunham, Gosewich, Gray, Guernsey, Haynel, Hull, Jeanes, Kitchen, Lippe, Neidhard, Pulte, Raue, Wells, Wesselhœft, Williamson and many others were always mentioned by him with respect and enthusiasm.

Dr. Hering's conversation, accustomed as he was to write with precision and brevity, was not constrained in private life. It was enlivened by piquant and witty remarks, and he sometimes employed sarcasm, although he rarely made use of this weapon. He enjoyed a joke, and his easy and natural narration of different events, joined to a slightly bantering air, lent a great charm to a sweet and sonorous voice.

Thus, for a half century, Dr. Hering worked, gathering together treasures of science, which he has bequeathed to us, as if the duty of doing good was the only thing which kept him on this earth. A man of a profound and sincere religious faith, as a Homœopath, having faith in the cause, and feeling himself endowed with a special mission, he has fulfilled his task, worthily, nobly, grandly, for the good of man and to the glory of God, in whose peace he is still living.

MEETING OF CANADIAN HOMŒOPATHIC INSTITUTE.

At a meeting of the Canadian Homœopathic Institute, held at St. Thomas, on Wednesday, October 27th, 1880, the President, Dr. John Hall, proposed that the sad subject of the demise of Dr. Constantine Hering be considered, and as an introductory read a most pleasing and touching memorial written by Dr. Edward Bayard, of New York, after which he offered the following resolutions which were unanimously carried:

WHEREAS, It has pleased the Almighty Disposer of all events to remove from his post of long and self-sacrificing labors our late venerable friend and colleague, Dr. Constantine Hering; and,

WHEREAS, He has been greatly endeared to us by his many qualities of mind and heart; by his eminent abilities and patient toil in searching after truth; by his keen faculty of observation and apprehension in its acquisition; by the tenacity, courage and ability with which he held and defended what he esteemed the truth; by his large accumulation of knowledge and extensive experience; by his noble simplicity of character and the unswerving devotion of his great talents and influence through a long life to the advocacy and extension of Homœopathy, agreeably to the principles and rules given us by the illustrious founder of our art in his *Organon;* wherefore be it

Resolved, That we and the homœopathic profession throughout the world have suffered by his death an incalculable loss; and,

Resolved, That at this first meeting of the Canadian Institute of Homœopathy since the decease of our departed friend, we tender our cordial expression of sorrow and sincere sympathy in this bereavement to the family and friends of the deceased.

MARYLAND STATE SOCIETY.

At the annual meeting of the Maryland State Homœopathic Medical Society, held in Baltimore, November 10th,

1880, Dr. F. R. McManus, of Baltimore, offered a motion that a committee of one be appointed by the president of the Society to prepare a proper notice and resolutions in regard to the loss the profession and humanity had sustained in the death of Dr. Constantine Hering. The motion was carried, and the president appointed Dr. F. R. McManus for that duty.

At the next meeting, November 11th, Dr. McManus said:

Mr. President and Gentlemen:—

Forty-three years ago, this very month of November, I had the pleasure to make the acquaintance of Constantine Hering, M.D., by calling upon him. I was then visiting Philadelphia preliminary to my investigation of Homœopathy. I explained to him the object of my visit, and was listened to with kind patience and advantage to myself; and I availed of and profited by the instructions I received from him. My visit having occurred during his office consultation hour, I noticed that he frequently made reference to his books for aid in the selection of his remedies. I mentioned this to him, and he replied, "You will find out that no man can carry Homœopathy in his head, every case being different and a subject for study." I oftentimes afterwards derived aid from his suggestions and advice when consulting him about serious and obstinate cases.

By the splendor of his mind, and his indefatigable labors in the cause of medical science, he has created his own monument, to perpetuate his fame and his worth to future ages, and a stimulus to ambition in all who are engaged in his high, honorable, and responsible calling.

It has often been remarked—in religion, in medicine, in law, in politics, in the arts and sciences—of some distinguished individual, that "*his* place can never be filled as *he* filled it." If ever such a remark proved to be true, it may be proclaimed in regard to our late distinguished colleague, Dr. Constantine Hering.

I beg to offer, in the name and behalf of this Society, the following resolutions:

Resolved, By the Maryland State Homœopathic Medical Society, that, in common with our medical colleagues of Philadelphia, and of the world, we have heard of the demise of our late colleague in the practice of medicine, the venerable Constantine Hering, M.D., who could justly be called "the Father of Homœopathy in America," who left us, filled with profound knowledge, and a master in his profession; and that we regard his loss not only as one to an especial locality, but to the whole medical world and to all suffering humanity.

Resolved, That our heartfelt sympathies be tendered to his bereaved surviving wife and relatives, and to his surviving medical colleagues of Philadelphia.

The resolutions were unanimously adopted.

WEST JERSEY SOCIETY MEETING.

At a meeting of the West Jersey Homœopathic Medical Society, held February 16th, 1881, the following preamble and resolutions were adopted as offered by a committee consisting of Drs. S. H. Quint, E. M. Howard, and M. F. Middleton:

WHEREAS, It has pleased an All-Wise Providence to remove by death, in the fulness of his years, our distinguished colleague, Dr. Constantine Hering,

Resolved, That the West Jersey Homœopathic Medical Society, in honor of his memory, place upon record our sincere appreciation of the very eminent services he has rendered to the cause of Homœopathy, and our deep sorrow that the medical profession has lost the counsels of so great and good a man.

Resolved, That we recognize in his life an example worthy of emulation in its devotion to the cause of science and Homœopathy, and in his death that of one who has filled the full period of man's life, with a noble life's work, which seems to have left nothing undone.

AMERICAN INSTITUTE MEMORIAL SERVICE.

At the thirty-fourth session of the American Institute of Homœopathy, held at Brighton Beach, N. Y., a special hour was set apart on the fourth day of the session, June 17th, 1881, for a memorial service in honor of Dr. Constantine Hering.

The necrologist, Dr. Henry D. Paine, of New York, had presented the following memoir:

Constantine Hering, M.D., of Philadelphia.

No memorial that can be embraced in the circumscribed limits of these brief chronicles of our departed colleagues, can adequately set forth the character and services of this eminent and venerable apostle of Homœopathy, whose death, since the last annual session of the Institute, has affected our whole fraternity with a profound emotion. Wherever Homœopathy has any standing in the community, the name of Dr. Hering has been known, for a generation at least, as that of one of its most distinguished expositors and propagandists, while thousands who have shared the privilege of his personal acquaintance, or having received instruction from his lips, not only venerate him as a master, but loved him as a friend and father.

To give a full account of his honorable career, or even a summary of his great services to the cause to which the greater part of his long life was devoted, would far exceed the object and the limits allowed to these reports, as well as the time and ability of the writer. An extended eulogium in this relation is unneccessary, in view of the memorial service which is to be held in his honor before the close of this meeting. All that will be attempted in these remarks is a brief sketch of the principal circumstances of the life of Dr. Hering, every turn of which must henceforth be of interest to every member of the Institute, with whose foundation and early history he was so closely identified. It was expected that, in the preparation of this narrative, the compiler would have had the assistance of some one whose knowledge of these events, derived from a long and intimate familiarity of them, would have more thoroughly secured its accurate performance. Although disappointed in this expectation, it is hoped that the following compendium, though imperfect, is substantially correct.

Constantine Hering was a native of Saxony, and first saw the light in the town of Oschatz, on New Year's day, 1800. His father was a man of liberal views on education, and an advocate of the system of instruction that has since become a characteristic of German educational policy. As may be supposed, young Constantine was given every advantage, and he worked his way through the successive grades of schools in a manner calculated to gain the highest praise of his preceptors. His inclination for the study of natural history was manifested at an early age. He even delighted in collecting, analyzing, and arranging specimens and examples from the different kingdoms of nature, some of which were thought worthy of acceptance by the public museums.

In due time he entered the University of Leipzig, intending to study especially with the view of becoming a physician. Having so strong a passion for the natural sciences, he soon became a favorite with some of the professors, who gave him every encouragement.

It was while resident at this seat of learning that his attention was first directed to the subject of Homœopathy, by a request from a large publishing house to write a refutation of the doctrines of Hahnemann, which were already stirring up no little commotion among the medical profession. Under the belief that this would be an easy task, and encouraged by the assurances of his teachers, he set about the work with ready confidence. The better to qualify himself for his undertaking, he wisely began by an examination of the tenets and methods that he was expected to demolish, as promulgated in Hahnemann's own writings. The result of this preliminary investigation was such as to cause his abandonment of the engagement, after a struggle of several months, greatly to the chagrin of his family and the disgust of his former medical friends. Further examination satisfied him of the truth of the new ideas and completed his conversion.

These proceedings sadly darkened his prospects at Leipzig, as they lost him the patronage he had enjoyed by the favor of his preceptors, and he became seriously embarrassed in the prosecution of his studies. Having, however, received from one of his family the means for the purpose, he removed to Würzburg, where, on the 22d of March, 1826, he succeeded in obtaining his degree, notwithstanding that in his inaugural thesis, "De Medicina Futura," he unhesitatingly espoused the cause of Homœopathy.

For some time after graduation he was occupied in teaching; but after some months he was offered an appointment as a member of a scientific expedition to South America, of which the King was patron. His love for natural history induced him to accept the position. While absent upon this expedition he fulfilled his scientific duties with entire satisfaction to the promoters of the scheme. At the same time, however, he did not neglect his study of Homœopathy—practicing his art as opportunity offered—but especially in making and conducting original provings of new drugs, in which work he had already done valuable service before leaving home. The accounts of his provings, etc., were sent to and published in the *Homœopathic Archives*. When this became known to the government an official intimation was dispatched that he should, in future, devote himself exclusively to the objects of the expedition. On receipt of this order he speedily resolved to sever his connection with the enterprise and devote himself to the practice and cultivation of Homœopathy. He remained six years in South America, during which time he diligently prosecuted the work he had taken in hand. Especially in the number and thoroughness of the provings that he then conducted, his characteristic industry and perseverance were remarkable. His reports of Lachesis, Theridion, Caladium, Spigelia, etc., are among the classics of our Materia Medica.

While practicing in Paramaribo he had for a patient a Moravian missionary, Dr. Bute, who had been sent to Surinam. He was dangerously ill with spotted fever—exceedingly dangerous in that climate—but recovered under Dr. Hering's treatment. He was so amazed at his own unexpected cure, and so grateful withal, that he began to crave a knowledge of the wonderful medical system, and from being a patient he became a student of his preserver. After his return to this country, in 1831, Dr. Bute practiced in Nazareth, Pa. On the outbreak of the cholera in Philadelphia in the following year, he went to that city to assist in the care of the sick.

Finding the demand for his services so great, he wrote to Dr. Hering, urging him to come and join him. The appeal was effectual, but Dr. Hering did not arrive till the spring of 1833. He associated himself with Dr. Bute in Vine street, Philadelphia, an arrangement which continued with mutual satisfaction until, from enfeebled health, Dr. Bute was obliged to retire, some years later. Dr. Hering did not introduce Homœopathy into Pennsylvania. This had already been done before his arrival by Dr. Detwiller, Dr. Ihm, Dr. Bute, Dr. Freytag, and others, and he found himself surrounded by a small but intelligent and earnest band of adherents of the system. His reputation had preceded his advent, and he was welcomed with great cordiality and enthusiasm. In December of the same year he joined with a number of others in organizing the first school of instruction in homœopathic therapeutics in the world, under the name of the "North American Academy of the Homœopathic Healing Art," to be located at Allentown. Dr. Hering was to be president and principal professor. A charter was obtained, funds were raised, buildings erected, a faculty appointed, students taught and graduated, and a vast deal of other work in behalf of the great medical reform, which cannot even be alluded to here. In all this, the leading spirit and the valiant hand was Dr. Hering's. The history of Homœopathy in this country cannot be fully understood without reading the narration of the "Allentown Academy," as it was generally called, of which an instructive sketch may be found in the second volume of the Transactions of the World's Convention of 1876. The faculty continued its labors till 1842, when, after a useful but brief career, the enterprise was discontinued. Dr. Hering returned to Philadelphia, but the same untiring zeal and industry never deserted him. He has ever striven with an earnest purpose and an intelligent judgment to develop and extend the resources of the Hahnemannian therapeutics. In 1844 he presided at the organization of the American Institute of Homœopathy, composed at first of a few but zealous converts, but which he lived to see embracing many hundreds of members.

Apart from his scientific, literary, and professional labors, his life during the last thirty years presents but few incidents of prominence. With strong domestic habits, and a deep conviction of his duty and mission, he was content to carry on the work of his vocation without ostentation, enjoying the respectful deference of his disciples, as they sought information or advice, more than the applause of the noisy multitude.

Our venerable colleague lived to a ripened age, and had seen rich fruits from his unselfish and sometimes unappreciated labors, and he finally sunk to his rest July 23d, 1880, with the calmness and composure of one who has performed his task with diligence and honesty of purpose.

The President, Dr. John W. Dowling, of New York, in his address at the opening of the session, concluded it with these words:

I cannot close without reference to the great loss the entire homœopathic profession throughout the world has met with in the death, since we last met, of Dr. Constantine Hering, President of the convention which originated the organization of the American Institute of Homœopathy. In the midst of labors from which, for over fifty years, he had never rested, he quietly fell asleep. I could hardly feel that this was an occasion for mourning, for he had been with us more than half a score of years beyond the allotted time of man; and this long, this spotless life had been one of usefulness and unremitting labor in the cause he loved to the very end. The results of the labor of his later years are living, and will live to aid us and those who come after us in the work to which our lives are being devoted. We should rejoice that through all his long and active life not a truthful word had ever been uttered that could reflect on his character as a man, as a Christian, and that at the last his death was peaceful, calm, and free from protracted suffering. We should rejoice that his troubles, for he had sorrows—sorrows hard to bear, too —are at an end, and that there is before him an eternity of happiness, for I believe of such as he is the Kingdom of Heaven. Others of us, noble men and true, dear to their families, friends and clientage, have died since we last met together, but this pioneer was dear to us all, honored by us all, and he will be remembered by us all, and our children will be taught to honor his memory.

At the opening of the memorial service, Dr. Henry D. Paine spoke as follows:

On this occasion our thoughts naturally recur to that great bereavement which our school, especially this Institute, has suffered since our last session, and in commemoration of which, it is understood, we are now called together. The name of Constantine Hering is so closely identified with the history of Homœopathy, his figure stands out so prominently in the progress of our art, and his writings have exerted so wide an influence in its development, that his death, though at the end of so long a career, could not but produce a profound impression throughout our extremest ranks. It is eminently proper that an event so important and impressive should be distinguished by a special solemnity. My feeble tribute to his memory has been already offered.

There are those present far better able to speak, not only of his public and lasting services to the cause to which so much of his life was devoted, but of those rare virtues that shone so conspicuously in his private relations. I am anxious to hear from them.

Dr. J. C. Morgan, of Philadelphia, then said:

Having already exhausted such reflections as seem worthy of our deceased colleague, Dr. Hering, in connection with our two Philadelphia meetings, I had thought to remain silent here. It may explain the backwardness of other Philadelphia members, perhaps, to say that this is the case with many of them: they feel, too, that they have passed the subject of his death into the more sacred precincts of the memory. The revival of it here by us, you will therefore understand, is attended with something like the pain that one has in the uncovering of an old and partly healed wound, or one, at least, which has become quiet; my colleagues from Philadelphia have, however, requested me to introduce this subject of such national interest. Permit me, then, to make reference to my personal acquaintance with Dr. Hering. I will commence with one point, very important to me personally, by saying that in boyhood, when Dr. Hering was yet in the vigor of his youth, I was taken to him for the purpose of medical treatment by a friend of his, one of his early supporters, and also a friend of my own, Mrs. Rev. Dr. Bedell, and my recollection of the prescriptions made by Dr. Hering is that they were eminently successful. We had no further personal relations for very many years. In the meantime I had become a physician of the old school, later of the homœopathic school. Even then my acquaintance with Dr. Hering was not renewed; this was partly owing to the fact that those from whom I had just derived my impressions of Homœopathy were his opponents; as Dr. Helmuth so finely mentioned last night in his poem, "They have had disagreements in Philadelphia, the city of brotherly love." It so happened that I learned my Homœopathy along with antagonism to Dr. Hering. I was taught to believe that he was a visionary, to use the words of my informant, "an eccentric." I, therefore, in all the pride of my youth, and with my but half regenerate allopathic mind, refrained from making his acquaintance, and I will add that I am heartily ashamed to have to say it. I was, however, introduced to Dr. Hering without my own knowledge, and in a way most characteristic of himself.

My home was in Illinois, a thousand miles from his. I made a two weeks' proving of Gelsemium, published in Dr. Shipman's *Journal of Materia Medica.* Dr. Hering's peculiarity was that he would seize upon provings wherever he found them, and with the skill of the anatomist would dissect them, and determine their essential points. It was my good fortune, therefore, to meet Dr. Hering's skill in the discussion of my proving of that drug. That is to say, he found therein the now historical symptom, viz., that depressing emotions produce a tendency to diarrhœic disturbance of the intestinal canal.

It was observed by me in April, 1861, on reading the telegrams of the firing on Fort Sumpter; these so disturbed me that I gave up the proving, and stated it as a fact that the telegrams produced the effect. But Dr. Hering, with the sagacity which was so peculiar to him, with that keen eye and that analytical skill in Materia Medica in which he was *facile princeps*, seized upon the very thing which I thought was vitiating the proving; said he, "There is the grand characteristic of the drug." Years later, after I had returned to Philadelphia and become acquainted with him and others associated with him, I found that it had been erected into what is now called a key-note. He gave me back my finding; and there are a thousand other such gems that we owe to Dr. Hering. In this way, then, he had become acquainted with me, and when I met him in the college, he was prepared, and I was prepared to form, as we did form, a warm and sympathetic friendship. I soon found out that I had been utterly misled in regard to the character—the intellectual character, I mean, of Dr. Hering; no one dared breathe anything other than profound respect for his moral character. I have to say here, ladies and gentlemen, that I believe Dr. Hering has been unfortunately misunderstood in this respect. He had his own peculiarities; to some he may have seemed, perhaps, sometimes disagreeable; those who have suffered from that have, no doubt, buried the recollection of it in his grave; but the idea of Dr. Hering being backward in attending to the progress of research and science, the idea that Dr. Hering was at all a visionary, in the bad sense, is a great mistake, a great unconscious slander upon the memory of his intellectual greatness. As a matter of fact, Dr. Hering was always foremost in our school in recognizing every forward movement. There is not a single one of the recent advances in science of which he had not, before any of his co-laborers, learned something, and it has commonly happened, during the past fifteen years, that when something new came up, and I have gone to his office, I found that he had already become cognizant of the details of the subject. Some of my first information in regard to the recent revelations of the spectroscope came, to my surprise, from his lips. Whatsoever had a bearing upon Homœopathy had for him a religious savor, and appeared to him in all the sanctity of a Divine revelation; so that if he were ever intolerant, it was with the inspiration of the Crusader, fighting for the Holy Sepulchre against the infidel, or of the Covenanter, defending his Bible in the mountain passes of his native land.

My acquaintance with Dr. Hering, in a social way, and more especially in relation to the college faculty, was exceedingly pleasant as a rule. We did not always agree, that could not be expected; but throughout we maintained that mutual respect and affection which I am glad to recall to-day. The faculty meetings, held usually in his office, in deference to his years, were really club meetings in their social aspect. They were all that we desire in a social club, and he was the illuminator of the club, always ready with some matter of interest and novelty, always ready to give of his rich store of medical information, always ready with some new point in general science with which to interest our minds, and valuable, either in society or in our professional duties; many a key-note, as we call, it in the Materia Medica, have I received from him in this way. Indeed, it was my practice, in these frequent convocations with Hering, Guernsey, Lippe, Raue, etc., to have a little memorandum book and my lead pencil ready, and often as these golden nuggets of homœopathic experience fell from the lips of these experts, I recorded them; and I think no one furnished them more frequently than Dr. Hering. This note-book became part and parcel of my capital in professional work. The matter that I am speaking of I would not part with for any consideration. Such, then, was our relation in the faculty. We all looked upon him, as a matter of course, as our *paterfamilias*, and he so regarded himself; would sometimes, indeed, claim a little supremacy, and thought that he might be privileged to talk to the rest of us as to the "youngsters of the faculty."

Once it was said to him, "Doctor Hering, these youngsters are all about forty years of age and upwards." "Boys of forty!" he exclaimed, in jocular contempt, and so gained his point; we were always willing enough to be considered by him as "boys of forty," and in this way we got along happily, yielding to his supremacy and always profiting by it. In his last days, fellow-members of the Institute, Dr. Hering's heart-life seemed to undergo a special development; the Philadelphia members here present understand what I mean. He was born with the century; the first day of January, 1800, witnessed his advent into this world; and as the year 1880 dawned, he reached his eightieth anniversary. Dr. Hering realized now that the end of his time was nearing. He made all arrangements in regard to his literary work—and that work, let me assure the profession, is in able hands, and will be issued as he would have it. This done, he seemed to cling, as never before, to those who had surrounded him during the past years. He desired that we should come often to see him; to some, as to me, he said, "Here is my study (many of you know it—on the second floor of his house), you have the entrée at all times—come right up stairs and knock." This was, of course, a great privilege, of which we were not slow to avail ourselves, and to myself they were occasions of great satisfaction. The clinging of the dear old man to these friends, and to me among the rest, at this time, was touching, and I, for one, tried to be faithful to his last days, my only regret being that I had not seen him for three weeks at the time of his decease. I think that every one of our members from Philadelphia will bear me out in saying that the kindliest recollections of Dr. Hering are those of the last six months of his life.

Dr. J. P. Dake, of Nashville, next spoke as follows, having first made a motion, which was carried, limiting each speaker to five minutes:

Mr. President:—I desire to say a few words in regard to the character and labors of our deceased brother, the father of Homœopathy in America, Dr. Constantine Hering. And in speaking with regard to him it is understood, perhaps, by all who are present, that I was among those who differed with Dr. Hering, pointedly and decidedly upon several matters, and I feel that it is therefore the more fitting that I should, upon this occasion, say something. In Dr. Hering I recognized, as I doubt not every one here present did recognize, a genius in medicine, and not only a genius in medicine, but a master-workman in medicine. Rich in new thoughts, he was industrious in the application and working out of those thoughts. Dr. Hering has added to our Materia Medica many things of great value. Those things will remain, and the passing years will increase their importance. They will be comprehended more and more. But Dr. Hering was mortal; Dr. Hering was fallible; not all of his opinions can we accept, nor can we appreciate the value of all that he has added to the Materia Medica; but we, in the homœopathic school, have been taught to think independently, to think for ourselves, to weigh all things and form our opinions in regard to them. We learned early, as did Hahnemann, who taught us to disregard authority when authority was not in accord with facts and with science. Therefore, in taking the works and products left to us by Dr. Hering, it becomes us not to accept them as revelations from above, as perfect in all respects, but to accept them as contributions to truth, and opinions put before us for our consideration and our use, in the light that is given us from all quarters. We are not expected, therefore, to accept all of Dr. Hering's works and all of his teachings as authoritative, not to be differed from at all. What was defective and erroneous in the opinions and works of Dr. Hering will pass away. No amount of veneration for him, no amount of appreciation for his genius, nor his industry, will require us to hold on to those things which experience and increasing light and knowledge do not endorse and sustain.

Dr. H. M. Smith, of New York City, was the next speaker; he said:

Dr. Dake seems to have been cut short in the expression of his feelings in regard to Dr. Hering. When he moved that the time be limited to five minutes to each speaker, he must have known that he could not have expressed his feelings in so short a time. I could not imagine any occasion on which I could not have something to say about Dr. Constantine Hering, but in five minutes I don't know where to begin any more than I know where I shall end. I can only give expression to my feelings and my veneration for that man. As a young man in the profession, I cannot but think kindly of the many happy and instructive interviews I have had with him. When the *American Homœopathic Review* was in existence, we received a great many contributions and a great deal of assistance from Dr. Hering, and it was our custom to spend one or two days with him every summer. Dr. Carroll Dunham, Dr. P. P. Wells and myself went on there to meet the homœopathic physicians from various sections of the country, and in his study, that Dr. Morgan speaks of, the recollections come back to me of many pleasant and instructive hours, and it is pleasant to recall the merry laugh and cheery face of Dr. Hering, when giving us some information or relating an anecdote. I went in one day to see him especially in regard to Digitalis. He had written an article in the *Review* on Digitalis, the second part of which was never published. He was never ready to publish it because some proofs were wanting he was obliged to get from a convent or monastery in Italy. After some casual remarks I said, "Dr. Hering, I came to see you especially in regard to that article on Digitalis; when can you give me half an hour?" "Quarter of four to-morrow morning," said he. Accordingly, the following morning I was in Dr. Hering's library. The old gentleman slept there. He had arisen from his couch, and was reading. He directed me to sit down, and to write what he dictated to me. That was the way that Dr. Hering worked, careful to obtain sufficient proof before making statements as facts, and always ready to assist everybody who sought information.

Dr. F. R. McManus, of Baltimore, said:

Mr. President and Gentlemen:

I wish to state a little incident that occurred in the early part of my homœopathic investigation and career. I went from Baltimore to Philadelphia in search of an allopathic physician who had practiced both systems, and I found one; I went to another physician afterwards, who was Dr. Hering. I introduced myself to Dr. Hering as Dr. McManus, of Baltimore. I told him the object of my visit, and he said, "I am very glad to see you, but you have happened to call at a time when I am attending to my consultations; take a seat there for a few moments, when I will talk to you." Well, I waited until he got through, and I said to him, "Doctor, I noticed you referring to your books and volumes from the library in every case in which you prescribe." "Yes," said he, "and no man will be the right kind of a homœopathic physician who does not do it, for there never was a brain, in my opinion, that could ever contain the one-hundredth part of what it ought to hold to enable one to practice without studying every case; every case is a new one." I told him it seemed to be a work of a great deal of labor. "Well," said he, "when you come to study Homœopathy, you will find out the difference in the two schools in regard to the means and facility to practice, because an allopathic physician can prescribe for forty cases where a homœopath would hardly be able to prescribe for two or three, or perhaps one." I merely mention this because it will stimulate the younger members of the profession to individualize and study their cases closely, as it has always stimulated me in my forty-three years of homœopathic investigation and practice. It has been to my advantage to do so, and, of course, much to the advantage of Homœopathy. I hold his memory in the sweetest recollection, and I am glad that I cannot say anything that will throw the slightest cloud upon his efficiency as a physician, or his adherence to Hahnemann as a homœopathist.

Dr. T. C. Duncan, of Chicago, next spoke as follows:

Mr. President and Gentlemen:

I cannot allow this opportunity to pass without presenting my deep regret for the death of our distinguished father of Homœopathy in the United States, and the impression made upon me by his loss will deepen as the years glide on. I think the one thing that will impress the profession more than anything else, is the exhaustive power of Dr. Hering in gathering together the fund of information that was scattered here and there in our medical writings. He was the one individual of the whole world of Homœopathy that gathered together all facts, and it is perfectly wonderful what he has accumulated, and it seems to me very proper that some one should take this up and continue it.

Various facts are coming out bearing upon Materia Medica and Therapeutics that will be lost except some one gather them together as did Hering. Dr. Hering has made a noble beginning. He has, I believe, in his library, or did have them at the time of the Centennial, every fact bearing upon Homœopathic Materia Medica extant. His memory will be bright forever. I hold him in high regard, and his influence upon the cause in the United States I think we cannot too highly appreciate.

Dr. Fisher, of Montreal, Canada, said:

I will not take up the time very long, but still, while we are on the subject, I may mention that before I commenced practice on this side of the Atlantic, on my way back from Europe, I called at Philadelphia and saw Dr. Hering, and one of the things which he then mentioned and which I thought characteristic, I was very much struck with, and I have often thought of it since. He said, "When I come to the bed-side of a patient I very often feel like a fool." Now, such has been the result of my own experience on many occasions. I have often looked back and thought of that fact, which has encouraged me to go on, notwithstanding I felt for a moment like a fool. There was another thing struck me at the time somewhat. We were speaking about somebody else, another medical man. "Well," said he, "he is a queer fellow, but we are all queer." Well, that also struck me, and I have often thought since that most of men are dreadfully frightened by what the world calls eccentricity. Now, it has often occurred to me that no man can be really original without being more or less eccentric. He may be eccentric without being original, but the effect of that eccentricity, no doubt, keeps a good many of us from doing things which we would otherwise like to do.

Dr. I. T. Talbot, of Boston, spoke next:

I cannot let an occasion like this go by without dropping one tribute of memory to a great man, for I believe Dr. Hering was really great. The memory of his kindness to students and young men, the memory of the kindness of Dr. Hering to myself, who had no special claims upon him in any way, is pleasant to contemplate. Soon after I had graduated, about to visit Europe, I was recommended by Dr. Carroll Dunham to get some letters from Dr. Hering to physicians living abroad, and assuring me that he would be willing to give them, I called upon him in Philadelphia. He was busy at the time, and said, "Come to me to-night and I will be happy to see you." "At what time shall I come?" "Well, I shall get through my work about 10 o'clock; come then." I went there. He had two friends with him who were also acquainted in Europe and whom he had brought there for the special purpose of seeing me. From 10 P.M. until 3 A.M. was spent in talking of European affairs—of what could be of benefit to me in my trip abroad—a sacrifice on his part of sleep, of rest, for an entire stranger, which we could hardly suppose any one would make on such an occasion. Having made a list of letters which he proposed to give, he the next day sent me six to prominent persons in Europe, old Dr. Stapf being one of them.

The letters were of great service to me, and the kindness extended by each of them I place as a tribute to the memory of Dr. Hering, and I venerate that great heart, that noble spirit, that could give so much to a young man without any claims upon him.

Dr. P. G. Valentine, of St. Louis, then rose and said:

It seems that what has been spoken in reference to Dr. Hering this morning has been mostly of the nature of personal reminiscences of him. I think that only once was it my pleasure to meet him, and that was when attending the Centennial meeting in Philadelphia. As he entered the door and passed down the aisle he was cheered by all the members present. He came upon the stand and took his seat beside the others there, the English gentlemen, etc. But my acquaintance with Dr. Hering was entirely through the Materia Medica. I wish to say that through that work I have learned to venerate and admire him. The question with us in St. Louis, when any point in Materia Materia is raised, is, what does Dr. Hering say? I have no personal recollections of him. The only way I learned to love him was through the Materia Medica.

Dr. M. M. Eaton, of Cincinnati, said:

It has not been my privilege to have had a personal acquaintance with Dr. Hering, and I can only say that I feel that one of our greatest men has passed away. I feel that he has left a record behind him worthy of emulation, and it struck me that we should profit by the example which he has set, that we should each endeavor to do something to add to the storehouse of knowledge for those who may come after. It strikes me that upon occasions of this kind we should make such resolves as to our future course as may benefit mankind.

Dr. S. R. Beckwith, of Cincinnati, said:

I would like to hear from our President.

Dr. J. W. Dowling, of New York, here said:

The President has already spoken in his Annual Address all that he can say on the subject of the death of our dear friend, Dr. Hering, and he has also alluded to others who have died. Those words are on record. I hardly think that I would say anything different or add anything to what I said upon that occasion.

This to me has been an exceedingly interesting and solemn service. I feel that it has been so to all, and I hope that when others of us depart, the members who are left behind will be able to say as many kind and good words with regard to us as have been said of Dr. Hering, our departed brother.

Dr. Wm. von Gottschalk, of Providence, was the last speaker; he said:

Mr. President and Fellow-Members:—

I wish to say a few words of Dr. Hering as a German. As there are no Germans here to speak about him or in his memory, I thought it was finally my duty, after so many different Americans have spoken in the praise of that most peculiar man, to give my tribute to his character in a different way. I saw Dr. Hering first in 1852, when I was an old school practitioner in the city of New York. I was then induced to try Homœopathy. I still looked upon Homœopathy as a peculiar quackery, and I wanted to see the greatest quack of them all. Dr. Hering being a countryman of mine, I visited him, and he struck me peculiarly. He encouraged me in Homœopathy more than any other man I ever met, and he probably was the sole cause of my becoming a complete homœopath, and I owe to him and to his influence my position in Homœopathy to-day. What I want to allude to now in particular is his distinguishing German characteristics. As a scholar he was a thorough German, and in his family relations he was a thorough German. I know that when in 1876 I came to his house, the moment I entered he called me by name. He called me the Yankee-Dutchman, and wanted me to sit down and take a glass of wine with him. Now, in response to his request, I went out into the back yard of his house, where there was a little arbor, and under this arbor the table spread for the family, and as a friend I sat down there to speak to him.

On the table were familiar German dishes, and the hospitality of a German was extended. It was a delight to be there and receive the hospitality of that man. He was a true German in all his habits to the very last moments of his life. I wish somebody else, better able and better qualified in the use of the English than I am, would pay a proper tribute to him in this regard. You see other Germans generally become Americanized. Dr. Hering always adhered to his Fatherland habits, a thing which I have not done. But I respect him for this peculiar characteristic, that in all his life he remained as he was born —a German.

TRIBUTE FROM ITALY.

Dr. Pompili, of Rome, on behalf of the Italian practitioners of Homœopathy, has requested the publication of the following tribute, to which is appended a translation kindly furnished by Dr. Horace Howard Furness:

Constantino Hering

Artis Medicæ Doctori eximio

post Hahnemannum Magistrum

suæ Scholæ principi ac decori præcipuo

qui

doctrina editisque de Homœopathia voluminibus

ubique terrarum

veri cupidos docuit, docet et docebit

Joachimus Pompilius in Urbe M.D.

suo Italiæque Homœopathicorum nomine

ob tantum Virum amissum mœrentissimus

Honoris Memoriæque ergo

inscribit et dicat.

To

CONSTANTINE HERING

THE EXCELLENT DOCTOR OF MEDICINE

NEXT AFTER THE MASTER, HAHNEMANN,

THE CHIEF AND PRE-EMINENT ORNAMENT OF HIS SCHOOL

WHO

IN WORD AND IN PRINT BY HIS DISCOVERIES IN HOMŒOPATHY

TEACHES, HAS TAUGHT AND WILL TEACH

ALL WHO ARE DESIROUS OF TRUTH THROUGHOUT THE WORLD

THIS TRIBUTE

TO THE HONOR AND TO THE MEMORY OF A MAN THUS LOST

AND

MOST DEEPLY MOURNED

IS BY

JOACHIM POMPILI, M.D.,

IN HIS OWN NAME AND IN THE NAME OF

THE PRACTITIONERS OF HOMŒOPATHY IN ITALY

INSCRIBED AND DEDICATED.

OBITUARY NOTICES.

Of the numerous obituary notices which appeared in the daily papers, and in the various medical journals throughout the world, only a few of the foreign ones are published as indicating the esteem and veneration in which the subject of this Memoir was held in other than the two great English-speaking nations, and especially in his own dear fatherland.

In *La Reforma Medica*, organ of the Mexican Homœopathic Institute, published in Mexico, the following* appeared in the issue of September 25th, 1880:

When, full of satisfaction, in the preceding number of this organ, we gave to our readers the statistical data showing the progressive march of Homœopathy in our neighboring Republic, how far were we from imagining, that at that time had already descended to the grave the illustrious physician, the venerable apostle, introducer and propagator of the medical reform in the United States, the eminent man, who, for his great works in behalf of our cause, was called the Hahnemann of America, and to whom the love and veneration of all the homœopathists of that nation had given the no less valuable and significant title of "Father Hering."

Constantine Hering died on the 23d of July, in the eighty-first year of his age. His name is intimately connected with the history of the introduction and development of the Hahnemannian doctrines in the United States, and to try to give here his biography would be as much as to write said history. There is not a city, town, village, or abode, where Homœopathy is known,

---

* Translated from the Spanish by Dr. E. Fornias, of Philadelphia.

which is not also familiar with the name of Dr. Hering, whose domestic work on Homœopathy, printed by the thousands and in numerous editions, translated into the principal languages, has contributed in a profitable manner to the diffusion of this modern system of medicine. His fruitful studies and experiments with the snake poisons, which, thanks to him, are to-day converted into valuable therapeutic agents; his constant efforts in the revision and perfection of our Materia Medica; his absolute devotion to the great work of medical regeneration and reform; his writings and works which may be called classic; his exemplary life and great civic virtues make Constantine Hering a grand figure in the school of homœopathic medicine, an example to follow, and his loss an irreparable one, which will be lamented by all who respect science and who care for the public welfare.

The Mexican Homœopathic Institute earnestly unites in condolence with the homœopathic profession, and offers its modest tribute to the imperishable name and memory of Dr. Constantine Hering.

In the *Allgemeine Homœopathische Zeitung*, published in Leipzig, in the issue of August 24th, 1880, appeared the following

Todesanzeige.

Was im Anfange dieses Jahres sich als falsches Gerücht erwies, ist jetzt zur traurigen Wirklichkeit geworden, der Altmeister Constantin Hering in Philadelphia hat der Natur seinen Tribut gezahlt. Er starb am Freitag, den 23. Juli, Abends 10 Uhr in seiner Wohnung, am Herzschlage, nachdem er noch wenige Stunden vorher Kranke empfangen hatte. Sein Name ist unzertrennlich mit der Geschichte der Homöopathie verwachsen. Ausgestattet mit ungewöhnlicher Geisteskraft und Energie, reich an Wissen, hat er, das glauben wir ohne Ueberhebung behaupten zu können, das Meiste zur Befestigung und

Verbreitung der von ihm erkannten homöopathischen Wahrheit beige=
tragen. Ein echter Paulus, zog er über den Ocean und unter Mühen
und Entbehrungen predigte er die neue Lehre. Und am Abend seines
Lebens hatte er die Freude, dieselbe in seinem neuen Vaterlande in
fester und geachteter Stellung und von Tausenden von Aerzten aus=
geübt zu sehen. Deß ungeachtet gönnte er sich keine Ruhe, sondern
war bis zum letzten Augenblicke unausgesetzt thätig. Der Tod über=
raschte ihn bei der Revision des dritten Bandes seines Hauptwerkes
"Guiding Symptoms." Sein Andenken wird, so lange es noch
homöopathische Aerzte giebt, ein unvergängliches sein. Von ihm gilt
vor Allen das Wort: „er ruhet aus von seiner Arbeit und seine
Werke folgen ihm nach!"

Einen ausführlicheren Nekrolog werden wir in einer der nächsten
Nummern bringen.

A week later appeared the following:

Nekrolog.

Einer der bedeutendsten und bekanntesten, wenn nicht berühmtesten
deutschen Bürger Philadelphias, Dr. Constantin Hering, ist am
Freitag, den 23. Juli, Abends 10 Uhr daselbst in seiner Wohnung am
Herzschlag gestorben, nur wenige Stunden nach der Krankenbehand=
lung in der Sprechstunde, also in voller Rüstung. Seit fast fünfzig
Jahren gehörte derselbe zu den hervorragendsten Männern der medi=
cinischen Wissenschaft in den Vereinigten Staaten, und nahm zugleich
in dem deutsch=amerikanischen Element eine hochgeachtete Stellung ein,
durch seine lebhafte und rastlose Theilnahme an Allem, was dessen
Stellung und Entwickelung fördern und heben konnte. Alle Bestre=
bungen im Allgemeinen für wissenschaftlichen, künstlerischen und
socialen Fortschritt hatten überhaupt in ihm einen enthusiastischen
Vertreter und thatkräftigen, liberalen Unterstützer.

Dr. Hering war am 1. Januar 1800 in Oschatz in Sachsen ge=
boren, also bei seinem Tod über 80 Jahre alt. Dabei aber war er
bis auf den letzten Tag rastlos in seinem Beruf und in seiner Wissen=

schaft thätig, und noch immer für alles Schöne, Wahre und Gute be=
geistert, wenn er sich auch in den letzten Jahren wegen Kränklichkeit
mehr als früher von dem öffentlichen Leben zurückgezogen hatte. Er
hatte sich seine geistige Jugendfrische bis zu seinem Tode erhalten.

Schon früh entwickelte der Verstorbene die größte Vorliebe für
Naturstudien, und widmete sich nach Absolvirung des Gymnasiums zu
Zittau auf der chirurgischen Akademie zu Dresden und auf der Univer=
sität Leipzig der Medicin. Die Aufgabe, eine Abhandlung g e g e n
die Homöopathie und gegen deren Hauptvertreter Hahnemann zu
schreiben, führte ihn zum tieferen Studium derselben und zur Bekeh=
rung dazu. In seiner Doktor=Dissertation "De Medicina Futura"
(über die Medicin der Zukunft) trat er für dieselbe auf. Am 23.
März 1826 wurde er Doktor der Medicin.

Er nahm alsdann eine Stelle als Lehrer der Mathematik und der
Naturwissenschaften beim Institut Blochmann zu Dresden an, erhielt
aber bald die Stelle eines Assistenten bei einer wissenschaftlichen Ex=
pedition nach Surinam in Süd=Amerika. Da ihm seine schriftstelleri=
sche Thätigkeit als Homöopath dabei untersagt wurde, resignirte er und
wurde praktischer Arzt in Paramaribo. Im Jahre 1833 auf einer
Besuchsreise nach Deutschland kam er nach Philadelphia und wurde
zum Dableiben veranlaßt, erhielt sofort eine gute Praxis und wurde
von dem deutschen Homöopathen Dr. Wesselhöft veranlaßt, mit ihm
eine homöopathische Anstalt zu Allentown zu gründen, wo er sich dann
mehrere Jahre lang aufhielt. Aus dieser Schule ging dann 1846 das
homöopathische College zu Philadelphia hervor.

Durch die Errichtung des letzteren wurde Dr. H e r i n g der eigent=
liche Begründer der Homöopathie in Amerika, unter deren Lehrern und
Schriftstellern er eine der ersten Stellungen einnahm. Er schrieb
„Ueber die Entstehung und den Fortschritt der Homöopathie" und war
Professor der Arzneikunde an jener Universität von 1846 bis 1869;
außerdem war er Gründer und Präsident des „Amerikanischen Insti=
tuts der Homöopathie." Durch seine Schrift „Der Hausarzt" machte
er sich sehr bekannt und populär. Sie war ursprünglich deutsch ge=
schrieben, wurde aber bald in das Englische, Französische, Spanische
und Italienische übersetzt. In 1869 errichtete er das amerikanische
Journal der homöopathischen "Materia Medica."

Sein Hauptwerk aber, an welchem er unausgesetzt arbeitete, führt den Titel "Guiding Symptoms" (Leitende Symptome) und soll die Charakteristik jedes Arzneimittels geben. Das Werk ist auf 12 bis 15 Bände berechnet und sind davon erst 2 Bände erschienen. Das Material für die übrigen ist aber der Art vorbereitet, daß dieselben von Anderen herausgegeben werden können. Dr. Hering war gerade mit der Revision des dritten Bandes beschäftigt, als ihn der Tod überraschte.

Der Verstorbene war ein wahres Universal=Genie und höchst originell in seinen Ansichten und Aeußerungen, dabei ein Mann strengster Ehrenhaftigkeit. An der Politik, an welcher er übrigens ebenso, wie an Allem, das größte Interesse hatte, nahm er activ wenig Antheil. Desto mehr lebte er der Wissenschaft und Kunst; mit höchster Liberalität eröffnete er sein Haus allen bedeutenden Männern der Wissenschaft und Kunst, das durch seine literarischen und musikalischen Unterhaltungen lange Zeit einen Mittelpunkt geistigen Lebens und Strebens bildete. Am alten Vaterland und an Allem, was Deutsch war, hing der Verstorbene mit enthusiastischer Vorliebe. Die deutschen Siege und die Errichtung des deutschen Reichs wurden von ihm durch ein großes Fest in seinem an einen geräumigen Garten stoßenden Haus, in der Zwölften Straße, oberhalb Arch, gefeiert.

Dr. Hering war dreimal verheirathet; seine erste Frau heirathete er in Surinam, wo sie starb und wo noch ein Sohn von ihm lebt. Seine zweite Frau war von Philadelphia, die ihm drei Kinder hinterließ, wovon noch eine Tochter lebt, die in Boston verheirathet ist. In 1845 heirathete er in Deutschland die Tochter von Dr. Buchheim, einem berühmten Arzt, die ihm acht Kinder schenkte, wovon ihn sechs nebst der Mutter überleben. Sein ältester, in Philadelphia lebender Sohn, Rudolf, ist Assistent=Ingenieur im städtischen Vermessungs= Department, und augenblicklich auf einer Reise in Europa, um die hiesigen Systeme städtischer Wasserleitungen zu studiren.

In the *Homöopathische Monatsblätter*, published in Stuttgart, the following notice appeared in the issue of October, 1880:

Nekrolog.

Mit wenigen Worten konnten wir vor vier Wochen unseren Lesern den am Abend des 23. Juli erfolgten Tod des Altmeisters der Homöopathie Dr. med. Constantin Hering mittheilen. Der Raum vieler Nummern unserer „Homöopatischen Monatsblätter" würde nicht hinreichen, um dieses Mannes Leben und Wirken, seine Verdienste um Ausbreitung und Ausbildung der Lehre Hahnemanns und seine rastlose aufopfernde Thätigkeit in dieser Richtung nach Gebühr zu beschreiben und zu würdigen.

Wir Laien haben noch dazu besondere Ursache, des Verstorbenen in dankbarer Anerkennung und Verehrung zu gedenken; denn er war es, der die Bedeutung des Laienelements in der Homöopathie aus langjähriger eigener Erfahrung kennen gelernt; er war es, der dieser seiner gewonnenen Ueberzeugung beredten Ausdruck gab in den Worten, die er der 14. Auflage seines Handbuchs, betitelt „Homöopathischer Hausarzt," voransetzte:

„Den Laienvereinen im deutschen Reiche, unserer großen Sache „größte Hoffnung, aus vollem Herzen gewidmet."

Constantin Hering war am 1. Januar 1800 in dem Städtchen Oschatz in Sachsen geboren, zeigte schon als Knabe eine große Vorliebe für Naturstudien und widmete sich, als er die Examina zur Universität bestanden hatte, dem Studium der Medicin, und zwar in Leipzig.

Hering ist einer der sehr wenigen Aerzte, welche schon mit dem Verlassen der Universität anfingen, für die Homöopathie zu wirken; veranlaßt dazu wurde er durch den bemerkenswerthen Umstand, daß er eine Abhandlung gegen die Homöopathie und gegen Hahnemann verfassen wollte. Die gründlichen Studien, die er zu diesem Zwecke machte, verwandelten den Saulus in einen Paulus und veranlaßten ihn, in seiner Doktor-Dissertation "de medicina futura" (über die zukünftige Medicin) offen für die Homöopathie aufzutreten. Trotzdem wurde er am 23. März 1826 zum Doktor der Medicin graduirt, was beiläufig gesagt heutigen Tages unter dem Regiment der „mehr wissenschaftlich gebildeten" Professoren der Medicin mit einer solchen Arbeit an keiner deutschen Universität möglich sein würde.

Sein Drang zum Reisen veranlaßte ihn, die Stelle eines Lehrers der Naturwissenschaften und Mathematik, die er in Dresden angenommen hatte, bald wieder aufzugeben und sich einer wissenschaftlichen Expedition nach Surinam in Südamerika anzuschließen. Er kehrte seinen Gefährten jedoch bald den Rücken und blieb als praktischer Arzt in Paramaribo. Im Jahre 1833 ließ er sich in Philadelphia nieder, wo er eine gute Praxis bekam. Im Jahre 1846 gründete er die erste homöopathische Bildungsanstalt für Mediciner, das homöopathische College in Philadelphia. Damit legte er den Grund zur erfolgreichen, nachhaltigen Verbreitung der Homöopathie in Amerika. Die Umstände brachten es mit sich, daß er mehr in englischer Sprache als in seiner Muttersprache schrieb, und während uns Deutschen nur sein „Hausarzt" als unvergängliches Andenken an den Verstorbenen bleibt, hat er vom Jahre 1869 an in dem amerikanischen Journal "Materia Medica" und noch mehr in seinem leider noch unvollendeten Hauptwerke "Guiding Symptoms" („Leitende Symptome") sich in Amerika ein Denkmal für alle Zukunft gesetzt.

Dr. Hering war dreimal verheirathet; seine erste Frau hatte er in Surinam kennen gelernt; sie starb bald und hinterließ ihm einen (noch lebenden) Sohn. Seine zweite Frau war von Philadelphia; eine Tochter aus dieser Ehe lebt verheirathet in Boston. Die dritte Frau, die er 1845 von Deutschland heimgeführt, betrauert mit 6 Kindern den Verlust des geliebten Gatten und Vaters.

Aber auch wir Andern alle empfinden den Hingang dieses Mannes als einen wahrhaft unersetzlichen Verlust! Wenn ihn Wohlwollen gegen seine Nebenmenschen, Rechtlichkeit und Gewissenhaftigkeit in den weitesten Kreisen bekannt und beliebt gemacht hatten, so schätzten die ihm näher Stehenden seine aufrichtige Frömmigkeit, seinen festen Glauben an ein Wiedersehen nach dem Tode als einen verehrungswürdigen Zug seines makellosen Charakters. Seine Leichenfeier, welcher die Fakultät des Hahnemann Medical College, sowie die Direktoren der American Homœopathic Publishing Society und zahlreiche Delegirte ärztlicher Vereine beiwohnten, war ein sprechendes

Zeugniß für die allgemeine Beliebtheit, deren sich dieser seltene Mann im Leben zu erfreuen hatte.

An uns Laien ist es, die großen Hoffnungen, die er auf unsere Vereine gesetzt, zu verwirklichen! Damit ehren wir am besten das Andenken an diesen eifrigsten und talentvollsten Schüler Hahnemanns.

In the *Populäre Zeitschrift für Homöopathie*, published in Leipzig, the following obituary notice appeared in the issue of September 1st, 1880:

Nekrolog.

Als wir in der am 1. Januar d. J. erschienenen Nummer der „Populären Zeitschrift für Homöopathie" das Portrait unseres ehrwürdigen Veteranen Professor Dr. Constantin Hering in Philadelphia brachten und den Jubilar zu seinem achtzigsten Geburtstage beglückwünschten, da ahnten wir nicht, daß das Bibelwort: „Des Menschen Leben währet siebenzig Jahre, und wenn's hoch kommt, so sind's achtzig, und ist es köstlich gewesen, so ist es Mühe und Arbeit gewesen," schon so bald an dem immer noch rüstigen und thätigen Greise sich bewahrheiten sollte. Ein Telegram aus Philadelphia, welches uns Herr Dr. Heermann von Hundermark in Paris übermittelte, meldete uns seinen am 23. Juli, Abends 10 Uhr erfolgten Tod, und heute, wo wir dieses schreiben, liegen uns zahlreiche amerikanische und deutsche Blätter vor mit den ehrenvollsten Nachrufen für „den bedeutendsten und bekanntesten, wenn nicht berühmtesten Bürger Philadelphias," den der Tod wenige Stunden nach seiner Rückkehr von einem Krankenbesuch, also in voller Rüstung, ereilte. Was Constantin Hering uns Homöopathen in dem Zeitraum eines halben Jahrhunderts als Schriftsteller und Arzt gewesen ist, das haben wir vor wenigen Monaten in der, seinem Portrait beigegebenen Biographie dargethan. Sein Hauptwerk, an welchem er bis zu seinem Tode arbeitete und dessen dritter Band von ihm soeben vollendet war, wird von seinen Schülern weiter herausgegeben werden.

Es führt den Titel "Guiding Symptoms" („Leitende Symptome"), ist auf 15 Bände berechnet, und enthält die Quintessenz der gesammten homöopathischen Arzneimittellehre. Das Material zu den noch fehlenden Bänden ist von dem Dahingeschiedenen derart geordnet hinterlassen worden, daß deren Herausgeber wenig Mühe haben werden.

Obgleich er die meisten neueren Werke in englischer Sprache publicirte, so hing er doch mit voller Liebe an seinem deutschen Vaterlande und stand mit den deutschen Homöopathen in regem Verkehr. Die deutschen Siege und die Errichtung des deutschen Reiches wurden von ihm durch ein großes Fest in seinem, an einen geräumigen Garten stoßenden Hause gefeiert. Letzteres war der Mittelpunkt des geistigen Lebens der Deutschen in Philadelphia und mit größter Liberalität allen Männern der Kunst und Wissenschaft zu jeder Stunde geöffnet. Rastlos nahm Hering an Allem Theil, was die Entwickelung des deutschen Elementes in Amerika fördern und heben konnte; und als Professor Reuleaux über die deutsche Industrie auf der Weltausstellung in Philadelphia das geflügelte Wort sprach: „Billig und schlecht!" da brauste er auf in einem an den Herausgeber d. Z. gerichteten Briefe: „daß Professor Reuleaux mit keinem Einzigen der achtbaren Deutschen in Philadelphia gesprochen, daß er in seinem Berichte verschwiegen hätte daß die Preise und Auszeichnungen vorzugsweise den Arbeiten von Deutschen in Philadelphia zugefallen seien, und daß den einzigen Preis, der die Homöopathie betraf, ein Deutscher erhielt."

Fern von seinem geliebten Vaterlande werden seine sterblichen Ueberreste in fremder Erde ruhen. Sein Geist aber wird fortleben in der Heilmethode Samuel Hahnemann's, diesem Kinde ächt deutschen Geistes, Fleißes und Strebens, und für immer wird sich an den Namen Constantin Hering die Erinnerung knüpfen, daß er nicht bloß der beste Kenner der homöopathischen Arzneimittellehre, sondern auch, nächst Hahnemann, deren eifrigster Förderer gewesen ist.

Ehre seinem Angedenken!
Friede seiner Asche!

INDEX.

Allen, Dr. H. C., remarks of, 272.
Allen, Dr. T. F., remarks of, 176.
Allgemeine Homœopathische Zeitung Todesanzeige, 353.
American Institute Memorial Service, 331.
Baxter, Dr. H. H., report by, 278.
Bayard, Dr. E., address by, 169.
" " remarks of, 188.
Beckwith, Dr. D. H., remarks of, 279.
Bigler, Dr. W. H., remarks of, 138.
Biographical Sketch by Dr. C. Gundelach, 234.
Bolles, Rev. Dr., remarks of, 276.
Boston, Meeting of Physicians of, 147.
Boyce, Dr. C. W., reminiscences by, 212.
British Homœopathic Congress, 162.
Burnham, Dr., remarks of, 283.
Canadian Homœopathic Institute Meeting, 327.
Carleton, Dr. E., Jr., remarks of, 185.
Carriere, Dr. Charles L., remarks of, 245.
Cleveland, Meeting in, 276.
Cole, Dr. A. L., remarks of, 285.
Dake, Dr. J. P., remarks of, 341.
Denver, Meeting in, 282.
Deschére, Dr. Martin, remarks of, 208.
Dowling, Dr. J. W., address by, 336.
" " remarks of, 181, 348.
Dudley, Dr. Pemberton, remarks of, 141.
Duncan, Dr. T. C., remarks of, 345.
Eastman, Dr. Emma, remarks of, 287.
Eaton, Dr. M. M., remarks of, 347.
Edmonds, Dr. W. A., remarks of, 237.
Eulogy by Dr. C. Heermann, Paris, 316.
Everett, Dr. Ambrose S., remarks of, 289
Finch, Dr. Joseph, remarks of, 179.
Fisher, Dr., remarks of, 345.

Franklin, Dr. E. C., remarks of, 262.
Frohne, Dr. J. P., remarks of, 244.
Funeral Sermon, 148.
" Services, 148.
Gause, Dr. O. B., remarks of, 132.
Gilbert, Dr. Charles B., remarks of, 211.
Goodman, Dr. C. H., incidents related by, 248.
Gottschalk, Dr. William von, remarks of, 348.
Guernsey, Dr. E., remarks of, 182.
" Dr. Henry N., address by, 195.
" Dr. Joseph C., remarks of, 228.
Gundelach, Dr. Charles, biographical sketch by, 234.
Hahnemann Medical College tribute, 188.
Hallock, Dr. L., remarks of, 184.
Hart, Dr. C. N., remarks of, 293.
Hills, Dr. Alfred K., remarks of, 184.
Inaugural Dissertation, 228.
Ingersoll, Dr. L. J., remarks of, 287.
Italy, Tribute from, 350.
James, Dr. Bushrod W., remarks of, 203.
Joslin, Dr. B. F., note from, 182.
Kansas City, Meeting in, 261.
" Physicians, memorial address to, 304.
Kershaw, Dr. J. Martin, tribute by, 242.
Korndœrfer, Dr. Augustus, remarks by, 136.
Lee, Dr. John K., address by, 167, 226.
" " remarks of, 142.
Liebold, Dr. C. Th., remarks of, 180.
Lilienthal, Dr. Samuel, remarks of, 163, 166, 174.
Lippe, Dr. A., address by, 129, 192.
" Dr. Constantine, remarks of, 210.
McClatchey, Dr. R. J., remarks of, 200.
McManus, Dr. F. R., remarks of, 329, 344.
Maryland State Society Meeting, 328.
Memorial Address to Kansas Physicians, 304.
" Committee, composition of, 144.
" Meetings, 158.
Mexican Homœopathic Institute tribute, 352.
Michigan College of Physicians and Surgeons, 161.
" University of, meeting, 261.
Minneapolis, Meeting in, 294.

Mohr, Dr. Charles, remarks of, 230.
Morgan, Dr. J. C., address by, 133.
" " eulogy by, 205.
" " remarks of, 337.
Necrology, 353, 357, 359.
Necrology by Dr. Henry D. Paine, 331.
Negendank, Dr. A., address by, 309.
New York City, Meeting of Physicians of, 145.
New York County Society Meeting, 169.
New York State Society Meeting, 163.
Northern New York Medical Society Meeting, 160.
Norton, Dr. George S., remarks of, 183.
Obituary Notices, 352.
Obituary Notice in the Allgemeine Hom. Zeitung, 354.
" " in the Homöopathische Monatsblätter, 357.
" " in La Reforma Medica, 352.
" " Populäre Zeitschrift für Homöopathie, 359.
Onondaga County Memorial Meeting, 158.
Paine, Dr. Henry D., Necrological Report by, 331.
" " remarks of, 336.
Pall Bearers, list of, 143.
Paris, Meeting in, 314.
Parsons, Dr S. B., remarks of, 240.
Pearson, Dr. C., remarks of, 189.
Pennsylvania State Medical Society Meeting, 166.
Philadelphia County Society tribute, 187.
" Meeting of Physicians of, 129.
" Memorial Meeting, 187.
Piepgras, Dr., remarks of, 291.
Poem by Dr. S. B. Parsons, 241.
Pompili, Dr. Joachim, tribute by, 350.
Post-mortem, account of, 138.
Reminiscences by Dr. C. W. Boyce, 212.
Resolutions adopted by the Boston Physicians, 147.
" " " British Homœopathic Congress, 162.
" " " Canadian Homœopathic Institute, 328.
" " " Cleveland Academy of Medicine, 278.
" " " Denver Physicians, 283.
" " " H. M. S. of Northern New York, 160.
" " " Kansas City Physicians, 261.
" " " Maryland State Society, 330.

Resolutions adopted by the Michigan College of Physicians and Surgeons, 162.
" " " New York State Society, 164.
" " " Onondaga County Society, 159.
" " " Pennsylvania State Society, 168.
" " " Philadelphia Physicians, 131.
" " " University of Michigan, 276.
" " " Washington Hom. Med. Society, 312.
" " " West Jersey Society, 330.
" passed by New York Physicians, 145.
Sanders, Dr. J. C., report by, 278.
Schleswig-Holstein, Meeting in, 314.
Seward, Rev. S. S., Funeral Sermon by, 148.
Smith, Dr. H. M., remarks of, 342.
Spalding, Dr. C. W., address by, 242.
Starritt, Dr. S. P., address by, 294.
St. Louis Memorial Services, 233.
Talbot, Dr. I. T., remarks of, 346.
Taylor, Dr. C. W., remarks of, 247.
Thesis, translation of graduation, 228.
Thomas, Dr. A. R., letter from, 140.
Tribute from Italy, 350.
Valentine, Dr. Philo G., original verses by, 249.
" " remarks of, 347.
Walker, Dr. G. S., Oration by, 252.
Washington, Meeting in, 312.
Wells, Dr. P. P., address by, 164.
Wilmington, Meeting in, 309.
Wilson, Dr. T. P., remarks of, 267.

www.ingramcontent.com/pod-product-compliance
Lightning Source LLC
Chambersburg PA
CBHW032045220426
43664CB00008B/873